Interpersonal: Do Self (I) to Other (You)		Interpersonal: Get Other (You) to Self (I)	
	See	**Want**	**See**	**Want**
Inclusion	I include you. 11	I want to include you. 12	You include me. 13	I want you to include me. 14
Control	I control you. 21	I want to control you. 22	You control me. 23	I want you to control me. 24
Openness	I am open with you. 31	I want to be open with you. 32	You are open with me. 33	I want you to be open with me. 34
Significance	I feel you are significant. 41	I want to feel you are significant. 42	You feel I am significant. 43	I want you to feel I am significant. 44
Competence	I feel you are competent. 51	I want to feel you are competent. 52	You feel I am competent. 53	I want you to feel I am competent. 54
Likability	I like you. 61	I want to like you. 62	You like me. 63	I want you to like me. 64

Periodic Table of the Human Elements

Individual Self (I) to Self (I)		Other Other (O) to Other (O)	
See	**Want**	**See**	**Want**
I am fully alive. 15	I want to be fully alive. 16	You are fully alive. 17	You want to be fully alive. 18
I determine my own life. 25	I want to determine my own life. 26	You determine your own life. 27	You want to determine your own life. 28
I am aware of myself. 35	I want to be aware of myself. 36	You are aware of yourself. 37	You want to be aware of yourself. 38
I feel significant. 45	I want to feel significant. 46	You feel significant. 47	You want to feel significant. 48
I feel competent. 55	I want to feel competent. 56	You feel competent. 57	You want to feel competent. 58
I like myself. 65	I want to like myself. 66	You like yourself. 67	You want to like yourself. 68

The Human Element

The Human Element

*Productivity, Self-Esteem,
and the Bottom Line*

WILL SCHUTZ

Library of Congress Cataloging-in-Publication Data

Schutz, Will.
    The human element : productivity, self-esteem, and the bottom line
/ Will Schutz. — 2nd ed.
      p. cm.
    Includes bibliographical references and index.
    ISBN 1-55542-612-3
      1. Personnel management. 2. Industrial management—Employee
participation. 3. Self-esteem. 4. Work groups. 5. Labor
productivity. I. Title. II. Series.
HF5549.S253 1994
658.3—dc20
                                         94-16107
                                         CIP

Credits are on p. 277

SECOND EDITION
SB Printing

 Business Consultants Network, Inc.

Contents

Preface to the Second Edition

I remember the day that my father told me he was going to leave Esalen Institute. We were in Carmel, California for the day, an hour's drive from the influential growth center where he had become synonymous with encounter groups. I was ten years old and I was crushed. I loved being at Esalen with my father and I was always taken with the energy of the place. It was magical, fascinating, and intense. He had come to be so much a part of the place, and the place so much of how I thought of him. I could not imagine him anywhere else.

It would take me years to understand fully why he left. For me, it was a home; for him, it was another step toward his goal of helping people to have joy and harmony in their lives. He had left a tenured position at the Albert Einstein School of Medicine in New York to move to Esalen, to explore and to learn. As a child, I absorbed the raw energy and emotional tone of the place and the time, but his scientific mind, honed over 20 years of teaching and conducting research as a university professor, had remained fully engaged. He participated in everything he could—encounter groups, gestalt therapy, Rolfing, transactional analysis, bioenergetics, tai chi, aikido, Feldenkrais, acupuncture, and lectures on everything from psychology to myth to spiritual practice—and methodically evaluated the results of each of these approaches for achieving human potential. He noted what was effective and not effective, useful and not useful, and distilled the essential principles of each one. While he found that many of these methods and ideas were extremely powerful and effected great change, they were often separate and unconnected. After eight years, he was ready to move on because he wanted to integrate the best of what he had learned to create something truly exceptional.

As usual, he did not know exactly where his path would lead. When he began consulting in corporate America he was as surprised as anyone. Someone asked him if he felt that he was selling out, considering that he was working for the "establishment". Wouldn't he rather be working with "real people" instead of those corporate types? His response, as was typical, was surprising and obvious at the same time: "I find that people in large organizations are a lot like, well, people."

This is what makes this book as relevant now as when it was first published. We are still, well, people. As a quick look at the news will show, we still have the same feelings, motivations, and creativity, and the same challenges and problems. Despite all our technical advances, it is still true that the most critical aspect of living and working together is understanding ourselves and relating to each other.

The Human Element is the culmination of my father's life's work. It combines the best of the scientific and the experiential to help people become more self-aware and improve how they relate to each other. It is elegant, powerful, enduring, and holistic, a principle that was very important to him. It is also a work in progress. He was never finished learning, experimenting with, editing, or road testing his ideas. In his words, he used a process of successive approximation—constant improvement and refinement, each iteration closer to the ideal. No matter how successful a particular workshop, presentation, or writing was, he remained focused on ways to make it even better. Every activity he designed, every piece that he wrote had a single, specific purpose. If an activity did not produce the reaction he expected from people, if they cried instead of laughed, he would refine it or discard it and try something new. If people misunderstood his written work, he would edit and reedit until it was crystal clear. He was never satisfied with filler pieces or parts that did not contribute clearly to the whole of the work.

As a result, every part of the work presented in this book has been distilled to a very simple concept or point. At the same time, each piece is very rich, and the fullness and depth emerges only through exploration over time. In short, the work is profoundly simple, a concept he explored in another one of his books *Profound Simplicity*.

His mastery, focus, and methods were very inspiring to me in my own life and work with The Human Element, though it was hard to tell early on. As many children of successful parents do, I initially pursued something entirely different from my father. I became an architect. I found, however, that I did not care very much about the buildings that I worked on. Instead, I was more interested in the process of getting people to work together who did not seem to want to, such as plumbers, electricians, city inspectors, engineers, and general contractors. After many years of feeling I wanted to do something else but not knowing what, I finally reached a point of clarity: what I really loved was helping people work together better. That sounded awfully familiar and I thought to myself, "Hey, I know someone I could talk to about this. Maybe I should call him!" So I did, and in that single phone call to my father I ended a decade of work in architecture and started down the path of learning and living The Human Element.

When my father died in 2002 he left a wealth of integrated Human Element material, writing, memories, and exceptionally large shoes to fill. As President of Business Consultants Network, Inc., the company that owns his work, my goal is to keep the original spirit and form of his work alive and healthy, while continuing to develop and expand it. In a larger sense, I am striving to create conditions—a business and a community—where The Human Element powers positive cultural change, in organizations and the world.

To date this book has been translated into 14 languages and The Human Element workshop is used in 18 countries worldwide in virtually all industries and sectors. It has been used to enhance teamwork, personal effectiveness, and leadership, and to foster collaboration, improve customer service, help people choose careers, promote creativity, and make difficult decisions. The Human Element functions as the engine that drives numerous other improvement efforts and makes them work better. These are "Powered by The Human Element".

Through the years a tremendous number of people have not only supported and practiced this work, but have committed their lives to living its principles. They are the heart and soul of The Human Element community that keeps this work alive and thriving. In particular, I would like to thank Mr. Shogo Saito, chairman of Business Consultants, Inc. Japan, who purchased my father's business shortly before his death. His belief in and commitment to the work and his trust and support of my father and of me personally has been exceptional.

Above all, The Human Element has helped people to change their own lives. This is what makes the work enduring. It addresses the core issues of who we are, who we want to be, and how we want to live our lives both individually and collectively. Its fundamental purpose is to help people realize their potential.

Not surprisingly, fulfilling one's potential was an important topic in my family. Quite often, I asked my father for advice or told him my thoughts to get his perspective. On one visit I was feeling particularly unsure of myself. I was planning to make a recording of a number of songs I had written, but I was stuck. "Whenever I work on a project like this I become obsessed," I said, jumping immediately to the difficult part. "I stop eating, sleeping, and seeing my friends. It feels terrible." My father paused to think for a moment and then said, "I feel obsessed in my own work as well, but I rather like it. It's very powerful. It helps me to engage fully and do my very best." I had to admit that I did my best work that way, too. "But when I get obsessed I feel lost and get afraid that I'll never come out of it," I objected. "I've reached that point before. Now I only want to work on tasks that don't require too much from me." He accepted this explanation of my victim-hood for a little while, and then offered, "I tell myself ahead of time that I'll become obsessed until I complete what I'm working on. Then I'm able to stop when I'm done."

His statement was profound, simple, and very powerful. I realized that I had choices in the situation that I had not seen before and I took the energy I was using to prevent myself from starting the project and used it to become wonderfully obsessed—for a time.

To practice The Human Element principles means to be truthful with oneself and others, to make choices consciously with awareness of the consequences, and to seek to increase personal awareness continuously. Imagine a world where everyone lived by these simple, powerful principles. My father imagined such a world, and I believe it can be real. We can achieve our highest potential. We are after all, well, people.

New York, New York   ETHAN SCHUTZ
September 2005

Preface

In the end all business operations can be reduced to three
words: people, product, and profit. People come first.
Unless you've got a good team, you can't do much with
the other two.
—*Lee Iacocca*[1]

If Iacocca is right, and I believe he is, let us take a deeper look at people and apply our modern understanding of people to organizations. We have learned a great deal about human behavior over the past few decades. Now is the time to apply it. Over the years, as a consultant, I have had the opportunity to observe people of all ranks in organizations. I have been impressed—and saddened—whenever I have seen the amount of pain that exists in organizational life. So many people are frightened of losing their jobs, of being inadequate, of being disrespected, of being overlooked, of being exposed, of just being known. So many have physical ailments, sometimes chronic, related to their livelihood. And the fear often carries over to their personal lives.

I don't like to see all this pain. I don't like to experience it myself, and it disturbs me to see it so widespread. The ramifications of high or low self-esteem are enormous and ubiquitous, and their extent is often underestimated. They affect every aspect of human personality and human interaction. They affect our productivity and ability to think creatively and logically. They are often the source of our social problems.

My personal and professional experiences have demonstrated that when people have sufficient self-awareness to have healthy self-esteem, and when organizations promote an open, honest climate, much pain can be eliminated. We can eliminate irrelevant arguments, wasted energy, withholding, lying, undermining, and other inefficient, misery-producing activity. The workplace can be transformed into an arena for expressing the best in ourselves and bringing out exceptional productivity.

Self-esteem also leads to the most fundamental methods for helping others. For me, the highest value is the full realization of myself and of all people. In fact, the most I can do for any other person is to help him or her become fully realized. I can do that only when I myself am unafraid and open.

I had a recurrent dream when I was a boy. I dreamed that I was a grown man, on the roof of a burning apartment building, and my children were on the ground, in the courtyard, frightened and needing my help. But I had an enormous feeling of frustration because up on the roof the bricks from the chimney were falling on me, and I had to keep dodging them myself in order to escape and help my children. The message of the dream was clear: I must free myself of threats to be of the most value to others.

What Is the Human Element Approach?

The Human Element model presents a well-tested theory and methods aimed at helping you increase your self-awareness, self-acceptance, and self-esteem and thus realize your full human potential, both individually and as a member of a group. If you are willing to open yourself to the ideas and experiences presented here and carry them into your organization, you'll help create a structure and conditions in which the following things can happen:

- Groups operate to their capacity because members choose to know and express themselves fully and to create a structure that elicits and uses everyone's contributions.

- Everyone tells the truth.
- Each person takes full responsibility for his or her behavior and feelings.

To the degree that these aims are realized, teams are most effective, organizations are most productive, and individuals are most accomplished. On the emotional level, human relationships in teams are personally satisfying, and individuals feel best about themselves. One observer, referring to an important experiment in the automotive field, put it more urgently: "No individual or group of individuals is smart enough to guide an organization today. The only way you can do it is to leverage all of your human resources, and that means minds as well as hands."[2]

Several fundamental principles lie behind *The Human Element*:

- At the heart of all human functioning is the self.
- Best solutions to organizational and leadership issues require self-awareness as an essential first step.
- Deeper self-awareness leads to self-acceptance and then self-esteem.
- As individuals gain self-awareness and self-esteem, they become more open and honest with their co-workers. They redirect the energy they now use for defensiveness, withholding, and other interpersonal struggles into productive work.

A phrase of Kurt Lewin's is justifiably famous: "There is nothing so practical as a good theory." Theory is usually the result of thinking through and understanding a phenomenon of interest. *The Human Element* presents a theory aimed at providing leaders with some simple and, I hope, profoundly effective tools that they can bring to any leadership dilemma. For example, if meetings are not efficient, the theory provides guidelines for noticing what is not being said and for knowing methods for eliciting what is hidden, thereby increasing group energy. If team members are not functioning well, the theory may direct the leader to several areas for solutions: Do team members not feel included? Do they feel disempowered? Disliked? Lied to? Ignored? Disrespected? If team members are not working together, is it because they are different in their orientations to work? Are they competing for the same role? Rigidly holding to their positions, since they feel threatened? Withholding feelings for fear of losing their jobs?

The purposes of the book are, first, to present a method for achieving cost-effective, productive work in organizations—the bottom line—through improving everyone's individual and team performance; second, to show how to accomplish this goal while supporting the personal growth and happiness of everyone in the organization; and, third, to teach people to be leaders who can guide their teams to accomplish their goals.

Who Should Read This Book?

I wrote this book for people interested in enhancing self-awareness and self-esteem. The people who share this interest include the following groups.

Leaders and Managers

As the people responsible for accomplishing the organization's goals, often in times of reduced resources and challenging expectations, managers know that the more time they can devote to solving work problems and creating successful products and services, the better they and the organization will do. The Human Element model provides a way for managers in organizations to learn about themselves in their roles and see ways of understanding and helping their subordinates. They can learn about their own self-concepts and self--esteem, about how people operate, and about new methods for dealing with such crucial issues as performance appraisal, job fit and satisfaction, teamwork, internal and external group dynamics, and individual and group problem solving and decision making. The book is a sourcebook for leaders on the human aspects of leadership.

Self-Directed Teams

Teams can also profit from the book, since its conception of leadership encourages the maximum participation of all members, which enhances everyone's feelings of responsibility and competence. (Chapter Three, devoted to teamwork, demonstrates how groups can come together to create healthy dynamics that lead to increased productivity.)

Professionals

Psychologists, social workers, counselors, nurses, and others in the helping professions may find many sections (such as those on the self and interpersonal behavior) of specific value. Those in sports organizations and the military should gain from the sections on leadership, teamwork, performance, and decision making.

Individuals

The Human Element approach fosters the idea that each individual mirrors the dynamics of groups within himself or herself, and so all the material on self-concept and self-esteem in organizational relationships also applies to the way each individual functions. The same principles of truth telling, choice, and self-awareness, plus those of teamwork and group problem solving and decision making, also apply to couples and families. The bottom line is that this approach can help you know yourself better and strengthen your self-esteem and thus make a difference in the quality and health of most of your relationships.

How to Read This Book

The Human Element is an invitation to you, the reader, to come with me on an intense journey. It will be quite demanding at times, requiring you to think about and react to your own and others' behavior and feelings, which may be difficult to acknowledge. You may find the ideas not only new but very different from what you've encountered before. You are faced with a choice: How much benefit are you willing to choose to get from this book? As you come across concepts that seem revolutionary, you may say, "That will never work in my organization. It's not realistic." I won't debate whether that's true; you are free to make your own choice. Instead, I want to point out that there are many ways to enhance or block the benefits of any learning tool, including this book. I promise you that if you choose to stay with this journey, you will gain insights and ideas that, as years of workshops based on these principles have shown, do make a tremendous difference in the quality of life and relationships in organizations. Because of the amount of material in the book and the length of some of the chapters, I suggest that you follow these steps:

- Begin by reading the book through once, quickly. Don't answer any queries or struggle over any parts that are unclear. Just concentrate on getting an overall feel for the book.
- Start again, and take one small part at a time. Let the material sink in. Note your responses. Connect the ideas to your own experiences, in your life and in your organization. Argue with the ideas, and challenge them—out loud, if you like. Try them out. Discuss them with people around you. Think about the methods and suggestions for action, and see how they might be useful. For you to get the most out of this book, the ideas in it have to become real to you, and your active engagement is the best way to make that happen.
- Respond completely and honestly to the Pause for Reflection sections interspersed throughout the chapters. The Pauses provide opportunities for you, the reader, to explore your personal relationship to the concepts and to devise a personal action plan. They give you a chance to increase your own self-awareness, self-acceptance, and self-esteem as well as to learn new ways of creating stronger teams and interpersonal relationships.

- Put the book down, reflect, and let what you have read settle in. When you have digested it, return to the book and take the next part. Then stop again and reflect. By taking bite-sized pieces, you will receive much more value from the book.
- If there are parts of particular interest, dwell on them longer. It will probably work better to stay in sequence, but if you have an overwhelming interest in one particular part, skip to it.
- When you have finished the second time, read through the whole book once more. You will probably get much more from it this time.

In addition to the Pause for Reflection sections, the book also features extended *cases* that are reports of the Human Element at work in a variety of organizations. In some instances, I wrote cases as reports of my experiences consulting with particular organizations. In other cases, the leader or manager of an organization writes about his or her experiences and those of the group. There are also shorter *case examples*, also drawn from real organizations, with episodes that are integrated into the chapters. Case examples are usually accompanied by analyses, to illustrate how the Human Element concepts apply to the examples.

Organization of the Book

The basis for organizing this book owes much to the many five-day workshops called *The Human Element*,[3] presented over the past dozen years, and to the late Ida Rolf, a magnificent woman who invented the method of deep massage called *Rolfing*.[4] Rolfing consists of a series of sessions administered in a specific sequence, each to a different area of the body. This "recipe," as Rolf called it, was designed so that after one part of the body (the top half, for example, in session one) was balanced, the client who was well aware of her body could sense where the next session would focus, since that part (the legs, in session two) would now be unbalanced. The sequence continues through ten sessions, with each session building awareness in the client and following logically and sensibly from those that have gone before. Similarly, as the Human Element workshops evolved, certain topics naturally followed from earlier ones. For example, to increase group effectiveness, it is essential for group members to understand and to have dealt with issues of self-concept and self-esteem.

The sequence of chapters in this book follows the organic evolution of Human Element concepts. The Introduction begins with an account of how my personal and professional experiences led to the development of the Human Element model and explains why I think it has such power and utility.

Part One presents two chapters designed to help the reader acquire more self-awareness. Chapter One introduces the Human Element theoretical framework for understanding the self, including behavior and feelings and how they affect relationships within groups. The chapter begins the process of developing self-awareness and is designed to answer several questions: How do I behave toward people? How do I feel toward others? How do people behave and feel toward me? What impact do I have on people? Chapter Two looks at perceptions of self (self-concept) and feelings about those perceptions (self-esteem), to help readers gain a more realistic view of themselves, which aids in self-acceptance. It answers these questions: Who am I? How do I see myself? How do I defend myself when I am threatened? What are my strong leadership traits, and how can I improve as a leader? How do I feel about myself? How much do I care about myself? How much do I respect and like myself? How can I increase my self-esteem? How do self-concept and self-esteem affect the organization?

Part Two, which comprises four chapters, applies the Human Element principles to major organizational issues. Chapter Three discusses group dynamics and presents a model for open and compatible teamwork. It explores these questions: How can I be a better team player? How do teams work? What blocks teamwork? How can I help my team work better? What motivates individuals? How can I help them work more effectively? How can I help my team manage its relations with outside forces and groups? It becomes clear that optimal teamwork requires optimal individual performance, and so Chapter Four looks at ways of enhancing individual performance through new approaches to performance appraisal, job satisfaction, and personal problem solving and decision making. Chapter Five turns to using the *concordance model* in building more efficient group-based decision making, including conflict resolution. It answers these questions: How can I better mobilize the resources on my team to help the members become more creative and logical problem solvers? How can we use the techniques to ensure that everyone has the opportunity to participate in all decisions? Chapter Six outlines the Human Element concept of the *leader as completer* and describes how such a leader can be encouraged and trained. The chapter concludes with a vision of the Human Element organization and what it takes to create one. The Conclusion, following Chapter Six, offers a few thoughts on change.

Style

Throughout this book, I have adopted a convention used in all my books written since 1973. For certain descriptions, to avoid sexist grammar and establish a direct writing style, *I* is used to designate the universal self or the universal employee, and *you* is used to designate the universal other. This convention avoids the cumbersome he-she-they and he/she locutions and the use of just *he* or *him* to represent both male and female. An exception to this practice occurs when I, the author, speak directly to you, the reader (this exception is usually made clear by the context). In addition to avoiding awkwardness, the universal *I* is designed to draw you, the reader, more deeply into the content and make it more immediate to you. It may take a while for you to get used to being included as *I*, rather than being addressed as *you* or included in what I consider a phony *we*, but I think you will find that it is well worth the effort.

Acknowledgments

I want to express my gratitude to the following people:

- The workshop trainers who contributed to this work, especially Judith Bell, Karen Copeland, Ron Luyet, Thompson Barton, Gary Copeland, Peggy O'Heron, Don White, and Nan Wydler
- Those from other countries who adapted the work to their culture, especially Rhonda Parkyns from Australia, Virginie Cornet from France, Jim Barrett and Roy Childs from Great Britain, Morio Itozu and Shogo Saito from Japan, Michele Branca from Italy, and Jorge and Monica Díaz from Mexico
- To my support staff: James Mellard, Jerry Miller, Elizabeth Pickens, Dean Radetsky, Maranne Thieme, and Ethan Schutz, my son, who contributed excellent background research
- To Warren Bennis, who championed the manuscript when others were skeptical and provided superb advice, conceptual editing, and general support
- To the folks at Jossey-Bass: Cedric Crocker, Marcella Friel, Bill Hicks, Sarah Miller, freelance copyeditor Patty Callahan, and especially freelance development editor Sheryl Fullerton
- To my wife, Ailish: strong partner, inspiration, colleague, defender, critic, comic, teacher, wonderful, generous spirit; the security that made my effort easier

Finally, it is with great sadness and pride that I dedicate this book to Joyce Feddon, who died during the writing. Joyce was extraordinarily bright, deeply human, and hilariously funny; she had a thorough understanding of the principles in this book and the ability to live them. Joyce spent over twenty years as a Catholic nun and wrote her master's thesis on the Bible and the Human Element. She was instrumental in launching this project and quickly became invaluable to its success. She was not only a marvelous colleague but one of my closest and most cherished friends. Joyce, this is for you.

Muir Beach, California   WILL SCHUTZ
May 1994

The Author

WILL SCHUTZ is one of the most respected leaders in the field of human relations. His FIRO-B questionnaire is internationally known as one of the most widely used approaches in the field.

Schutz has served on the faculties of Harvard University, the University of California at Berkeley, and the University of Chicago, among others. In addition, he created and chaired the graduate department of holistic studies at Antioch University, San Francisco.

As a consultant, Schutz has worked extensively with organizations in both the private and the public sector. These organizations include such Fortune 500 companies as American Express, AT&T, Boeing, Coca-Cola, IBM, Intel, Levi Strauss, Procter & Gamble, and Xerox; government agencies such as the Federal Aviation Ad-min-i-stration, the Indian Health Service, NASA, the Office of the Comp-troller of the Currency, U.S. Army Intelligence, and the World Bank; hospitals, such as Baylor in Texas and Mercy in Iowa; universities, such as Northwestern and Rochester; and nonprofit organizations, such as Bread and Roses and the Urban League. He has led workshops in many countries, and his work has been translated into French, German, Swedish, Italian, Japanese, and Spanish.

Schutz is author and developer of *The Human Element*, an integrated series of modules that addresses all phases of organizational development. He has written eight books, including the best-selling book *Joy* (1967). His most recent book, *The Truth Option* (1984), presents a combination of scientific and experiential methods for self-empowerment.

The Human Element

INTRODUCTION

The Heart and Power of the Human Element

All the greatest and most important problems of life are fundamentally insoluble.... They can never be solved but only outgrown. This "outgrowing" proves on further investigation to require a new level of consciousness.... It is not solved logically in its own terms but fades when confronted with a new and stronger life force.

—Carl Jung[1]

Jung's statement expresses one of the cardinal points of this book. The new consciousness that is needed to solve many personal, professional, international, and organizational problems is, I believe, self-consciousness or self-awareness, which is directly related to self-esteem. The magnitude of those problems—from war to crime to divorce to hunger to terrorism to pollution and far beyond—has created a shared urgency for finding new paradigms to help "reinvent" organizations and governments. People now are ready to understand themselves at a much deeper level and, through that understanding, gain a new and more powerful set of tools to deal with major issues. What began with the giant strides made in the human potential movement[2] has led to ideas and techniques that provide the ingredients for a fresh approach to solving problems. On the organizational level, many consultants and organizational leaders have pointed for years to the need for more attention to the "human side of enterprise"[3] and, in selected realms, have made a noticeable impact.

My plan for this book is to select from the most useful of the new and the best of the old but neglected ideas developed about individual, group, and organizational behavior, bring them together into one theoretical model, and present specific methods for making these ideas practical. This selective and integrative process represents what has grown to be an imperative in my professional and personal life. I have been intent on integrating the personal with the professional, the old with the new, the scientific with the experiential, for well over thirty years. This integrative drive also comes from another of my fundamental beliefs: in *holism*, the idea that body and mind, thoughts and feelings, are intimately intertwined.

To understand more fully the bases of the theoretical and practical ideas in this book, I hope you will indulge me as I share some of my personal history. I tell this story to provide some sense of the origins of, and some context for, what may at times seem like radical alternatives.

A Bit of Autobiography

As virtually any eldest son in a Jewish family will attest, the family push is toward accomplishment: "First become president, then make something of yourself." And each accomplishment is never quite good enough. As a dutiful son, I went to a respectable university (UCLA), received a Ph.D. at a young age, and proceeded to do everything my Jewish mother wanted me to do, so I would "be happy" and so she could tell her Mah-Jongg and canasta partners about her successful son. (I later found out that these values are not confined to Jews or to mothers.)

For twenty years, I taught and did research at Harvard, the University of Chicago, the University of California at Berkeley, and other prestigious institutions. I concentrated in psychology but studied virtually just as much philosophy—in particular, the scientific method, the philosophy of science, logical empiricism, and research design (with the distinguished philosophers Hans Reichenbach and Abraham Kaplan). I taught statistics, produced a dissertation in which I created a new statistic, attended a summer workshop on mathematics for social scientists at Stanford, and worked with Paul Lazarsfeld, the well-known sociologist and methodologist, on a fellowship that resulted in an article in *Psychometrika*.[4] Even during my stint in the Navy, I did research on understanding and predicting how any given group of men would work together, especially in the Combat Information Center of a large ship. In short, I became a "scientist."

I thoroughly enjoyed the pleasure, respectability, and elite status that came from knowing about numbers. My first book, *FIRO: A Three-Dimensional Theory of Interpersonal Behavior* (1958),[5] was based on my Navy research and presented the Fundamental Interpersonal Relations Orientation theory and several measuring instruments. It included FIRO-B, an instrument designed to predict interaction between two people. It was the climax of what I've since come to see as my first scientific phase.

The next few years continued to be outwardly quite successful, but something was wrong. I was straining at the edges of traditional techniques. Although I loved the classroom and the teaching process, I never felt fully adequate. I felt phony. I assigned my classes the second-best book in the field while I read ahead in the best book and lectured from it. I did not feel I *knew* anything from my own experience.

Soon after, I came into my first contact with a psychotherapeutic group, while doing research at the Massachusetts Mental Health Center, in Boston. The process group for young psychiatrists, designed to help them learn more about themselves before they started helping others, was led by Elvin Semrad, a brilliant, earthy psychoanalyst who became my main mentor about groups. After observing and doing research on the group for a year, I finally became a member. And there I found what I had been missing. As a group member, I was admonished to tell the truth, hear feedback from others about how they really felt about me, and open myself to the world of feelings. Since my scientific bent had held me to appreciate only the logical—in fact, to feel a bit superior to those who "wallowed" in emotion—the discovery of the world of feelings was a frightening delight. In addition to letting me gain personal growth, the group experience helped reduce (but did not eliminate) my feeling of being a phony in my teaching. Groups became a source of intellectual knowledge and of personal growth. I became fascinated by them, a fascination that continues to this day.

In the mid-1960s I studied clinical behavior in a day hospital at the Albert Einstein Medical School, in the Bronx, New York, a widely respected, avant-garde institution. Under the supervision of an eminent psychoanalyst, I watched psychiatrists run psychotherapy groups. At the same time, I began to conduct T-groups ("T" for training) for the National Training Laboratories (NTL)[6] at Bethel, Maine. T-groups were being conducted by many people who, from the traditional-professional viewpoint, were "unqualified," used "untested" methods for "too short a time," with "inadequate screening and follow-up." In short, they were "outlaws"—and they intrigued me.

I puzzled over my simultaneous experiences at Einstein and NTL. Maybe it was youth and naïveté, but I thought the outlaws' work and the results they obtained seemed more creative, deeper, faster, and more effective than what was being done in the heart of the psychiatric establishment. At Einstein, for example, a male psychiatrist had a lengthy discussion with a patient about whether she trusted men, and especially him. She insisted that she did, and that it was "no problem." The psychiatrist then put a great deal of energy into trying to convince the patient that she did have trouble with trust, and she continued to deny it. In the T-group, when a similar issue of trust arose, the group leader did not argue. He simply invited the participant to stand up, turn around, and fall backwards, to see if she would trust him to catch her. Several unsuccessful tries at letting go made the point. After a few rationalizations about strength, weight, and so on, this participant was willing to acknowledge her lack of trust, especially of men.

In an attempt to learn more, from 1963 to 1967 I went to all the many seminars and meetings then available in New York, to learn about new techniques in human behavior. I spent a year with psychosynthesis, a spiritually oriented technique involving imagery, devised by an Italian contemporary of Freud named Roberto Assagioli.[7] I experienced psychodrama with Hannah Weiner,[8] bio-energetics with Alexander Lowen and John Pierrakos,[9] Rolfing with Ida Rolf,[10] and gestalt therapy with Paul Goodman.[11] All these methods seemed rich and effective. They had in common the use of nonverbal methods, especially movement and imagery. These non-traditional methods appeared to work. I began to incorporate parts of them into my own group techniques, with exciting results. I felt I was acquiring many methods, from the traditional to the new. My challenge now was to know when to use each most appropriately.

All the while I was soaking up these trends in human behavior, I was also consulting with various organizations and corporations. I presented workshops on creativity, team building, communication, or whatever other topic was currently popular. To judge by the participants' high ratings, these workshops were reasonably successful. But even as I read the evaluations, typically computed the mean (average), and smiled at my success, a vague discomfort nagged me. If I returned to the same organization two weeks later and asked the participants what they had learned from the workshop, I received answers like "Wait just a minute—let me find my notes." Apparently my work had no lasting effect. I would smile weakly, leave, and rush home to the solace of rereading the postworkshop evaluations, trying to put the follow-up comments out of my head. Clearly, though, something was not working, and I wanted to know what. It would take me twenty years to find out.

At the same time, I had a decade birthday that felt like Judgment Day. I asked myself, "Are you living where you want to be living? Are you married to the woman you want to be married to? Are you doing the kind of work you want to be doing?" The answer to all of these questions was a resounding *no*. I had found little energy for my last two jobs and felt a deadness going to work. The same was true in my home life. I longed for an environment where I would feel stimulated and excited and motivated to use my creativity. So, even though I had just been promoted to associate professor at the Einstein Medical School—a coup for a nonmedical doctor—my heart was elsewhere.

As I pondered alternatives, I recalled an offer made by a man named Michael Murphy. I had met Michael while I was teaching at the University of California at Berkeley, from 1958 to 1962, through a student, Fred Weaver, who felt we had similar ideas. Michael had started something called a growth center, the Esalen Institute, at Big Sur, California. He made me an unusual offer. He said he could not pay me, but I could offer three workshops, and if anyone came I would make some money. He could not provide a place to live; there was a garage where I could put a sleeping bag. But he could give me a title, any title I chose. I found this offer irresistible, and so I became the first Emperor of Esalen (in my own mind). In 1967, I resigned from Einstein, got divorced, put my belongings in a Volkswagen, and headed west to Big Sur.

At Esalen, I entered the heart of the human potential movement. I studied and experienced a variety of approaches, drawn from many periods of history and from many countries, to developing the full potential of each person and each interaction between people. I tried everything physical, psychological, and spiritual—all diets, all therapies, all body methods, jogging, meditating, visiting a guru in India, and fasting for thirty-four days on water. These experiences counterbalanced my twenty years in science and left me with a strong desire to integrate the scientific with the experiential.

I tried to accomplish this integration through my research and writing. In my first years at Esalen, I wrote a great deal. Before moving to Esalen, I had written *Joy: Expanding Human Awareness* (1967),[12] which, fortunately, became a best-seller and helped fill my workshops at Esalen. *Joy* summarized what I had done with all the techniques I had been learning during my five years in New York. It described some of those methods, as well as others I had devised, and told how to use them. *Here Comes Everybody* (1971)[13] was a follow-up to *Joy*, reflecting my early experiences at Esalen. The principles of encounter groups were chronicled in *Elements of Encounter* (1973).[14] *Leaders of Schools* (1977)[15] was the last hurrah of my second scientific era. It reported on a large research study of school administrators done earlier at Berkeley. Later came *Body Fantasy* (1977),[16] a case study for a new body-mind therapy I had developed, combining Rolfing and imagery.

In 1979, I published *Profound Simplicity*,[17] a book about the fascinating near-decade of experiences at Esalen that had so widened my perspective on people and human interaction. *Profound Simplicity* communicated my realization that no matter where I began my investigation of human beings—with individuals, or with such interpersonal methods as encounter groups, imagery, gestalt therapy, or psychodrama; with such body techniques as acupuncture, bioenergetics, Rolfing, or the Feldenkrais method[18]; with such energy approaches as aikido or t'ai chi; or with spiritual orientations—if I could understand what all these approaches were saying at a deep enough level, they were all talking about the same thing. Psychologists, for example, talked about realizing the full human potential; the spiritually oriented spoke of finding the God within. When I explored more closely, it seemed to me that they were talking about almost the same thing, but in different language. In *Profound Simplicity*, I described the seven principles of human functioning (truth, choice, simplicity, limitlessness, holism, completion, and dimensions) toward which I felt all approaches to human experiences—psychological, spiritual, physical, and energy-based—were converging.

At the same time, during the late 1970s, American organizations were becoming aware of the benefits of tapping more of the potential within their employees. This awareness was spurred by (among other influences) the spectacular success of Japanese production, an achievement often attributed in part to Japanese management techniques, such as quality circles, and the familylike atmosphere of Japanese business organizations. In response to these changes in business, I became motivated to develop some materials systematically for organizations, based on my human-potential experience and on my work with FIRO theory and the FIRO scales.

In late 1975, I left Esalen. Over the next four years, I undertook the fascinating task of trying to integrate the scientific with the experiential. After dozens of revisions, based on administering the new materials to about two hundred people from many organizations (Kodak, Esso, Ampex, Mattel, United Biscuit, the U.S. Army), several modules emerged. They were called, collectively, *The Human Element*.[19] They were first published in 1981, in workbook form, and were to be administered by qualified trainers in a workshop setting.

In the beginning, I had very little experience working in organizations; as I have said, my professional life had been spent chiefly in teaching and doing research in universities, doing therapy in hospitals, conducting therapy and encounter groups, and creating and experiencing methods for realizing the full human potential. My only hope for success as a consultant was that my "outsider" perspective would lead to some fresh insights into how organizations work and how they could be improved.

My first organizational test was very surprising and encouraging. During a team-building session, a first-level manager said he was having trouble with someone at work and did not know how to handle it. I asked if that someone was in the workshop group. With great anguish, he acknowledged that she was. I suggested that he tell that person directly what the difficulty was. (She turned out to be his boss. Later, I was informed that this was seen as an unusual request, since the more accepted method of dealing with such a problem was to collect a list of anonymous comments made by the boss's subordinates, collate them, and present them to her in random order.) The manager accepted my invitation and was surprised to discover that his boss was aware of his trouble. When a short discussion cleared up a long misunderstanding, everyone treated me like a magician. What a clever technique—talking directly! I felt embarrassed, since this "technique" was the most elementary type of communication in the world I had just come from.

Emboldened by this "success," I decided to apply the principles from *Profound Simplicity* to organizations and started testing them.

For example, "tell the truth," or "be open," is one of these principles (I use the terms *truth* and *openness* synonymously). I told my consulting colleagues that I was going to go to my next client and suggest that the team members try solving their problems by simply telling the truth to each other. My friends smiled and thought that was very quaint: "You've been away quite a while. You see, in organizations we tell the judicious truth, or partial truths, or what people need to know. We rarely tell the whole truth. It isn't...well... professional."

They were right. I had a great deal of difficulty persuading executives or anyone else of the value of telling the truth. But, every now and then, someone was willing to give truth a chance, and the results were amazingly effective. Over the years, truth emerged for me as the great simplifier. It seemed to be the universal tool for dealing with most, perhaps all, human problems.

Over the next several years, I had an opportunity to try out my ideas about human behavior in many organizations of various types and to observe how truth affected productivity. In all these diverse places, the phenomena were virtually the same. People spent (and wasted) an overwhelming amount of time not telling the truth. They were devoting energy to deciding to lie, figuring out how to present the lies, remembering what not to say and what subjects not to discuss, trying to figure out other people's lies, avoiding situations where lies might be revealed, and reconstructing the surrounding situations to make the lies plausible. And this activity did not even include two other pernicious kinds of lies—not saying anything (withholding), and fooling oneself (self-deception). My consulting experiences confirmed the notion that not telling the truth is a tremendous drain on productivity.

In addition to truth, choice (the second principle from *Profound Simplicity*, also called *self-determination*) emerged as a key concept for me in organizations. It is at the heart of the buzzword *empowerment*: if I do not feel I am determining my own life, I am limited in how empowered I feel. Stressing this concept led to a dramatic reduction in blaming in organizations.[20] The practice of choice leads to greater productivity as people shift their energy away from blaming and toward figuring out how to do the work.

The principles of truth and choice proved very useful, but there was one more I wanted to add. I became more and more attracted to the idea of self-concept as the key to solving organizational problems, and to universal self-esteem as the human goal for the organization. This formulation helped me understand my uneasiness of twenty years earlier, when I had first done a small amount of organizational consulting and returned a week later to see that the impact of my "splendid" work was close to nil. At that time, when I had presented the five rules of teamwork, or the seven principles of leadership, or whatever, I had described each item on the list; I did not help the participants find out why they were not embodying those principles in the first place. I neglected the self-concept. In other words, I ignored the *human element* —personal fears, rigidities, defenses, and all the other real reasons why human events do not take place more smoothly in organizations.

As I continued to develop my thinking and my workshops and to experience some success with my approach, I still feared that my offerings were too psychological and not sufficiently business-oriented, and so my first seminars were choppy. The first module I presented was on truth, which I quickly followed with one on teamwork, as if to say, "Don't go away—all this truth and self-awareness stuff really *is* relevant to organizations." Then we'd do a module on behavior, with one on job fit coming right after it. The result was that people went away feeling that these were "good and useful" workshops.

But I wanted a different outcome. I was used to seeing people emerge from encounter groups truly moved and changed, feeling emotional growth as well as having had an intellectual experience. Although the Human Element workshop was and is not an encounter group, I felt that it might be more effective if it went beyond the intellectual level. It needed the emotional, personal-change component. I decided to take a chance.

At the next seminar, I announced, "The first part of this seminar is devoted to personal awareness and creating an open atmosphere. After that, we shall turn to applications using what we have learned in the first part. I would like you to trust me that everything we do will eventually have a practical application." To my delight, the participants had no trouble accepting my request, and I found that even the applications sections of the workshop improved. From then on, people in the seminars invariably ended with a feeling of both intellectual stimulation and personal growth. People appreciated the importance of personal factors more than I had given them credit for.

As I experienced success in the Human Element seminars, I gained confidence that I did have something to offer. I learned to acknowledge my lack of expertise in those aspects of organizations (financial, technological, legal) where I was ignorant, but my understanding of people was relevant. I now believed that organizations were mainly people. Likewise, the aim of training the human element in organizations became clear: to help all employees realize their full potential and increase their self-esteem. In that way, all individuals were fully motivated, creative, and logical. They could get the most out of their experience, work best with others, create a workplace people looked forward to coming to, support each other, help each other reach their potential, identify with the organization out of desire rather than coercion—and maximize profits.

Equally important, I saw that self-esteem had a great deal to do with effective leadership, and that the success of any organization was directly related to its leadership. Indeed, I have come to believe that the success of the leadership and the success of the organization are identical; any approach to organizational effectiveness must include leadership at its core.

As I observed various attempts to define and strengthen leadership among professionals and practitioners, I remembered a concept introduced by Elvin Semrad, my mentor at the Massachusetts Mental Health Center. During a seminar that Semrad was conducting for a group of professionals, he introduced the notion of the *leader as completer*. By that phrase, Semrad meant that the leader's role is to ensure that all the functions necessary to successfully carry out the team's mission are accomplished well, regardless of who does them. This concept made clear why different people succeed in some places and not in others. It made clear the centrality of self-awareness for the leader, in knowing what to do himself or herself and what to have other people do. It also made clear why many different styles can work. (Chapter Six discusses this model of leadership in more depth.)

In the past, I had found that to write a book was not simply to record what I already knew; it had always turned out to be a more creative experience, one in which new correlations emerged, new associations were made, and new simplifications appeared. In short, I usually had a much better idea of what I had been doing all those years after I finished. At this point in my journey, it seemed appropriate to pause, reflect, and write about my experiences over the past dozen years or so. This book is the result of that pause.

Graphic Representation of the Human Element

The Human Element is a holistic, overarching model that presents an integrated approach to all the human issues in an organization. To show its range and scope, Figure I.1 displays the sequence of topics covered in this book and shows how they are related to one another. The circle in the center of the octagon represents a human being. Circle 1, Person to Self, covers areas such as self-esteem and self-concept, while its partner on the diagonal, Circle 2, represents the long-term aspects such as personal growth. Circle 3, Person to People, covers areas such as communication and leadership, while its long-term counterpart, Circle 4, deals with team building and decision making. Circle 5, Person to Job, includes job fit and job placement, while Circle 6 covers career planning, the long-range aspect. Circle 7, Person to Health, relates to fitness and illness. The long-term aspect is covered by Circle 8, general health and health plans.

Figure I.1. The Human Element in Organizations.

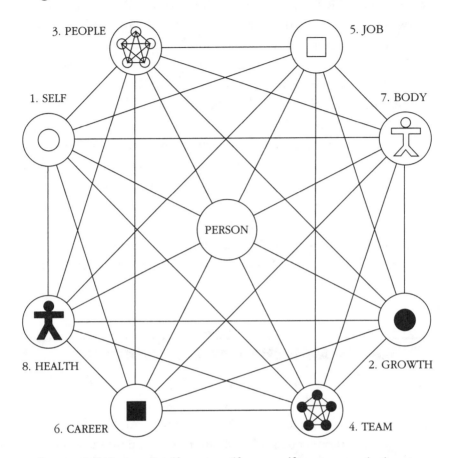

1. Person to Self (short term): self-concept, self-esteem, self-awareness, motivation, stress (Chapters 1, 2, 4)
2. Person to Self (long term): personal growth, realizing full potential (Chapters 1, 2, 4)
3. Person to People (short term): communication, leadership, teamwork (Chapters 3, 4, 5, 6)
4. Person to People (long term): team building, decision making (Chapters 3, 5)
5. Person to Job (short term): job fit, job satisfaction, relation of person to organization (Chapter 4)
6. Person to Job (long term): career planning (Chapter 4)
7. Person to Health (short term): fitness, illness, energy level
8. Person to Health (long term): general health

(In the interest of keeping a clear focus, these two areas are not dealt with here.) The Human Element framework allows the relations between the various human aspects to be dealt with precisely, since each circle is described with the same dimensions (inclusion, control, and openness, to be discussed in detail in Chapter One). For example, the dimensions used for job satisfaction are the same as those used for exploring decision making. This simplification makes it easier to relate all the human activities. Learning about one area leads to simultaneous insights about all the others. In addition, the representation of the octagon as totally connected conveys the interrelations among all areas. Changes in self-esteem, for example, may affect the process of team building. Conflicts about liking myself may help explain my difficulties in being a firm leader and how these in turn impede teamwork. Improved job satisfaction affects communication. Self-awareness affects the quality of decision making, and so on.

Pause for Reflection: Group Lifeline

As already described in the Preface, the Pause for Reflection sections offer opportunities for you to consolidate your learning of the material and apply the material to yourself. When you do, you are likely both to learn more about yourself and to understand the material at a deeper level. (From here on, the pronoun *I* is used throughout for the "universal self"; see the note on style in the Preface.)[21]

This first Pause for Reflection reviews my role in group situations throughout my lifetime. One of the first things I must know about myself as a leader is what kinds of roles I am familiar with, which ones I can carry out comfortably and well, which ones I am inexperienced or uncomfortable in, and, at this point, which ones I probably do not perform very well. I will then be better able to find my place on my team or in my group by continuing what I do best and, as time goes by, strengthening my performance in my weaker roles.

I think about myself—or, better, draw a picture of myself—as far back as I can remember. I shut my eyes and picture myself at the very earliest age I can recall. Now I open my eyes and draw myself through my lifetime, using the following guidelines:

- *In my family:* Where am I in the birth order? What was my role in the family when my parents were home? when they were not home? when no one was home?

- *With my playmates:* Was I a leader? dominant? shy? well liked? ignored? rejected? admired? good at sports? good at school? rebellious? What else?

- Was my size a factor? my appearance? my abilities or lack of abilities? my gender? my ethnic group? Did I have a nickname?

- Was there a change in me when the other sex was present? when dating began? Was I popular? unwanted? a loner? a party-goer? sought out? ignored?

I now reflect on how much of my present behavior is more understandable in light of these early events.

- Now I think about and then draw all my social groups throughout my life—first with people older than I, then with peers, then with people younger than I or with people of lower status or position. When I complete these drawings, I stand back and observe the evolutionary lines. What roles have I typically played? Which am I good at? Which am I poor at? Which do I enjoy? Which do I avoid?

- How do people typically treat me? In what ways do all people treat me the same? In what ways do certain types of people (of a particular age, gender, and so on) treat me the same?

- How do I expect people to respond to me? What types of reactions do I typically elicit (fatherly, sexual, sisterly, competitive, sympathetic, motherly, helpful, victimized, nasty, critical)?

- Given these memories, I describe the type of leader I would be in order to make the best use of my strengths and most familiar roles.

- As a leader, what would I (initially, at least) want others to take over?

- I keep these pictures in mind as I read the rest of the book.

PART ONE

Developing the Human Element

To begin helping you understand how the Human Element model provides both theory and methods for promoting self-awareness in organizations, Chapter One discusses the model's basic assumptions and its three main dimensions—inclusion, control, and openness. Chapter Two extends those discussions into an exploration of the role that the dimensions play in self-concept (the perceptions I have of myself) and self-esteem (my feelings about those perceptions). Part One sets the stage for seeing how those dimensions of personal behavior and feelings—and the desire to defend them at times—can be used to improve individual performance and group decision making and teamwork, as discussed in Part Two.

1

A New Way of Making Sense of Ourselves and Our Relationships: Inclusion, Control, and Openness

Out beyond ideas of right-doing and wrong-doing.
there is a field. I'll meet you there.   —*Rumi*[1]

The first proposal I submitted for my dissertation at UCLA was to write a theory of personality. My chairman, a kindly man, smiled benignly and told me that perhaps this was a bit ambitious for a young graduate student.

Chagrined, I accepted his verdict and changed my topic, but not my desire. It resurfaced later, when I had a chance to begin to formulate a theory in my research on group dynamics for the Navy during the Korean War.

As I pondered the reasons for the persistence of my interest in overarching theory, I had an interesting memory. When I was around eight years old, I was a rabid baseball fan, as was my father. My hero was Lou Gehrig. I would approach my father in an attempt to prove to him how good Gehrig really was: "He hit .363, had 49 home runs, batted in 165 runs. He's terrific!" My father's response caught me off guard: "Yes, but he can't field." I wasn't prepared for that. From then on, my way of coping with my father's responses was to make sure I knew everything about any topic I wanted to talk to him about. Partly as a defense, I became a holist. I had to make sure I had accounted for everything.

Since my initial attempts at devising a theory of interpersonal behavior, I have been expanding, revising, sharpening, and simplifying it. I find that my understanding goes through three stages. The first is simplistic: *I think the problem is simple because I do not really understand its complexities and subtleties; I was at that stage in graduate school. The next stage is when I appreciate how* complex *the problem is and do complex experiments, trying to take account of many variables all at the same time. Finally, if I study the problem enough and begin to see how it works, the many facets seem to simplify themselves again, in time becoming* profoundly simple; *I believe I am now beginning to catch glimpses of this level in the Human Element theory of human personality and relationships.*

At Esalen and elsewhere, I learned that theory is of scant value unless it works. My quest, parallel to the theoretical one, was to live my ideas. It's fine, for example, to prescribe truth telling as the best mode, but what happens when I try that with my wife? Does it work? Is truth telling just a cute idea that wreaks havoc when actually tried? Living the theory is an ongoing journey, a fascinating one that I suspect will be a part of me from now on. When an idea does not work in my life, I discard it as a theoretical concept. When it does work, I make it part of the theory and test its universality. That's part of holism, and part of the back-and-forth that's so intriguing in the abstraction of theory and the reality of life. Moreover, living the concepts of the theory is a requirement for teaching them to others.

The purpose of this chapter is to present the dimensions of the Human Element model. The chapter begins with a discussion of the model's basic assumptions, drawn from the principles (with one addition) of the human potential movement that I wrote of in Profound Simplicity. *The chapter then examines the three central dimensions of the model and of human functioning—inclusion, control, and openness—which in turn are essential to any understanding of how self-awareness and self-esteem can be enhanced in organizational settings. A case example of an organizational situation illustrates how each dimension operates. Then the chapter explores the role of the dimension within behavior in interpersonal relations and looks at associated feelings. Each of the three "dimension" sections ends with a summary and a Pause for Reflection that asks readers to respond to and think more deeply about the particular dimension and its applicability to their own work and personal lives.*

What's Behind the Human Element Model?

Truth. Truth is the grand simplifier. Relationships—in the long run and, usually, in the short run—are greatly simplified, energized, and clarified when they exist in an atmosphere of truth.

Choice. I choose my own life—my thoughts, feelings, sensations, memories, health, everything—or I choose not to know I have a choice.

Simplicity. The most profound solutions are simple. Simplest is best.[2]

Limitlessness. Human beings have no limits to their potential. Our only limits are limits of belief.

Holism. All aspects of a person (thoughts, behavior, feelings, and the body) are interrelated.

Completion. Effectiveness and joy are enhanced by the completion of unfinished experiences.

Dimensions. The basic dimensions of human functioning are inclusion, control, and openness.

Self-esteem. All behavior derives from self-esteem.

These principles are stated starkly here, without texture, but will be elaborated throughout the book. To illustrate some consequences of these assumptions for organizational life, the next section compares the operating procedures that these principles generate with some current common assumptions and beliefs. The beliefs, though common, are not necessarily shared universally; exceptions occur in some organizations, in parts of some organizations, and among individual leaders and managers. Human relations consultants often recommend practices that are based on the Human Element assumptions described in the following sections, but organizations have generally been slow to adopt those practices.

Self-Esteem

Common belief: Focusing on self-esteem,[3] per se drains energy from productive work. Feel-good activities should be conducted, if at all, on the employee's own time. Work is a place to concentrate on the job, not on personalities.

Human Element assumption: Self-esteem is the core of each person, the center from which all creativity, motivation, and productive work issue. A major aim of the organization is to optimize self-esteem for all employees.

Truth

Common belief: People should tell the truth as they know it, judiciously, taking care to not hurt others' feelings, to preserve privacy, and to avoid vulnerability. Many people can't handle the truth. They become angry, belligerent, or devastated. Managers should avoid telling the direct truth about personnel matters, salaries, imminent firings, and organizational secrets.

Human Element assumption: In most organizations, the number of legitimate organizational secrets is minimal. There are far fewer legitimate secrets than is usually believed. Secrets are poison. The more the organization tells the whole truth, the healthier and more productive it is. People are better able to handle the truth than they are given credit for.

Teamwork

Common belief: Team building is accomplished through the clarifying of team goals and missions, through appreciation and recognition of the validity of a variety of roles (gatekeeper, idea generator, and so on), and styles (analytical, emotive, and so on), and through improved communication and negotiating skills.

Human Element assumption: Poor teamwork does not arise primarily from differences among members but rather from rigidities (that is, attitudes held to rigidly). Rigidities result when people have low self-esteem, are defensive, and are fearful (for example, of being incompetent). To dissolve rigidities and improve teamwork, fears are best dealt with openly and truthfully.

Empowerment

Common belief: Participative management, in which everyone has input into a decision that a leader then makes, is a mechanism for empowering employees.

Human Element assumption: Empowerment is accomplished only through giving power. "Empowerees" participate equally with the leader and the final decision is made only when all agree.

Accountability

Common belief: It is important to have someone accountable for each task. Then responsibility and blame can be assigned when something goes wrong, and the problem can be fixed more quickly.

Human Element assumption: When anything goes wrong, everyone involved is 100 percent responsible, and no one is to blame. Then everyone is on the same team, trying to solve the problem.

Performance Appraisal

Common belief: The manager works with an employee to improve the employee's performance by negotiating the expectations of employment, writing out appraisal criteria, conducting a direct and supportive feedback session, and discussing behavior rather than the person.

Human Element assumption: An employee's performance is largely a function of the relationship between the employee and the manager. Therefore, improvement of performance is more effectively accomplished if the relationship between the two people is improved first.

Change

Common belief: To bring about change, enroll employees in a formal or informal program, set goals, make deadlines, plan procedures, create milestones, build in safeguards, and reward success along the way.

Human Element assumption: These change methods all work if everyone involved has made the basic decision to change. If not, then it's the "diet plan" phenomenon (lose twenty pounds and gain back more). People must learn why they have not wanted to change, what the payoff is for not changing, and what they fear about the new state. If they are clear about all of that and then decide to change, the program will work.

Ethics

Common belief: People act ethically if they avoid temptation, if they are rewarded for ethical behavior, and if they are severely punished for transgressions. Ethics is a matter of character and internal moral fiber, motivated by internal values and authority.

Human Element assumption: If people feel good about themselves, they act ethically and feel pleasure from acting ethically. Ethical behavior that stems from fear is unstable and vulnerable to temptation.

Stress

Common belief: Stress is decreased through reduced workloads, time off, meditation, biofeedback, and psychotherapy. Special consideration should be given to people in high-stress jobs.

Human Element assumption: While these are all useful techniques, they do not reach the central issue: namely, why people choose to feel stress. Some people feel stress in everything they do; others in the same jobs never feel stress. When people become aware that they are choosing stress and uncover the payoff for feeling stressed, they may decide to make a different choice.

Decision Making

Common belief: Decisions should be made objectively, not subjectively. Everyone is to act "professionally" (that is, to overcome feelings).

Human Element assumption: Feelings exist. When everyone handles feelings by being aware of them, expressing them, including them in final decisions, and being conscious of when they are useful and of when they distort, feelings lead to improved creativity.

Leadership

Common belief: The leader should have a vision, enlist people behind the vision, and act decisively and quickly.

Human Element assumption: Leaders should mobilize all the talents of a group, including their own talents. The people most qualified and most affected by a decision make the best decisions, and these decisions are implemented quickly and with a minimum of resistance.

What Are the Basic Dimensions of the Human Element Model?

To make the Human Element assumptions more than just statements, it's important to understand inclusion, control, and openness, the three dimensions central to understanding interpersonal relations and self-concept, and the relations between the two. First, however, let me establish a common fundamental vocabulary for talking about all these concepts.

As I work in organizations, I often feel that there are many different ways to do training and many facets of organizational life, but a few underlying principles can be used to simplify all that variety into a manageable framework. The language that describes self-concept and the relations among people identifies the building blocks of human functioning so that they can be identified, assessed, and perhaps even measured. The language introduced in this section provides the vocabulary for later discussion and application of those building blocks.

There are several candidates for the rubric of "fundamental dimensions of organizational phenomena." Warren Bennis[4] speaks of the importance of feeling *significant* and *competent* and of the central role of *self-esteem* as a trait of leaders. The Johari Window[5] delineates four types of information: what *I know and you know*; what *I know and you do not know*; what *you know and I do not know*; and what *I do not know and you do not know.* The Myers-Briggs type indicator[6] uses the dimensions of *introversion-extroversion, thinking-feeling, perceiving-judging,* and *intuiting-sensing.* Ouchi's Theory Z[7] describes Japanese *consensus decision making.* Robert Blake and Jane Mouton's Managerial Grid[8] includes *concern for production* and *concern for people.* Steven Covey[9] lists the seven habits of effective people: *be proactive, begin with the end in mind, put first things first, think win-win, seek first to understand and then be understood, synergize,* and *sharpen the saw.* Peter Senge[10] describes five disciplines: *systems thinking, personal mastery, mental models, shared vision,* and *team learning.* Statistical approaches to describing the fundamental personality traits now speak of the Big Five (*neuroticism, extraversion, openness, agreeableness,* and *conscientiousness*). Are all these concepts completely different? Is there any overlap? Are different theorists simply looking at different aspects of the same situation? Experience and research have led to the discovery of an underlying set of dimensions that can generate all these management concepts and demonstrate their interconnection. One tool used to help discover underlying dimensions is called *facet design.*[11] Facet design looks for the facets that underlie many different concepts. To illustrate, introversion (Myers-Briggs) and extraversion (Big Five) are *behaviors.* Significance (Bennis) and part of openness (Big Five) are *feelings,* as is concern for production (Blake and Mouton). Concern for people (Blake and Mouton) and shared vision (Senge) are *relationships* between one person and others. Intuiting (Myers-Briggs) is a *decision-making method.* Thus the facets underlying these various concepts and theories include at least the following: behavior, feelings, relationships, and decision-making methods.

As someone trying to develop a theory, I wanted to know whether an underlying structure could show the relationship of all these concepts to each other. I concluded that just as physical space can be described with the use of three dimensions, so also can the human "space" of individuals, relationships, and organizations be described by means of the three dimensions that I have called inclusion, control, *and* openness.[12]

Inclusion: Am I In or Out?

Case Example   While I was consulting at a large paper plant, Irving, a worker on the night shift, was caught asleep. The plant manager was furious and about to fire him. We prevailed on the plant manager to use some of the Human Element methods and call a meeting of all the people affected by this act, in order to come to some agreement about a course of action.

The plant manager, the employee, and the people on his shift all appeared. The discussion revealed that everyone on Irving's shift was having trouble with Irving. Each person had a different complaint.

The group members decided to ask Irving to spend an hour with each person he worked with, hear his or her reactions to him, and work out the problems. If Irving was willing to do that, he would not be fired but would only be docked a day's pay. Irving agreed gladly.

The manager sat back in surprise. He had not known about

these difficulties or about the intense interest in and caring for Irving shown by his co-workers' willingness to help him. When I returned, three months later, Irving came running up to me and gave me a big smile and a hug. He was in charge of the day's schedule. Later I was told that Irving was now one of the most productive workers on any shift and frequently worked extra, on his own time.

Inclusion and Interpersonal Relations

Inclusion, as a concept in interpersonal relations, refers to associations between and among people: the desire to be given attention, to interact, to belong, to be unique. Being unique implies that you are interested enough in me to discover who I am. (Here, let us begin again to use the universal *I*, as discussed in the Preface: "I may be silent and withdrawn" means "Anyone in this situation may be silent and withdrawn.") In the initial testing of a relationship, I present myself to you, to discover what part of myself will interest you. If I'm not sure you care about what I say, I may be silent and withdrawn. Inclusion does not entail strong emotional involvements with individuals. My concern over being included is a preoccupation with prominence, rather than with dominance. Because inclusion is crucial to the process of group formation, it is usually the earliest interpersonal issue in the life of the group. My first decision is whether I want to be a part of the group—whether I want to be *in* or *out*.

My inclusion behavior is a function of two aspects: the rational and the defensive. The rational aspect represents my preference for contact with others. The defensive aspect represents my anxiety about inclusion. The rational aspect is flexible and can adapt to the situation. The defensive aspect is rigid—that is, it does not vary in response to situations—and results in inappropriate behavior (such as the coping and defense mechanisms discussed later in this chapter). I am a mixture of the rational and the defensive, depending on how I feel about myself. The healthier my self-esteem and the greater my self-awareness, the larger role my rational part will play.

When my relations are *undersocial* (characterized by rigid—that is, unvarying—low inclusion, through defensiveness), I am introverted and withdrawn. I want to maintain distance between myself and others. I do not want to become enmeshed with people and thereby lose my privacy. My greatest fear is that people will ignore or abandon me. My deepest anxiety is that I am worthless, insignificant, and unimportant. My unconscious attitude is "Because no one is interested in me, I am not going to risk being ignored. I will ignore them first and get along by myself." Behind my withdrawal is the private feeling that people do not understand me. Unconsciously, I feel that no one has ever considered me important enough to give me attention, and so I must be of little value. I abdicate the pursuit of being *in*.

In contrast, when my relations are *oversocial* (characterized by rigidly high inclusion, through defensiveness), I am extroverted. I seek people incessantly, and I want them to seek me out. I would enjoy going every night to a bar where everybody knows my name. My fear is that people will ignore me. My unconscious attitude is "Although no one is interested in me, I will force them to pay attention to me in any way I can." I seek contact because I cannot bear to be alone. My behavior is designed to focus attention on myself, to make people notice me, to make me prominent. My *direct* method of getting included is to be intense, exhibitionistic, and participative. My *subtle* method is to seek to be powerful, or to be well liked, and to use those traits to gain attention. My anxiety leads me to vacillate between the extremes of being undersocial and oversocial. In a meeting, for example, either I want to be the one presenting the report or I lose interest and may even fall asleep.

When my relations are *social* (characterized by appropriate inclusion), my inclusion problems have been resolved, and my contacts with people present no problems. I am comfortable being with people, and I also enjoy being alone. I am capable of strong commitment to a group, and I can also deal comfortably at a distance when that is appropriate.

Case Example   Before he fell asleep on duty, Irving had felt ignored by his co-workers, and he dealt with this feeling by acting undersocial (although, as later events demonstrated, this was not his preferred mode; he liked being with people, and his undersocial behavior was a defense against his anticipation of being ignored). Having a meeting devoted to him—whether the attention was positive or negative was less important than having people include him—was exhilarating for Irving, and he began to change his attitude toward his co-workers. He felt included at work for the first time.

Inclusion and Feelings of Significance and Aliveness

Underlying my inclusion behavior is the feeling that accompanies my experience of *significance*, as expressed to and received from those around me. I feel that you are significant when you exist for me, are important to me, and have meaning for me. I indicate that I feel you are significant when I pay attention to you, notice your absence, and take account of you. As a person and as a fellow worker, I feel that you regard me as significant when you consider me, talk to me, recognize me, acknowledge me, and act toward me as if I make a difference. Feeling that you think I am significant does not necessarily mean feeling that you regard me as competent or that you like me; for example, there is such a thing as an unpleasant (unlikable), ineffective (incompetent), but significant boss. My fear associated with feeling insignificant is being *ignored,* or abandoned. If you don't think I'm significant, why would you pay any attention to me?

Case Example   The fact that so many people took time off for the meeting and cared enough about Irving to tell him about how they reacted to him (and, obviously, about how they wanted to improve their relations with him and even wanted to help him preserve his job), showed Irving that they felt he was significant. With his low feelings of self-significance, Irving had experienced difficulty seeing that people thought he was important, even when they gave him clear signals to that effect. His inner feeling that he was insignificant had led him to interpret any overtures toward him as negative. His co-workers' caring, and the many who came to express it, surprised Irving but finally broke through to him. It became a source of Irving's greatly increased aliveness, feelings of significance, and motivation to work more effectively. It released abilities that Irving had never revealed before.

When I feel significant within myself, I know that I make a difference, am an important person, am meaningful and worthwhile. When I do not feel significant, I feel unimportant and meaningless; if I lived or died, it would make no difference. My feelings about myself, how I feel about other people, and how I behave toward other people are all connected. To the degree that I feel insignificant, I fear and anticipate that I will be ignored and abandoned: other people can have no interest in such an unimportant person as myself and will therefore act as if I don't exist. This feeling of insignificance is so painful that I often put it out of my consciousness, or I express it unconsciously in my body, through a variety of illnesses.

Feeling insignificant is not the same as other people's feeling that I am insignificant (or, if there were some objective measure, as actually *being* insignificant). I react in terms of my own perceptions of how I feel, regardless of how close they are to other people's perceptions or to how significant I "really" am. Feelings of insignificance come, in large part, from my early years and do not necessarily change as a result of external conditions, since they originate in my own perceptions.

In a class I was teaching, we were discussing self-concept. I mentioned that my chief problem was in the area of significance. I did not feel significant, and I could not ever remember feeling significant. The class members expressed great surprise: "Here you are, a university professor, getting to be known on campus and being important to many students. How could you not feel significant?" In essence, they were right. I was far from a celebrated figure, but I was paid a certain amount of attention, and some people were interested in knowing more about me. Still, I did not feel important. Then I remembered my feelings in high school, when I really was insignificant, as evidenced by the fact that no one had remembered me at the last high school reunion I had attended. Apparently, my perception was stuck in the teenage years, a time when the self-concept frequently solidifies.

When employees feel personally insignificant, and when an organization does not regard them as significant, serious morale problems can result. For example, during a Human Element workshop at a biscuit company in England, it was discovered that all the people in the finance department felt insignificant at work: "The boss never says anything to me in the morning. He just walks right by my desk." The boss, who was in the group, was astonished to hear this: "I didn't know you cared whether I said good morning. I thought you would think I was interfering with your work." It was a problem simple to fix. The boss was delighted to say hello, and the employees were delighted to be greeted. Neither they nor he had recognized the importance of simply being recognized and acknowledged.

Besides knowing that I am significant to others and to myself, to some degree I also experience my own significance as a living being, including my thoughts, feelings, sensations, and movements. This dimension is called *aliveness*. My quest is to be optimally alive—to experience myself so that I can feel the joy that comes from using myself fully, while at the same time choosing to avoid painful experiences as much as possible. If I stop thinking, suppress my feelings, am unaware of my sensations, or do not use my muscles, I limit my experience and am not fully alive. Sometimes I am not as alive as I want to be. I have a dead or tired or blank feeling. When nothing stimulates me, or when I am bored or insensitive to my environment or do not differentiate my sensations, I may take "uppers" in an attempt to feel something and avoid malaise, the feeling of deadness.

At other times, I feel more alive than I want to. Life is too painful. Thinking is too difficult, too unrewarding. Feelings of jealousy, anger, rejection, or humiliation are too much to handle. Sensations are unpleasant. My body hurts, aches, or pains me and is not responsive to what I want it to do. I may take "downers" to zone out and escape my unpleasant experiences. I ask myself, "When was the last time I felt fully alive?" I may answer sadly, "A long time ago." That moment may have been in childhood, or in sports, or in some adventure where there was great and even life-threatening risk. Perhaps this is one reason for the immense popularity of sports and violent, action-oriented movies and entertainment. For many people, peaceful living engenders boredom and lifelessness, which must be compensated for through fantasy. The constancy of war may be attributable to the same phenomenon: unconsciously, we long for enlivening experiences.

When I was a boy, I joined my friends playing football on the corner lot. I would play many hours in the rain, getting injured, bruised, bloodied, and exhausted, and my team would lose. I would elicit no sympathy from my parents. A thoroughly negative experience, right? It hurt, and I lost, and so there was no pleasure of triumph, and there were no accolades. The peculiar thing was, it would never occur to me not to play the next day. Why? Because when I played I felt alive. I was using myself. I was exerting myself physically. I was experiencing a wide range of emotions, more than at almost any other time in my life. I was not motivated by glory or affection. Those motives were there sometimes, but more often they were not. The sense of aliveness is what was compelling.

Sources of aliveness are not limited to active movement. Many people feel most alive when they are meditating, praying, thinking, being in nature, or being alone. Full aliveness can also be present in peace and silence.

Too few organizational climates encourage aliveness. Sadly, few people who are asked, "When was the last time you felt fully alive?"

answer any time when they were at work. Organizations may fail to support aliveness fully because their leaders believe that discipline is difficult to maintain in the midst of aliveness, and that chaos may result. In the former USSR, for example, when Mikhail Gorbachev reduced the traditional forms of suppression, the citizens wanted to become totally free. That energy surge forced Gorbachev out, brought Boris Yeltsin in, and then threatened Yeltsin. As of this writing, Russia still faces the problem of how to allow its citizens to express their long-suppressed energy and channel that force into an effective new pattern without destroying the country.

When organizations encourage creativity and risk taking, the usual methods for maintaining order and decorum are indeed shaken. The issue for the organization, as for each individual, is to achieve a balance between allowing full aliveness and harnessing it in service of orderly procedures. The most pertinent single statement reflecting positive organizational policy and practice regarding aliveness is this one: "I look forward to coming to work." If I look forward to work partly because I feel that I am using my capacities to the fullest and am therefore growing, I feel a certain excitement that is very enlivening. And that has a significant impact on morale, productivity, and the bottom line.

Case Example   When Irving fell asleep, he felt no aliveness: "Nothing meant anything to me. I didn't care what happened to me or to the plant." The meeting with his co-workers energized him and propelled him into feeling more aliveness. Irving's elation at the meeting was due partly to his reassessment of how significant he was. Getting attention from co-workers does not automatically bestow higher self-esteem, but it usually gives pause for thought. Irving began looking to his past, when he had belonged to what was an ethnic minority in his neighborhood. His unstable home life had also led him to believe that he was of no importance. He still had a long way to go, but he began to strengthen his self-concept and to test himself more by taking on and even volunteering for many new tasks and challenges. What had begun as a personal disaster evolved into a growth experience for Irving. As he came to be included in the life of the company and of his co-workers, his interpersonal relations, his feelings of significance, and his sense of aliveness began to change for the better.

Summary of Inclusion

Issue	*In* or *out* (prominence)
Behavior with others	Inclusion
Behavior toward self	Aliveness
Underlying feeling	Significance
Interaction	Encountering or meeting
Interpersonal fear	Being ignored or abandoned
Personal fear	Being insignificant, unimportant, or worthless

Pause for Reflection: Inclusion

The following questions invite me to apply the principle of inclusion to my thinking about the preceding section, my organization, and myself. There are no right or wrong answers. The object is greater awareness.

1. How would my organization have dealt with Irving?
2. How do I feel about the way Irving was treated?
3. How would I describe my organization's approach to inclusion? (High inclusion = many meetings, easy access to others, open spaces; low inclusion = private offices, many walls, few face-to-face meetings.)
4. What are the advantages and disadvantages of the way my organization approaches inclusion? How do I feel that approach should be changed?

5. How important is the issue of significance in my organization? How is it affecting our productivity?

6. How do people react when they first meet me? Do they change over time? If so, how? Why is that?

7. When people react to me as they do to someone in a family, which family member does it tend to be (father, sister, uncle, mother)? What are the characteristics of that family member (a stern father, a supportive mother, a younger sister)?

8. How do others' reactions help me be effective? How do they hinder my effectiveness? (This question asks me to think about significance.)

9. How might I reflect on those patterns? What would I like to change?

10. What do I think of this statement? "People who vacillate between the extremes of calling attention to themselves and of withdrawing, and who have difficulty simply being regular participants, may be concerned about their own significance." Have I ever known anyone like that?

Control: Am I on Top or on the Bottom?

Case Example   A prominent bank lost millions of dollars on bad loans and sent its entire credit department off on a retreat to discover what had gone wrong. Corwin, the deputy director of the department, soon became the center of attention. It was clear to everyone that he was an extremely able man who was often arrogant about his own abilities, as compared to those of the others. He manifested this attitude by micromanaging and by doing virtually everything himself.

Corwin's obvious competence had allowed him to get away with micromanaging for a while, at little cost to productivity. As time went on, however, his subordinates were given no responsibility, so they did not improve their skills, and they began to lose interest in their jobs.

The department members finally expressed this feeling at the retreat. Everyone began to see that the ramifications of Corwin's micromanaging were central to the failure of the department. The work (such as that involved in the bad loans) had become too large and complex for one man to handle, especially since Corwin had been ill during crucial phases of the loan negotiations, and his absence had meant that several normal safeguards were neglected.

When the department members finally acknowledged the issue, they decided to promote a well-liked person to the post of co–deputy director and have that person assign work within the department. Further, in recognition of Corwin's ability, they asked him to turn over one aspect of his job every six months to one of the other members of the department. This would put him in a teaching role. Corwin quietly—and reluctantly—agreed.

After six months, no transfer of Corwin's work had occurred. Corwin was rarely seen around the office, and he finally relocated.

Control and Interpersonal Relations

Control refers to relations of power, influence, and authority between people. If, in an argument, I am seeking inclusion, then I want to be one of the participants in the argument. If I seek control, then I want dominance: I want to be the winner or at least on the winning side. If forced to choose, the inclusion seeker prefers to be a losing participant; the control seeker prefers to be a winning nonparticipant, someone content to observe while fellow team members secure the victory.

Control behavior does not require prominence; inclusion behavior does not require dominance. Control behavior may also be manifested in a person's degree of resistance to being controlled. Expressions of independence or rebellion indicate resistance. Compliance, submission, and willingness to take orders indicate acceptance of being controlled.

Preferences for controlling others and for being controlled are not necessarily related. I may be a "company man" who prefers both to control my subordinates and to be controlled by my superiors. I may prefer to control and not be controlled, like an authoritarian middle manager who rebels against top management. I may prefer a flat power structure, where no one gives anyone orders. I may prefer to follow orders but be reluctant to give them. Sometimes a subordinate prefers to be the "power behind the throne," simultaneously fulfilling the desires for control and low inclusion (conversely, the office comedian is an example of a high-inclusion person with a low desire for control).

Control problems usually arise after a group has formed and relationships have begun to develop. People seek or take different roles (leader, helper, joker, opponent, conciliator), and power struggles, competition, and influence become central issues. Typical interactions around control involve confrontation or deliberate avoidance of confrontation. Most problems in organizations initially appear to be control issues — power struggles, turf protection, factions, undermining — but these symptoms often turn out to be, at bottom, issues of either inclusion or openness.

As with inclusion, there is a rational and a defensive aspect to my behavior with control. The rational part involves my preference for a certain amount of control over my life; the defensive part comes from my fear of being helpless or of being overwhelmed with responsibility. The rational part is flexible and can adapt to the situation. The defensive part is rigid, regardless of circumstances. I am a mixture of rational and defensive. The higher my self-awareness and self-esteem, the more my behavior is rational and not defensive.

When I am an *abdicrat* (rigidly low in control, through defensiveness), I abdicate my power. I take a subordinate position, in which I will not be expected to take responsibility or make decisions. I want other people to relieve me of my obligations. I don't control others, even when that would be appropriate. If I'm the boss, for example, I don't do what is necessary to correct the parts of my operation that aren't working. I delay and procrastinate. I never make a decision that I can "kick upstairs," and the buck never stops with me.

When I am an *autocrat* (rigidly high in control, through defensiveness), I am dominating in the extreme. My *direct* method is to seek power and compete. I am afraid that others will not be influenced by me—that they will in fact dominate me. My underlying feeling is the same as that of the abdicrat: I am not capable. To compensate for this feeling, I keep trying to prove that I *am* capable, with the result that I take on too much responsibility and am frequently burned out. My *indirect* method for getting control is to be wily, seductive, or misleading.

When I am a *democrat* (appropriate in control), it is because in my childhood I successfully resolved my issues with control, so that power and control present no problems. I feel comfortable giving or not giving orders, taking or not taking orders—whatever is appropriate to the situation. Unlike the abdicrat and the autocrat, I am not preoccupied with fears of my own helplessness, stupidity, or incompetence. I feel competent, and I am confident that other people trust my ability to make decisions.

Case Example   After the retreat, discussions with Corwin revealed that, contrary to his outward appearance, he was insecure about his competence. His father had held him to high standards, which Corwin had internalized, along with the belief that he could never meet those standards. Corwin's way of dealing with his anxiety was a common response. First, he tried to run everything—micromanage—in a desperate attempt to convince everyone, primarily himself, that he was indeed competent. Corwin became an autocrat, with the almost inevitable burnout that being an autocrat eventually entails. When he failed, he went to the other end of the continuum and became an abdicrat, doing nothing that might reveal any weakness in his abilities, and finally leaving the department. Neither response was appropriate to the situation.

Control and Feelings of Competence and Choice

Competence   Underlying control behavior is the experience that accompanies feeling or not feeling competent. *Competence* typically has to do with the ability to make decisions and solve problems. I am competent if I have the capacity to cope with the world, satisfy my desires, avoid catastrophes, hold a job, be self-sufficient, and acquire sufficient material goods. I feel that you regard me as competent when you give me responsibility and allow me to undertake difficult tasks on my own. Awards, as well as compliments on the quality of my work and accomplishments, tell me that you feel I am competent. Feeling that you regard me as competent does not necessarily mean feeling that you regard me as significant or likable. For example, there are obnoxious yet efficient clerks.

The fear associated with feeling incompetent is the fear of being humiliated, embarrassed, or vulnerable. When I feel competent, I feel intelligent, strong, harmonious, and capable of coping with the issues of living. When I feel incompetent, I feel the opposite: weak, chaotic, impotent, and unable to cope with life. I feel that I need a great deal of help and direction from others if I am going to make it in the world, and even then I am unsure. To the degree that I feel incompetent, I fear and anticipate being humiliated as soon as people find out (as they inevitably will) that I am a phony: I don't know what I should know, I can't do what I should be able to do, and people can't rely on me. Like feelings of insignificance, the feeling of incompetence and the fear of humiliation may be so great that I put some of those feelings into my unconscious and defend myself from awareness of them. Feeling competent must come from inside. Having reinforcement from outside helps, but it does not get to the heart of my feelings of incompetence.

Case Example   Corwin was stuck. His underlying feelings of being incompetent, which were not objectively justified, led him to identify every idea he proposed as *his* idea, not just one possible solution. It was vital for him to be right all the time, since being wrong immediately reinforced his unconscious belief that he was incompetent. With that much anxiety about his performance, it was very difficult for Corwin to look at each problem on its own and see that sometimes he did have the best idea, but if someone else did, that did not mean that Corwin was inadequate. Rigidity and defensiveness like Corwin's play a very large role in organizational conflict and inefficiency, since competence is so often the currency of social interaction.

Choice Central to the dimension of control is *choice* (also called *self-determination*, or *autonomy*). I am fully self-determining when I choose my whole life—my behavior, my thoughts, my feelings, my illnesses, my body, and my reactions. I am not self-determining when I act as if my life were decided by external forces—luck, coincidence, fate, synchronicity, the economy, the environment, society, my parents, heredity, my childhood, the law, predestination, my boss, the organization.

Sometimes I wish something or someone would tell me what to do. I feel overburdened. I would prefer to be more like a child and less like a responsible adult: "Please offer me a job, and choose my career path for me." "Please initiate a divorce, and relieve me of the guilt of initiating it."

Sometimes I feel that I do not choose my life enough. I never seem to be doing what I want to be doing. I feel under obligation to someone or something. I feel blocked from getting what I want by someone or something stronger than I am.

No one has yet tested the limits of human capacity, but a key factor in extending capacity is to assume that I determine my own life and am capable of making any changes I wish in myself, in my relationships, and in my work situation. As a pragmatic statement, this gives me a way of operating that can allow me to avoid and transcend self-imposed limitations. If I preclude nothing, then I put my energy into figuring out how to succeed. As Henry Ford once said, "If you think you can, or you think you can't, you're right." If I start out by assuming some things are unchangeable, then I am imposing limitations before I even try.

The concept of choice has nothing to do with morality; self-determination is not being considered here in the context of what is good or proper or moral or responsible or right. Instead, the focus is on the consequences of choice. What is the result of assuming that I determine what happens? Consider the results of this assumption: "I choose my own life, and I always have. I choose my behavior, my feelings, my thoughts, my fears, my stresses, my body, my illnesses, my reactions, and my emotions, including what I think of as spontaneous responses, such as anger."

Case Example   Corwin vacillated between feeling omnipotent (he could do anything) and discouraged (people would not let him do what he wanted to). He had not yet reached the point of looking inside himself and discovering how he was choosing his situation. He was subject to a common confusion, probably resulting from his relationship with his father: he confused being *able* to do something with being *required* to do it. He didn't realize that even though he was capable of doing a particular job, he didn't have to do it. This confusion helped lead Corwin to his micromanaging. With no concept of choice, he was seeing himself as a victim of his situation.

The aspects of choice are worth considering in some depth because they affect behavior so dramatically. Since my choices can be conscious or unconscious, I may choose not to be aware of feelings that I do not want to deal with, or of unacceptable thoughts, or of connections between events (for example, feeling tired after not expressing my feelings). I may hide my true feelings from myself by relegating them to my unconscious.

The unconscious (or the unaware) is simply all those events, feelings, traits, and defenses I choose not to be aware of. Unconscious choice works like a program that I install in my computer and then forget about. From that moment on, the program can affect every output—and not in ways I would anticipate. The computer keeps running the program, whether I use it deliberately or forget that I've installed it.

To make sense of the output (my behavior and feelings), I must find a way to remember (become aware of) the forgotten program. Since I choose my unconscious, I also can choose to make it conscious—that is, to deal directly with issues, feelings, and behavior that I might prefer not to address. I can then either remove the program of unconscious choice or take it into account in everything I do from now on.

Once I accept that I determine my own life, everything is different. I accept my power. I am in control of my life. If I assume the concept of choice, I must alter my understanding of many key concepts, such as group pressure, manipulation, using people, brainwashing, and scapegoating. All these terms imply that something is being done to me; but, according to the choice principle, I am *allowing* something to be done to me. I may use these terms to blame others for what I allow to be done to myself, but in fact I cannot be pressured or brainwashed or manipulated or used unless I allow myself to be.

This point of view has profound implications for work relations and especially for conflicts. If I feel that my boss is manipulating me—for example, making me feel guilty for not taking on a particular assignment—I can take an extra step. I can ask myself, "What am I doing to allow my boss to make me feel guilty? What am I getting out of feeling guilty?" I may conclude that I am choosing to feel guilty because that lets me feel like a conscientious employee who wants to do a good job; the alternative is to feel slothful and indifferent to my performance.

If these statements seem strong, consider again the reasons for assuming self-determination. Choice is a pragmatic operating principle that allows me to devote all my energy to doing what I want to do, rather than wasting it on finding reasons for why I'm not doing what I want to do. As a practical matter, it can provide options that may not have occurred to me before. If I find these assumptions about choice unacceptable, I can simply reject them, and I'll be back where I began.

From the standpoint of the choice principle, fears can be seen in a different way. I may say that I am afraid of my boss, or of rejection, or of sharks. But, to be consistent with the principle of choice, I cannot really say that I'm afraid of those external threats. Rather, I am afraid of my inability to cope with my boss, or rejection, or sharks. As long as I see you as the cause of my fear, I spend my time trying to change, criticize, avoid, or destroy you—all actions that are unproductive. Suppose I dread seeing you come into my office because you talk all the time. In truth, I really dread your visit because I don't feel able to cope with you. Once I am willing to ask you to leave when I do not want you there, my dread disappears. Once I see that my fear is in me, I can work to improve my ability to cope or to become aware of other choices.

Similarly, stress is not only a function of "stressors" (events in the environment that supposedly cause stress, such as heavy workloads, deadlines, loud noises, and conflicting demands) but also a function of how I interpret and react to them. There is nothing inherent in my life situation that requires me to feel pressure. I choose to interpret what I experience as stress. Whatever my circumstances are, they just are. I'm the one who labels them as stressful. Nothing is stressful to me unless I interpret it as stressful. If I feel I'm responsible for everyone around me, I quickly burn out. I have difficulty delegating or letting my children decide for themselves. I keep all decisions to myself, including decisions I am not aware of. Understanding clearly where choice resides in each situation is one of the surest ways to reduce stress.

Example   Eddie Murray, the baseball player, was asked by a reporter how he handled the stress and pressure of the pennant race and the World Series.

"Everyone is counting on you, Eddie, to come through for the team," the reporter said. "You know that if you don't, your job, your salary, and your career may be in jeopardy. When it comes down to September and October, every game, every time you are at bat, may make the difference between winning the championship and being a loser."

"I make my own pressure," Murray answered.

Or, as the basketball player Charles Barkley replied to a similar question, "Pressure is in tires."

One of the biggest benefits of an organization's adopting the choice principle is a change in how members of the organization view accountability. Differences of opinion about what is wrong in work situations usually evolve into blaming. The boss blames the worker for doing a sloppy job. Marketing blames the mailroom for inefficiency. Middle management blames the president for poor organization. Stockholders blame the board for lack of long-range planning. All this energy spent on assigning blame is rarely productive, because workers defend their own behavior and find as much fault as possible with others' actions. When people spend their energy assigning and avoiding blame, they do not have energy to devote to being more creative and productive.

But if everyone is choosing, then anything that happens between us is the result of a collusion[13] between us, and so blaming is irrelevant. Accountability takes on a different meaning when it is assumed that everyone involved in any given situation is 100 percent responsible for whatever has happened, and that no one is to blame. Each person involved in an outcome could have done something that would have led to a more positive result, and each relationship could have been changed to lead to a more favorable outcome.

Accepting responsibility without assigning blame is crucial to conflict resolution. It allows us to look objectively at each person's contribution to the outcome of any given situation. If I am aware of the effect of my feelings and actions on our situation, then I can see my contribution to our difficulties more clearly. We both can see a difficulty between us as a problem to be solved, not as a situation for which to assign blame. We see ourselves as being on the same side, against a common enemy—the problem. We can then figure out how to modify our positions and improve the situation, rather than attacking each other and defending ourselves. As Michael Crichton's narrator observes in the novel *Rising Sun,* "The Japanese try to fix the problem; the Americans try to fix the blame."

Example   A lending company rewarded its employees with individual bonuses that were based on management's judgment of how each person had performed. The result was fierce competition and undercutting. When a loan fell through, the marketing department blamed the credit department for being too conservative. The credit department accused the accounting department of taking too long to provide the needed data. Accounting accused marketing of cutting corners to make the loan. Accusations filled the air.

The suggestion was made that bonuses be assigned equally to all personnel, depending on the productivity of the company as a whole. Immediately the atmosphere changed. After considerable discussion, some people in marketing acknowledged that they did sometimes go ahead a bit recklessly to please customers and receive commissions. Credit personnel admitted that they sometimes were overcautious because they were afraid of being fired. Several people in accounting conceded that they felt ignored and therefore dragged their feet as a way of getting even.

As soon as all the people involved acknowledged their part, an air of enthusiasm took over, and new procedures evolved. Marketing and credit scheduled regular meetings to balance risk taking with caution. Procedures were developed on the assumption that it was to everyone's advantage for the whole team to be productive. Some of the problems were individual (marketing's desire to please, credit's fear of being fired), and some were relational (accounting's fear of being ignored by marketing, credit's feeling of being held back by accounting). All problems were minimized when the change in the reward system reduced blaming.

The concept that all choices have payoffs is basic to self-determination. Even when I'm not entirely aware of it, I make a particular choice because I anticipate a particular payoff. I may feel guilty because guilt makes me appear to be responsible and to care about the consequences of my actions. When I feel guilty for taking a vacation and leaving my children with a relative, I may be striving unconsciously to look like a conscientious and caring parent. I may choose to feel confused about an important business decision because, unconsciously, I will feel relieved of the responsibility to make a decision and thereby alienate some people. Typical payoffs in a work situation involve gaining sympathy from others, being held to lower work expectations, and looking better.

The choice principle reorients my search for solutions. Before when things did not go well, I blamed others and cursed the fate that made me a victim of circumstances. When I assume that I choose a situation, I go beyond blaming. I look for the payoffs I get for creating the situation in which I find myself. I do not blame myself. I simply look for what I'm getting out of the situation, whether I think the payoff is positive or negative.

Summary of Control

Issue	*Top* or *bottom* (dominance)
Behavior with others	Control
Behavior toward self	Self-determination, choice
Underlying feeling	Competence
Interaction	Confronting
Interpersonal fear	Being humiliated, embarrassed, vulnerable
Personal fear	Being incompetent, incapable, phony

Pause for Reflection: Control

1. In my organization, do I know someone like Corwin?

2. How has my organization dealt with individuals like Corwin? How would I deal with Corwin?

3. How would I describe my organization's approach to issues of control? Does it have an atmosphere of high control—strict hierarchy, decisions from the top, tight schedules, enforcement of rules? Or does it have an atmosphere of low control—relaxed atmosphere, distributed decision making, consensus-type management? What are the advantages and disadvantages of the type of atmosphere in my organization?

4. What are the main reactions that others have to my competence when they first meet me? Do these reactions change over time? If so, how?

5. Has anyone ever said that I am too controlling? What truth is there in that observation? If I feel that it is not true, why do I think someone else thought it was?

6. Has anyone ever said that I am not controlling enough? What truth is there in that observation? If I feel that it is not true, why do I think someone else thought it was?

7. How important is the issue of competence in my organization? How does it affect productivity?

8. Do I ever diminish my own competence through some emotional concern I have? How and why?

9. What are five stresses and problems in my life that I could eliminate by adopting the principle of choice or self-determination?

10. What do I think of this statement? "People who vacillate between the extremes of taking responsibility for almost everything and taking responsibility for nothing, and who have difficulty simply taking their share of responsibility, may be concerned about their own competence." Have I ever known anyone like that?

Openness: Am I Open or Closed?

Case Example   Ophelia was technically very competent, but her managerial skills were strangely deficient. Her team members were never clear about what she wanted. She gave them leeway to use their own judgment and creativity, and she did not dictate what they were to do. That sounded good to her team members, but something just wasn't working well. Nevertheless, they all agreed not to discuss the problems, because they all liked Ophelia and didn't want to hurt her feelings.

Then a crisis arose. Owen, a programmer, was doing a terrible job and dragging morale down. He lied, did not keep his agreements, missed work, and attacked other people on the job with outrageous charges about their behavior. Owen felt that everyone else was against him and that he was completely misunderstood, just as he had been on his last job. Ophelia did not want to make an issue of Owen, and so she offered him the opportunity for more training, which he refused. Ophelia continued to befriend Owen and give him encouragement, but she was unwilling to take any strong action to remedy the situation. Morale continued to go down, and confusion about the team's mission continued.

Ophelia felt bad about the situation and tried to make it better by having a party for everyone. The party was an embarrassing failure. Fewer than half of the group appeared, and those who did come left early. Owen did not appear. Ophelia did not know what to do next.

Openness and Interpersonal Relations

The third basic dimension of the Human Element is *openness*— that is, the degree to which I am willing to be open to another person. Openness varies across time, among individuals, and within relationships.

Sometimes I enjoy a relationship in which you and I share our feelings, our secrets, and our innermost thoughts. I enjoy having one person—or, at most, a few people—in whom I confide.

At other times I avoid being open with others. I would rather keep things impersonal, and I prefer to have acquaintances rather than a few close friends. I have some desire both for open relations and for more privacy.

Because openness is based on building deeper ties, it usually is the last phase to emerge in the development of a human relationship or of relations within a group. Inclusion involves how much we want to encounter each other, as well as our decision to continue our relationship or not. Control issues are concerned with the degree to which we confront one another and work out how we will relate. As the relationship continues, openness has to do with the degree to which we literally or figuratively embrace each other.

As with inclusion and control, my behavior with openness is a function of two aspects: the rational and the defensive. The rational part results from my preference for a certain amount of openness in my life. The defensive aspect results from my fear of being too open and thus vulnerable to being rejected and unloved. When I am flexible and rational, I can adapt to different situations. When I am rigid and defensive, I react the same way to all circumstances. I am some mixture of the rational and the defensive, depending on how I feel about myself. The worse I feel, the more defensive I am.

When my interpersonal relations are *underpersonal* (rigidly low in openness, through defensiveness), I avoid revealing myself to others. I maintain one-to-one relationships on a superficial, distant level, and I am most comfortable when other people do the same with me. I maintain emotional distance and do not become emotionally involved. I am afraid that no one likes me, and I anticipate not being liked. I have great difficulty genuinely liking people, and I distrust their feelings toward me. My unconscious attitude is "Openness in my life has led to very painful rejections. Therefore, I shall avoid that pain by not opening up in the future." My *direct* technique is to avoid closeness, by being antagonistic and rejecting if necessary. My *subtle* technique is to be superficially friendly to everyone, even seeking to be "popular," with my popularity acting as a safeguard against my becoming especially open to any one person.

When I am *overpersonal* (rigidly high in openness, through defensiveness), I tell everyone about my feelings, and I want everyone to do the same with me. My unconscious feeling is "My first experiences with openness were painful, but perhaps if I try again they will turn out better." Being liked is essential to me. My *direct* technique is to attempt to gain approval by being extremely personal, ingratiating, intimate, and confiding. My *subtle* technique is to be manipulative and possessive as I punish any attempts my friends make to establish other friendships.

When I am *personal* (appropriately open) and have successfully resolved issues of openness in childhood, my level of interaction with others varies with the individual and the circumstances. I am comfortable in a close relationship, as well as in a situation that requires distance. I feel comfortable both giving and receiving affection. I enjoy being liked, but if I am not liked, I can accept that this simply means that someone does not like me; I do not generalize from this one reaction and conclude that I am unlovable.

Case Example   Owen exhibited underpersonal behavior in the sense of pushing people away by being antagonistic. In response, the group did the same thing by avoiding him. By not dealing directly with the issue that was preoccupying everyone, the group maintained a facade of peace. In fact, however, everyone was quite unhappy, angry, irritated with Owen, and disappointed in Ophelia. But no one said anything.

Openness and Feelings of Self-Liking

When I like myself, I enjoy my own company. I feel good about who I am, and I feel that if people knew everything about me, they would like who I am.

When I do not like myself, I do not enjoy who I am. I am ashamed of how I behave and how I feel. My impulses and desires are unacceptable, and I believe that anyone who knew everything about me would be revolted and would despise me. To the degree that I feel unlikable (or unlovable), I fear and anticipate rejection. I fear that the more people get to know me, the more they will not like me. Keeping a personal distance from people and keeping secrets feels safer — temporarily, at least.

To some degree, I feel somewhat likable and somewhat unlikable. Often I suppress the parts of myself I do not like, including feelings, thoughts, past events, and such desires as lust and violence, and I put them in my unconscious. Suppression is painful, and the experience of it usually leads me to avoid situations in which I must confront undesirable feelings. My attempts to avoid the pain of experiencing the negative self-concept give rise to defensive behavior and, in many cases, to illness.

Example   As a manager, Eric was a constant source of frustration and anger. He was dictatorial, curt, rigid, personally remote, and unapproachable. Every once in a while, he would smile or attempt a joke. All his employees would feel elated, only to be deflated in the next moment by more of Eric's rejecting behavior.

A long campaign convinced Eric to attend a workshop. After fierce resistance, he settled down and began to listen to how his behavior was affecting everyone else. He seemed truly sad and stunned. He felt that no one liked him, but he believed it really did not matter how he behaved, so long as he did his job.

As the workshop progressed, Eric told about his relationship with his father, who had always been too busy for him, and whom he saw as constantly rejecting him. This and other earlier experiences had led Eric to feel very unlovable.

The workshop went deep enough for Eric to safely reevaluate himself and see that he was not nearly as bad as he had thought he was. His group reinforced this perception and was rewarded by seeing more and more of the smiling, joking, considerate Eric. The quality of the group's work improved dramatically. A few months later, Eric was selected to lead the project on which the future of the company depended.

Likability and lovability are areas that often overlap with home life. Hard-driving executives who have always felt that business was no place for emotions and close friendships, and who pride themselves on their objectivity, often become motivated to look at themselves and their impact on others only after they are divorced or have problems with their children. They realize that feelings have a strong impact on behavior. Working (and living) with a self-loathing person can be very toxic, as well as extremely inefficient and unproductive.

Openness and Truth

Underlying the behavior of openness is the feeling of being likable or unlikable, lovable or unlovable. I find you likable if I like myself in your presence, if you create an atmosphere within which I like myself. I feel you like me when you confide in me, are friendly toward me, respond warmly to my overtures, and seek my friendship. When I feel that you like me, I do not necessarily feel that you regard me as significant or competent. For example, there exist charming and attractive (likable) people who are inept (incompetent) and unemployed (socially less significant). The fear associated with feeling unlikable or unlovable is the fear of being rejected, disliked, or despised.

Issues of openness to myself (that is, my self-awareness) and my openness to others are strongly intertwined. I can't be open with you meaningfully if I'm not open to myself. If I don't know what is happening within me, I can hardly communicate it to you accurately. I may be open to myself, but not to you, if I fear being vulnerable or rejected. If I persist in this stance, I may get out of touch with my own truth, through dissembling: I may distort or withhold so much that I no longer know my own feelings.

Self-awareness requires that I allow myself to know and be conscious of everything I am experiencing. I do not censor my experience when it does not fit my picture of myself.

Sometimes I am too aware. I may have experiences—for example, knowing I have been fired for incompetence, even though I have been told that the reason is economic conditions—when I would prefer not to be aware of my pain and discomfort. At other times, I feel too unaware. Things happen that I don't understand. I feel I'm deluding myself. I tell myself I'm one kind of person, and yet I seem to act in quite the opposite way in many circumstances.

In organizations, lack of openness leads to enormous inefficiency and reduced productivity. Human Element consulting experiences indicate that about 80 percent of work problems are not real problems at all. They are simply the results of not being open—of distorting or withholding. This realization is shocking, since the conventional organizational wisdom assumes that getting along means being strategic, judicious, discreet, and selective about being truthful, especially when it comes to such issues as salaries.

Example A large division of a finance company was in trouble. The division's productivity and morale were very low. Management called in a consultant.

The major complaint of the vice president heading this division was the salary procedure. Each year, the seven managers under him would march individually into his office and present evidence to show why they should receive higher salaries. The vice president in turn would marshal his forces to show them why their raises should be somewhat lower. This process took several months and frequently ended with some of the managers feeling bitter and resentful. "Truly," the vice president said, "this whole process is a nightmare, probably the worst part of my job."

Since everyone in the division agreed that this was the major problem, the consultant decided to focus on resolving it in the three days allotted for the consultation. He began by asking the managers if they would be willing to be open about their salaries: "Would each of you be willing to tell how much you make?" The response was a resounding *no*. The consultant had asked them to violate one of the cardinal rules of organizational life: "It's a private matter. It's nobody's business. I don't even tell my wife." And so on.

Much of this resistance came from the managers' claim that they could have no idea of how much everyone else was worth, since, after all, they did not work very closely together. Finally, however, they agreed to try determining everyone's worth.

They started with criteria and constructed many lists of traits for determining worth. None of the lists helped. After two and a half days, the consultant suggested a compromise. Everyone knew the total amount of money that was available for salaries for the seven managers and the vice president. The consultant asked if everyone would be willing to write down privately how he or she would divide the total among these eight people. Everyone agreed. The consultant collected the written allocations and wrote the results on a blackboard for everyone to see.

Everyone was astonished. With two minor differences, everyone agreed almost exactly on the salary that each person should get. After a brief discussion, the group adjusted the salary of a modest manager upward and that of an overambitious one downward, with all the managers in agreement.

The group stared at the board for several minutes. Slowly, the members began to realize what they had accomplished. In thirty minutes, through being open about their attitudes toward salaries, they had solved their horrendous, constant "problem." In the process, they discovered several things. First, revealing their salaries was not threatening. Second, everyone knew everyone else's salary anyway, within a few thousand dollars. Third, being open about how they felt about their own worth and that of others led to better working relationships. Fourth, they were all aware of how much they felt each person was worth.

This procedure allowed them to realize how they felt—it increased their self-awareness. Their openness had the effect of freeing up great amounts of company time and energy, and it all but eliminated resentment and deception. This "nightmare" of a problem would actually require only about thirty minutes a year to solve, if they were willing to be open.

Case Example   Self-deception was a very large factor with Owen and Ophelia, and it was also something of a factor with the other group members. Owen apparently had little or no awareness of how he antagonized other people and came to be misunderstood so often. Instead of acquiring more self-insight, he spent much of his energy blaming and being angry. The key to his becoming a valuable team member would be his willingness to become more aware—to tell himself the truth about his own contribution to his dismal situation. Ophelia didn't want to see what was happening, because then she would have to take an action that was even more difficult for her. She was operating from great personal fear. The team members, too, were refusing to look at their own impotent behavior and at what might have been preventing them from taking action.

Self-Awareness and Truth Telling

The rest of this section explores self-awareness as an aspect of truth and openness, in order to make a case for why openness, along with choice, is central to the Human Element approach. Here are some pertinent terms (some of them have been defined before):

- *Experience* is the state of every cell of my body—my memories, my thoughts, my feelings, my sensations. I'm *open* to myself when I allow myself to know my experience, and I am open to others when I tell them my experience.

- *Self-awareness* is the extent to which I let myself know my own experience. If I'm afraid of, ashamed of, or guilty about some things that have to do with me, I may repress or deny them. The part of my experience that I choose not to let myself know about can be called my unaware part, or my *unconscious*. When I'm aware of my experience, I can decide consciously what I want to do. When I'm not aware of my experience, it may control me in a way I do not understand. Bringing my unconscious experience into my awareness is one of my objectives in reading and working with this book.

- If I choose to tell you about what I am aware of, I am *self-disclosing*. If I choose to tell you something contrary to my awareness (that is, something that I do not believe is true), I am *distorting* or *lying*. If I choose not to tell you something I am aware of, I am *withholding*.

- To be fully *open* or *truthful* and thus communicate my experience to you, I must be both self-aware and self-disclosing. Self-disclosure without self-awareness is what can be called the "sincere politician" syndrome: I self-disclose but have not allowed myself much self-awareness, and so what comes out is usually boring; I do not present myself fully because I am not aware of my total experience. For instance, if I tell you (and have convinced myself) that I believe strongly in wide participation in decision making, but everyone sees my authoritarian behavior, I come across as unreal.

- Self-awareness without self-disclosure is what can be called the "whatever it takes to win" syndrome: I am quite aware of myself and my desires, but I choose not to be open with other people. To give myself an advantage, I lie about or withhold what I do know.

Telling the truth sounds like a good idea. It has been espoused for millennia. But most people do not believe in it for an instant, and they make their way through this contradiction by inventing euphemisms and rationales for lying: *tact, diplomacy, white lies, business is business, spin control,* and *being realistic*. Manners and protocol systems discourage self-disclosure: "Act in the prescribed way, whether or not you really feel like it." Lack of truth telling is even justified with a bit of moralizing: "Don't hurt people's feelings." Even as truth is espoused, the implication is that withholding and distorting are the preferred forms of communication. Society reinforces lying and the idea that human beings are too weak to deal with the truth. But wherever the Human Element workshop has been tried and deeper levels of truth have been reached, it has become quite clear that people can handle far more truth than is generally believed, and with very profitable results.

The current, ongoing controversy over ethics and credibility in organizations is really an issue of truth or openness. After years of tolerating distortion and secrecy in all aspects of organizational life—governmental, religious, corporate—the public is becoming more alert to and intolerant of such behavior. With the resurrection of the truth principle in organizations, ethical deficiencies may be greatly reduced, and organizations may become more profitable, more fair, and more pleasant to work in. The breakthrough in this area is twofold. First, many old clichés turn out to be absolutely correct. The truth *does* set me free—organizationally, interpersonally, personally, and bodily. Second, the tools and techniques—specifically, feedback, imagery, and understanding of the body—are available to test the effects of self-disclosure and of withholding on the body, on relationships, and on performance in organizations. When I am open, my body feels good. Distortion or withholding expresses itself in my body as some form of discomfort—shortness of breath, neck pain, tightness in the stomach, sweaty palms, a dry throat, a headache—and expresses itself as well by creating distance in relationships, loss of motivation, burnout, illness, absenteeism, and declining productivity on the job. The more open I am, the healthier I am. As I become more alert to how much I pay for lying and withholding, in terms of energy, health, and mental clarity, I open myself to the possibility of an atmosphere of greater truth.

Truth telling is probably the single most cost-effective and simplest way to make major leaps in organizational productivity and worker satisfaction. But many people in organizations find the prospect of increased truth telling ridiculous: "If I ever told people, especially my boss, what I really think of them, I would be long gone." That's probably correct if truth telling, as is commonly thought, means name calling—saying what someone else (like a boss) is really like, and if the message is negative. We often turn to tact: "If the message is conveyed in a softened, sensitive, politically astute manner, I can tell my boss what I want without getting fired." Being tactful often means shading the truth, so that it is not quite as clear to the listener as it is to the speaker.

But name calling isn't really about a very deep truth. In fact, the most superficial level of truth is what *I* say about *you*. I can deepen the truth that I tell by moving away from naming your faults and toward paying attention to what *I* experience—that is, toward more self-awareness. The most superficial levels of truth are *self-deception* (no self-awareness) and *withholding* (no self-disclosure). Neither level expresses any openness at all. In self-deception, I don't tell you, and I don't tell myself. In withholding, I let myself know, but I don't tell you. These two levels account for such an extraordinarily high percentage of communication that reducing their prevalence alone would lead to much straighter communication and higher productivity.

To move to deeper levels of truth and openness, you and I must learn to speak to each other about the feelings we have *at each level.* Then we can move more quickly toward greater depth of self-awareness and self-disclosure and get to the feelings that are causing our conflict or disagreement (see Table 1.1).

Here is an example that shows the practical importance of the levels of truth or openness. Suppose a colleague parks in my parking space. I am inconvenienced and very angry with her. I believe that the problem is largely her fault, and that the resolution will come if I can show her that what she did was wrong and convince her to apologize and change. She, by contrast, is equally convinced that she was justified in parking there, and she wants to help me see the error of my ways. This scenario is frequent in disagreements, from international affairs to labor-management differences to work struggles to marital squabbles, but it has never led to notably successful resolutions. One major reason is that neither side exhibits much self-awareness. But if I have more self-awareness, I realize how likely it is that I'm not *all* right and that my colleague is not *all* wrong. Further, I understand that when our disagreement arouses strong feelings in

Table 1.1. Levels of Truth.

Level	Indication	Description
− 1	Self-deception	State of withholding my experience from both you and myself. The unconscious level—all that I choose not to let myself know and therefore can't tell you.
0	Withholding (silence)	I am aware of something important but do not express it directly to you. This is the overwhelming proportion of my feelings. Many rationalizations—"It's not tactful." "It wouldn't do any good." "I might get fired." "He can't do anything about it anyway." "I may be wrong." "It's none of your business." "I don't want to hurt you."
1	"You are . . . (. . . a jerk)."	Expressing an opinion about you, even name calling, is a step toward openness. I focus on *you*. I am a critic, but I am showing more self-awareness. If I stop here, though, I'm likely to get into trouble.
2	"Toward you I feel . . . (. . . dislike)."	I express my feelings toward you, which requires self-awareness. I switch focus from what *you do* to how *I feel* toward you. I could still get into trouble.

3	"Because you . . . (. . . don't answer calls)."	The rational and rationalizations level. I report *your* action that is the basis for *my* feeling; it explains and justifies me. Here, I can begin a dialogue with you, and so there is less threat.
4	"I think you feel I . . . (. . . am insignificant)."	I generalize and imagine that you feel I am insignificant, incompetent, or unlikable. I am not fully aware of that feeling but am *becoming* more self-aware. I often feel that I am a victim, but there is now a real possibility for us to align our perceptions through useful dialogue.
5	"I fear I am . . . (. . . insignificant)."	I recognize *my fears about myself* (feeling insignificant, incompetent, and/or unlikable). I perceive that *this is how I feel about myself* (before this level, I preferred to attribute that feeling to you, rather than to myself). If I have this much self-awareness, I probably will not get into trouble with you, because I recognize that my negative feeling has to do primarily with myself, not with you.

me, there are probably other factors operating than the narrow ones involved in this incident. If my colleague and I continue to discuss my parking space, however, we are both in for a long harangue.

Breaking through the bickering, I realize I feel she is *very thought-less* (level 1 — "You are . . . ") and *I do not like that* about her (level 2 —

"Toward you I feel . . ."). Further, this is not the first incident of this type. *I can recite at least three more* to make my case (level 3— "Because you . . ."). Continuing to examine my inner feelings, I discover that I feel hurt by her behavior; it makes me feel that *she does not regard me very highly* (level 4— "I think you feel I . . ."). She treats me thoughtlessly because I am of no importance to her. If I were a big shot, she would never do these things to me. At any point during my ruminations, I can tell her what I am feeling. If I do, it may get us both off our self-righteous positions and open up a dialogue. If I still feel preoccupied, disturbed, and uncomfortable, I may look to the next level of insight. My disturbance stems not only from my perception that she feels I am insignificant but also from the feeling that *she is right, and I am an insignificant person* (level 5— "I fear I am . . ."), at least in this situation, and perhaps more generally. This deepest level of insight requires a well-developed self-awareness and often taps into what has been an unconscious part of my self-concept.

To the degree that I do indeed have some feelings of insignificance, my argument with my colleague about my parking space is doomed to go on endlessly, because the parking space is not the issue. This point is dramatically illustrated by how quickly we resolve the parking problem when, in the course of our dialogue, I learn that she really does regard me as important. Level 5 is particularly applicable when I find that an issue is preoccupying me, when I complain to my spouse and my colleagues, and when I lose sleep. These are signs that I'm afraid my adversary is right; if an adversary says something negative about me that I'm sure is inaccurate, I don't usually get upset. I go to great lengths to avoid feeling bad about myself, and so I'm very sensitive to anything that may lead me to look at my negative self-concept. Without self-awareness, I transfer my self-dislike to you. As I become more self-aware—that is, reach a deeper level of truth—I see the situation more clearly.

Thus a key vehicle for resolving arguments is self-awareness. Unfortunately, however, the practice of arguing vehemently about issues that are irrelevant to the real feelings is widespread. The most effective way of breaking through such impasses is to acquire more self-awareness and be willing to express it to others. Withholding, lying, distorting, and "softening" the truth are not necessary. When an organization establishes an atmosphere of truth and openness, every disagreement is looked upon as a problem to be solved, not as an opportunity to assign blame or to be right.

Case Example   Ophelia, Owen, and their team members had not progressed very far in the levels of truth, either in their dealings with one another or in their self-awareness, and so they made little progress. Few of their real feelings were being acknowledged or even recognized, and so it was unlikely they would solve their problems. Most of their communication was at the levels of self-deception and withholding. Owen and Ophelia were not aware of their personal fears in this setting. Moreover, even the factors they were aware of (such as Ophelia's seeing the trouble with Owen but not dealing directly with it) were withheld from the group. Here's what their situation looked like (see Table 1.1):

Level 1: "You are..." Owen operated at this level when he accused and abused his co-workers. Ophelia had not reached even this level; she held back from expressing dissatisfaction with anyone.

Level 2: "Toward you I feel..." Owen may have tapped into this level from time to time when he expressed how he felt about the situation, rather than engaging in name calling.

Level 3: "Because you..." Since the group had tacitly agreed *not* to bring up specific grievances, the members had not tapped into this level.

Level 4: "I think you feel I..." The group had barely reached level 3, and so there was no activity at all on this level either. If there had been, Owen would have said, "I think you don't like me (*I am unlovable*)." Ophelia would have said, "I think you feel that I am unlikable (*therefore, I won't antagonize you*)." The group members, taking their cue from Ophelia's behavior, might have said, "I think you feel that we are not nice (*unlovable*) if we criticize you, or that we are not important enough for you to notice what we say."

Level 5: "I fear I am…" Like level 4, this level requires more self-awareness than the group members had reached. If they had, both Owen and Ophelia and the group members would have been able to say, "I fear I am unlikable." The group members might also have said, "We fear we are insignificant."

Pause for Reflection: Levels of Truth

The following questions are designed to increase my awareness of my behavior and to reveal my attitudes toward the levels of truth. These questions are aimed at my achieving more clarity; they are not evaluations. *I choose* whether to change.

1. On which level of truth do I usually operate? On which one would I like to operate?

2. Does the concept of the levels of truth help me clarify any situation at work? Which one? How?

3. How would I describe a work setting where everyone operated on level 1?

4. How would a work setting be where levels 4 and 5 were used regularly?

5. How might the levels of truth be used in labor-management negotiations?

6. How might the levels of truth be used in technical disagreements?

7. How might the levels of truth be used in personal disputes?

8. How would I implement the levels of truth in my workplace? Am I willing to do it?

9. What do I see as the relationship between the levels of truth and the bottom line (profitability)?

10. Is it a good idea to be truthful in the workplace? Why?

The levels of truth can be extended to another important part of communication: listening (see Table 1.2).[14] The levels of listening correspond to the levels of truth, but here I can analyze what I do or say in response to your initiation, as well as what I feel underneath my own behavior.

The Limits of Openness

Complete and constant openness is a notion that can be reduced to absurdity. Am I required to stop everyone on the street and tell them my reaction to their appearance? Must I spend half an hour telling a waitress my feelings about her competence, instead of being on time for an important meeting? No. Even though I may be willing to tell the waitress my feelings, I may choose instead to spend my time elsewhere.

At the heart of this issue is relevance—and it is more troubling in the abstract than in practice. Take the example of a work situation where I am struggling with whether to tell a co-worker that her smoking bothers me.

"It's really trivial," I say to myself. "I can't tell her every little thing that bugs me. Besides, I can tell her tomorrow."

The practical solution in such a situation is this: if I am trying to decide whether I should or should not tell something, then I should. If the issue were really irrelevant, it probably never would have entered my mind. The dilemma is usually this: I know that it is important to tell, and I want a reason not to.

Another limit to openness concerns extreme, life-threatening situations. For example, if the Nazis had stormed into my house and

Table 1.2. Levels of Listening.

Level of Truth		What I Say/Do	What I Want/Feel Underneath
− 1	Self-deception	"I didn't know you wanted to talk to me."	"I don't want you to talk to me."
		In this state, I keep myself unaware of your overtures because I do not want to deal with you.	
0	Withholding	"I'm not listening to you."	"I don't want to listen to you."
		I am aware that I do not want to hear you, and so I deliberately do not listen.	
1	"You are..."	"I'm not what you said I am."	"I want to deny what you said and defend myself."
		I anticipate being attacked and blamed, and so I listen to you only enough to deny what you say and prepare to defend myself.	
2	"Toward you I feel..."	"You are wrong."	"I want to attack you and discredit you."
		I do not like what you are saying, and so I will try to discredit you, even distort a bit, and attack you.	

3	"Because you..."	"...are wrong, and I am right."	"I want *you* to hear *me*. I listen to you only to find an opening to counterattack."
		I interrupt because I do not want to hear you. I want you to hear me. I want to convince you that I am right and you are wrong.	
4	"I think you feel I..."	"I listen until I understand what you are saying."	"I want to understand what you are saying."
		I really want to understand what you are saying. I will ask you to clarify or elaborate if I do not understand.	
5	"I fear I am..."	"...misunderstanding you, and so I will listen."	"I want to understand what you are saying and how you are feeling."
		I want to hear not only the words but also the music.	

demanded to know the whereabouts of my children, for the purpose of shooting them, I would *not* have said, "They are in the closet." I would not even have said, "I won't tell you." Such situations, however, must be extreme to qualify as exceptions to the principle of openness.

Case Example   Ophelia, Owen, and the other group members who attended a workshop began to look inside themselves for some of the answers to their difficulties with themselves and one another. As in most other groups, everyone had concerns about inclusion (significance) and control (competence), but the main anxiety for both Ophelia and Owen was being liked.

Ophelia had confused being clear about what she wanted from the team with being authoritarian. She was so afraid that people would see her as an autocratic leader that she bent over backwards, to the point of not initiating anything. She was afraid that if she took strong action against Owen, he and the other team members would be offended and would dislike her. That led to confusion and indecision. The team members assured Ophelia that if she told them what she wanted, it would help them. They could always disagree and work out a better solution.

Owen, when he finally was told about the negative reactions of the other team members, was relieved. He had always known (or at least suspected, anyway). He softened and began talking about his background and about how it had left him feeling very unlikable. In new situations, he always assumed that people would eventually reject him. He saw that his obnoxious behavior was an attempt to reject people before they could reject him.

The other team members recognized their reluctance to complain as their fear of being disliked by Ophelia and the other members and, perhaps, of losing their jobs. In terms of the levels of truth, their answer to both "I think you feel I am . . . " and "I fear I am . . . " was "unlikable." When the team members reached the deepest level of truth, they had the ability to be honest with each other and with themselves, and the beginnings of an understanding of themselves and one another. These were the tools they needed to begin solving their problems.

Ophelia vowed to be clear about what she wanted. The team members promised to object if they disagreed with Ophelia and to work out a better solution with her. Owen would be told when he was annoying others, and he would also be coached and instructed in his weak areas. All the members of the group would speak up whenever anything was bothering them, and they designated a particular time each week for this activity. The group's productivity began to rise.

Summary of Openness

Issue	*Open* or *closed*
Behavior with others	Openness
Behavior toward self	Self-awareness
Underlying feeling	Likability, lovability
Interaction	Embracing
Interpersonal fear	Being rejected, disliked, despised
Personal fear	Being unlikable, unlovable

Pause for Reflection: Openness

1. In my organization, do I have a situation like the one with Ophelia and Owen?

2. How did the levels of truth help resolve that situation?

3. How would I describe my organization's level of openness? Is it an atmosphere of high openness (open communication, no secrets, no withholding, honest feedback)? Or is it an atmosphere of low openness (respect for privacy, judicious communication on a need-to-know basis, care not to hurt people's feelings)? How would I like to see it change, if at all?

4. What are the advantages and disadvantages of each type of organizational approach to openness?

5. Do people like me when they first meet me? Does this reaction change over time? If so, how?

6. Has anyone ever said that I am too open? What truth is there in that observation? If it is not true, why do I think that someone else thought it was?

7. Has anyone ever said that I am not open enough? What truth is there in that observation? If it is not true, why do I think that someone else thought it was?

8. In my experience, how important is the issue of being liked in organizations? How does it affect productivity?

9. Do I ever reduce my own likability through some fear I have? When and how?

10. What do I think of this statement? "People who vacillate between the extremes of being open with everyone and being personally closed to everyone, and who have difficulty simply being appropriately close, may be concerned about their own likability." Have I ever known anyone like that?

2

The Basis for Personal and Professional Effectiveness: Self-Concept and Self-Esteem

Do you want to be a positive influence in the world? First, get your own life in order. —*Tao Te Ching*[1]

From the basics of the Human Element approach—inclusion, control, and openness—this chapter turns to the *self-concept* (my individual sense of how I experience myself, how I perceive myself) and to *self-esteem* (the way I feel about my self-concept). When I feel good about my self-concept, I have strong self-esteem. For instance, if I see myself as aggressive (self-concept), I may be proud of that trait (self-esteem).

Self-concept and self-esteem are crucial to personal and professional effectiveness because if they are not fully positive, I may act in mystifying and sometimes destructive ways. Not until I become more aware of the origins of my behavior can I be effective when I choose to change. Teams, groups, and entire organizations, with greater awareness of the dynamics of self-concept and self-esteem, can look forward to more productive and certainly more pleasant working relationships.

This chapter carries forward the quest for self-awareness, first by further exploring how the basic dimensions of self-esteem (inclusion, control, and openness) are related to each other and pointing out some implications and applications, and then by presenting a fuller discussion of the Human Element model, which will be a vehicle for defining the self-concept more precisely. The chapter goes on to describe the coping and defense mechanisms that come into play when the self-concept is threatened. Finally, it discusses the interplay between self-concept and self-esteem and what can be done in organizations to improve both.

Self-Concept and Inclusion, Control, and Openness

To provide a richer understanding of the content of inclusion, control, and openness, this section looks at the concepts from different viewpoints: historical origins, childhood studies, and stages of group development.

Early Origins and Childhood

The dominant human relationship in the first stages of life is *inclusion*. When I am born, to survive I must make contact with other humans; it is well established that lack of human contact for very young infants may lead to retardation, illness, and death.[2]

Following the period of inclusion, I enter an era of socialization (between the ages of two and four). In this period, my primary human relationships center on *control* (that is, on how much I run my own life and how much I obey the orders of parents and other adults).

As I mature, issues of *openness* emerge (between the ages of four and six), and the expression of deeper feelings, love, and affection becomes the central interpersonal issue. Sacrifice, jealousy of my mother's relationship with my father, sibling rivalry, friendships with playmates—all these issues present themselves. The central interpersonal and personal event at this point is the openness with which I deal with these issues. Discovering who I am and how we relate will require a decision about how open both my parents and I will be about expressing our true feelings.

Studies of childhood, although varying in the terminology they use, also indicate the importance of inclusion, control, and openness in development. In these studies, inclusion is also called *parent-child interaction, stimulation,* and, in the extreme, *indulgence.* High inclusion in the parent-child relationship is characterized by a child-centered home, where I, as the child, am constantly given attention, concern, a high level of activity, and intense and frequent contact with both parents. Low inclusion is characterized by an adult-centered home, in which I am left to my own devices, neglected, ignored, and understimulated, and where my interaction with my parents is low even for discipline, and I do not get attention even when I engage in such disapproved activities as neglect of my chores, disobedience, and masturbation.

In the context of the parent-child relationship, control is also spoken of in terms of *democracy* and *promotion of independence.* A low-control relationship includes my freedom to choose, decide, originate, and reject—that is, my freedom from arbitrary control. My parents typically justify their policies, decide democratically, explain readily, answer my questions about sex, take me on picnics, provide spending money, and do not interfere with my fights. Under high control, I am strictly restrained, my obedience is demanded, I am given orders, and regulations are typically restrictive.

In studies, openness is also called *affectionateness, approval,* and *acceptance.* High openness includes behavior that is encouraging and facilitating. In a low-openness family, I am blamed, discouraged, disapproved, rejected, inhibited, and not given affection.

Reinforcing the importance of inclusion, control, and openness in child-family interactions is Eleanor and Sydney Glueck's classic study of delinquency,[3] which found that issues of inclusion, control, and openness are powerful predictors of which children eventually become delinquent. The Gluecks used the factors of cohesiveness of the family (inclusion), discipline by the father and supervision by the mother (control), and affection of the father and the mother (openness).

Group Development

The inclusion, control, and openness phases of group development parallel those for child development. In forming a new group or an organization, the members establish boundaries to make clear who is in and who is out. In ancient and some modern tribes, initiation rites—rites of passage—establish tribal membership. In modern organizations there are similar ceremonies: voting, paying dues, passing tests, having a certain lineage, promising to uphold certain principles, successfully completing interviews. Whatever the criteria, the group uses a specific procedure to define *inclusion* for each of the group members. When a group already exists and someone is added or leaves, the group applies the inclusion procedures to deal with the change.

Once formed, the group or organization turns to *control* issues to differentiate roles and distribute power. Tribes often established a leader through tests of strength, or through age. Families determine the relationships of members to one another on the basis of sex roles, age, or abilities. Modern organizations use elections, bylaws, appointments, special skills, power, money, lineage, likability, or "who you know" to allocate tasks and establish power relationships among members.

At this point, the organization or group must make a decision about *openness:* either we will be a businesslike group that does not bring up personal feelings, or we will be open with one another and discuss how we feel, both individually and about each other. We usually have strong feelings about openness. Some of us are not interested in remaining in the group if feelings are not expressed, since that limits our personal closeness too much. With perhaps equally strong convictions, others among us will not stay if the group allows that type of discussion. Sometimes the group dynamics change if the leader changes. If the previous leader encouraged an open atmosphere, but the new leader prefers a more closed one, that can create stress in the organization, especially if the issue is not directly addressed. (Chapter Three, on teamwork, goes into much greater depth on group dynamics.)

A Model for Understanding Self-Concept

The three dimensions of inclusion, control, and openness can be assembled into a model that will integrate and sharpen the concepts and make them easier to apply. The *Periodic Table of the Human Elements* (see Table 2.1) is important for organizations because it can help in forming a clear, complete picture of the ingredients of the Human Element approach in general and the self-concept (and self-esteem) in particular. Self-concept is the basis of self-awareness and thus of the ability to choose change in behavior and feelings, which in turn is central to improving the quality of life in organizations.

The model discussed in this section has several advantages. It is comprehensive, showing all factors and aspects in summary form, without duplication, and it allows the integration of all approaches to organizational problems, since they all can be expressed in the same terms. The highlighting of different sections of the Periodic Table also allows concentration on specific concerns, behavior, and feelings.

Human behavior is vastly complex. Or is it? I observe an infinite variety of behavior each day, and I often give up the possibility of understanding it all. It's just too much. But perhaps the three dimensions we have been discussing can provide a way to simplify my understanding. The method called *facet design*, mentioned earlier, is very helpful in the simplification process. If I can find the principles or factors—that is, the *facets*—that underlie all behavior and then find the ways these facets combine, I may be able to cut through some of the apparent human chaos.

Deepak Chopra invites us to "imagine that a violin is enclosed out of sight in a box. As its strings vibrate, different pitches, chords, sequences of notes, and timbres are produced. If you were an alien who did not know what music is, you would find each of these things different from one another.... Only by opening the box and seeing that indeed every sound came from one violin would you be convinced that they had a unified source."[4]

As another example, the discovery that the myriad colors in the world all derive from three primary colors—red, yellow, and blue—

Table 2.1.
Periodic Table of the Human Elements.

	Interpersonal: Do Self (I) to Other (You)		Interpersonal: Get Other (You) to Self (I)	
	See	Want	See	Want
Inclusion	I include you. 11	I want to include you. 12	You include me. 13	I want you to include me. 14
Control	I control you. 21	I want to control you. 22	You control me. 23	I want you to control me. 24
Openness	I am open with you. 31	I want to be open with you. 32	You are open with me. 33	I want you to be open with me. 34
Significance	I feel you are significant. 41	I want to feel you are significant. 42	You feel I am significant. 43	I want you to feel I am significant. 44
Competence	I feel you are competent. 51	I want to feel you are competent. 52	You feel I am competent. 53	I want you to feel I am competent. 54
Likability	I like you. 61	I want to like you. 62	You like me. 63	I want you to like me. 64

is an instance of simplification through the discovery of basic underlying facets. Combining the three colors (the facets) in various ways—instances of an *operation* performed on those colors—produces hundreds of other colors. Other operations produce other effects. For instance, juxtaposing one color with another changes the

Individual Self (I) to Self (I)		Other Other (O) to Other (O)	
See	Want	See	Want
I am fully alive. <div align="right">15</div>	I want to be fully alive. <div align="right">16</div>	You are fully alive. <div align="right">17</div>	You want to be fully alive. <div align="right">18</div>
I determine my own life. <div align="right">25</div>	I want to determine my own life. <div align="right">26</div>	You deter- mine your own life. <div align="right">27</div>	You want to determine your own life. <div align="right">28</div>
I am aware of myself. <div align="right">35</div>	I want to be aware of myself. <div align="right">36</div>	You are aware of yourself. <div align="right">37</div>	You want to be aware of yourself. <div align="right">38</div>
I feel significant. <div align="right">45</div>	I want to feel significant. <div align="right">46</div>	You feel significant. <div align="right">47</div>	You want to feel significant. <div align="right">48</div>
I feel competent. <div align="right">55</div>	I want to feel competent. <div align="right">56</div>	You feel competent. <div align="right">57</div>	You want to feel competent. <div align="right">58</div>
I like myself. <div align="right">65</div>	I want to like myself. <div align="right">66</div>	You like yourself. <div align="right">67</div>	You want to like yourself. <div align="right">68</div>

intensity and appearance of the first. In addition, various classifications of color, such as "earth colors," "hot colors," or "cool colors," can be defined precisely through selection of subgroups of all colors. The facets—the primary colors—provide an intellectual structure that simplifies our understanding of all colors and provides tools for exploring their properties and relationships. Likewise, inclusion, control, and openness provide the basis of a design that simplifies understanding of human behavior by showing the underlying facets and then adding operations to generate more complexity.

There are three sets of facets in the Periodic Table of the Human Elements, as follows:

- *Psychological* facets (six dimensions). On the level of behavior, there are three facets: inclusion, control, and openness. On the level of feelings, there are also three facets: significance, competence, and likability.

- *Directional* facets (four dimensions). In interpersonal relations, there is an initiator and a receiver of behavior or feelings. When I am both initiator and receiver, I am exploring my self-concept. The facets here are Self (*I*) to Other (*you*); Other (*you*) to Self (*I*); Self (*I*) to Self (*I*); and Other (*you*) to Other (*you*).

- *Aspect*-related facets (two dimensions). Whether I perceive (*see*) or want (*want*) a feeling or a behavior constitutes another facet. The difference between these two aspects measures my satisfaction with myself. When what I *see* (self-concept) and what I *want* are the same, I have strong self-esteem. For example, if I see myself as high on controlling people and I like that about myself, my self-esteem on that dimension is high.

The six psychological facets are listed down the left side of Table 2.1. The four directional facets are arrayed across the top. The two aspect-related facets are placed under each of the directions. The chart's forty-eight cells represent all possible combinations of all the facets. To make them easier to refer to, I have given each cell a two-digit number. The first digit is the *row* number; the second is the *column* number. For example, *I want you to be open with me* is in the third row and the fourth column; therefore, it is in cell 34. Important concepts can be expressed as combinations of cells. The self-concept, for example, can be expressed with six cells in column five (15, 25, 35, 45, 55, 65) and six cells in column six (16, 26, 36, 46, 56, 66).

Operations within the Periodic Table describe certain ways each cell can be used. For example, in order to measure degrees of *agreement*, each cell can be regarded as incorporating a scale that runs from +9 ("I strongly agree with this statement") to 0 ("I strongly disagree") to −9 ("I strongly agree with the negative of this statement"). I may like you very much (+9 on cell 61), or I may not like you (0 on cell 61), or I may hate you (−9 on cell 61). Each cell may also be regarded as incorporating a continuum that runs from full *awareness* to total *unawareness* (in other words, from conscious to unconscious). I may consciously feel very competent (+8 on cell 55), but unconsciously I may have serious doubts about my competence (−8 on cell 55), yet I do not allow myself to be aware of that feeling.

When I have assigned numerical values to each cell—using test scores, ratings, or such objective measures as achievement of a quantitative goal—the cells can be combined, or other cells can be added or subtracted. Any operation can be applied to any cell. The Pauses for Reflection throughout the rest of this book provide opportunities for assigning values that reflect current situations.

Pause for Reflection: Defining My Self-Concept

This Pause for Reflection has three parts: one on inclusion, one on control, and one on openness.[5] Each part features highlighted sections of the Periodic Table, followed by a questionnaire. By answering the questionnaires, I can establish numerical values for each of the major behavioral and feeling dimensions and begin to define my self-concept at this point in time. As I rate myself on each cell, I have the opportunity to understand my interpersonal relations, gain knowledge of myself, and begin to increase my self-awareness.

Cells 11, 12, 13, 14: Inclusion with others

Inclusion

	Interpersonal: Do Self (I) to Other (You)		Interpersonal: Get Other (You) to Self (I)		Individual Self (I) to Self (I)		Other Other (O) to Other (O)	
	See	Want	See	Want	See	Want	See	Want
Inclusion	I include you. 11	I want to include you. 12	You include me. 13	I want you to include me. 14	I am fully alive. 15	I want to be fully alive. 16	17	18
Control	21	22	23	24	25	26	27	28
Openness	31	32	33	34	35	36	37	38
Significance	I feel you are significant. 41	I want to feel you are significant. 42	You feel I am significant. 43	I want you to feel I am significant. 44	I feel significant. 45	I want to feel significant. 46	47	48
Competence	51	52	53	54	55	56	57	58
Likability	61	62	63	64	65	66	67	68

Cells 41, 42, 43, 44: Significance with others

Cells 15 and 16: Inclusion of the self, or aliveness

Cells 45 and 46: Self-significance

Circle one number for each of the highlighted cells, using a scale of 0 (disagree) to 9 (agree). *You* is the generalized other person in the interaction.

Cell 11. **I include you.**
disagree   0   1   2   3   4   5   6   7   8   9   agree

Cell 12. **I want to include you.**
disagree   0   1   2   3   4   5   6   7   8   9   agree

Cell 13. You include me.
disagree   0   1   2   3   4   5   6   7   8   9   agree

Cell 14. I want you to include me.
disagree   0   1   2   3   4   5   6   7   8   9   agree

Cell 15. I am fully alive.
disagree   0   1   2   3   4   5   6   7   8   9   agree

Cell 16. I want to be fully alive.
disagree   0   1   2   3   4   5   6   7   8   9   agree

Cell 41. I feel you are significant.
disagree   0   1   2   3   4   5   6   7   8   9   agree

Cell 42. I want to feel you are significant.
disagree   0   1   2   3   4   5   6   7   8   9   agree

Cell 43. You feel I am significant.
disagree   0   1   2   3   4   5   6   7   8   9   agree

Cell 44. I want you to feel I am significant.
disagree   0   1   2   3   4   5   6   7   8   9   agree

Cell 45. I feel significant.
disagree   0   1   2   3   4   5   6   7   8   9   agree

Cell 46. I want to feel significant.
disagree   0   1   2   3   4   5   6   7   8   9   agree

Control

Cells 21, 22, 23, 24: Control with others

Cells 51, 52, 53, 54: Competence with others

Cells 25 and 26: Control of the self, or self-determination

Cells 55 and 56: Self-competence

	Interpersonal: Do Self (I) to Other (You)		Interpersonal: Get Other (You) to Self (I)		Individual Self (I) to Self (I)		Other Other (O) to Other (O)	
	See	Want	See	Want	See	Want	See	Want
Inclusion								
	11	12	13	14	15	16	17	18
Control	I control you.	I want to control you.	You control me.	I want you to control me.	I determine my own life.	I want to determine my own life.		
	21	22	23	24	25	26	27	28
Openness								
	31	32	33	34	35	36	37	38
Significance								
	41	42	43	44	45	46	47	48
Competence	I feel you are competent.	I want to feel you are competent.	You feel I am competent.	I want you to feel I am competent.	I feel competent.	I want to feel competent.		
	51	52	53	54	55	56	57	58
Likability								
	61	62	63	64	65	66	67	68

Circle one number for each of the highlighted cells, using a scale of 0 (disagree) to 9 (agree). *You* is the generalized other person in the interaction.

Cell 21. **I control you.**
disagree   0   1   2   3   4   5   6   7   8   9   agree

Cell 22. **I want to control you.**
disagree   0   1   2   3   4   5   6   7   8   9   agree

Cell 23. **You control me.**
disagree   0   1   2   3   4   5   6   7   8   9   agree

Cell 24. **I want you to control me.**
disagree   0   1   2   3   4   5   6   7   8   9   agree

Cell 25. **I determine my own life.**
disagree   0   1   2   3   4   5   6   7   8   9   agree

Cell 26. **I want to determine my own life.**
disagree   0   1   2   3   4   5   6   7   8   9   agree

Cell 51. I feel you are competent.

disagree   0   1   2   3   4   5   6   7   8   9   agree

Cell 52. I want to feel you are competent.

disagree   0   1   2   3   4   5   6   7   8   9   agree

Cell 53. You feel I am competent.

disagree   0   1   2   3   4   5   6   7   8   9   agree

Cell 54. I want you to feel I am competent.

disagree   0   1   2   3   4   5   6   7   8   9   agree

Cell 55. I feel competent.

disagree   0   1   2   3   4   5   6   7   8   9   agree

Cell 56. I want to feel competent.

disagree   0   1   2   3   4   5   6   7   8   9   agree

Openness

	Interpersonal: Do Self (I) to Other (You)		Interpersonal: Get Other (You) to Self (I)		Individual Self (I) to Self (I)		Other Other (O) to Other (O)	
	See	Want	See	Want	See	Want	See	Want
Inclusion								
	11	12	13	14	15	16	17	18
Control								
	21	22	23	24	25	26	27	28
Openness	I am open with you.	I want to be open with you.	You are open with me.	I want you to be open with me.	I am aware of myself.	I want to be aware of myself.		
	31	32	33	34	35	36	37	38
Significance								
	41	42	43	44	45	46	47	48
Competence								
	51	52	53	54	55	56	57	58
Likability	I like you.	I want to like you.	You like me.	I want you to like me.	I like myself.	I want to like myself.		
	61	62	63	64	65	66	67	68

Cells 31, 32, 33, 34: Openness with others

Cells 61, 62, 63, 64: Liking with others

Cells 35 and 36: Openness to the self, or self-awareness

Cells 65 and 66: Self-liking

Circle one number for each of the highlighted cells, using a scale of 0 (disagree) to 9 (agree). *You* is the generalized other person in the interaction.

Cell 31. I am open with you.
disagree   0   1   2   3   4   5   6   7   8   9   agree

Cell 32. I want to be open with you.
disagree   0   1   2   3   4   5   6   7   8   9   agree

Cell 33. You are open with me.
disagree   0   1   2   3   4   5   6   7   8   9   agree

Cell 34. I want you to be open with me.
disagree   0   1   2   3   4   5   6   7   8   9   agree

Cell 35. I am aware of myself.
disagree   0   1   2   3   4   5   6   7   8   9   agree

Cell 36. I want to be aware of myself.
disagree   0   1   2   3   4   5   6   7   8   9   agree

Cell 61. I like you.
disagree   0   1   2   3   4   5   6   7   8   9   agree

Cell 62. I want to like you.
disagree   0   1   2   3   4   5   6   7   8   9   agree

Cell 63. You like me.
disagree   0   1   2   3   4   5   6   7   8   9   agree

Cell 64. I want you to like me.
disagree   0   1   2   3   4   5   6   7   8   9   agree

Cell 65. I like myself.
disagree   0   1   2   3   4   5   6   7   8   9   agree

Cell 66. I want to like myself.
disagree   0   1   2   3   4   5   6   7   8   9   agree

Coping with Threats to the Self-Concept

Just as it is important, in understanding self-concept, to have a holistic picture of the dynamic dimensions of the Human Element model, it's vital to understand the processes by which self-awareness is blocked. I unconsciously hide from myself the parts of my self-concept that I have not accepted, by using defense (or coping) mechanisms. Those parts—motivated by feelings of insignificance, incompetence, and unlikability and by fears of being ignored, humiliated, and rejected—are so painful that I go to great lengths to avoid feeling them. I distort my reality. I invent philosophies of how things should be. I try to get other people to do things for me, and I even express my conflicts in my body. My reluctance to look at myself clearly leads me to use other people to avoid my own reality. For example, it is easier to be critical of others than to deal with self-criticism.

This section describes the kinds of defenses I use to avoid the pain of such unpleasant feelings. The defenses, by definition, are used only when these feelings are unconscious; if I am aware of my feelings toward myself, I can choose how I want to deal with them. If the feelings are unconscious, however, I am on automatic pilot, and I am not sure why I do many of the things I do. For example, if I dislike my boss and think I should not, I try to reconcile my feelings and my thoughts and proceed toward a "rational" solution. I talk to friends, read books, occupy myself elsewhere, or go to sleep. At bottom, though, my conflict concerns *how I feel about myself.* It is not so much my feelings for my boss that bother me; it is that I dislike myself for disliking him, and I feel unlikable for having that feeling.

I want to avoid the feeling of not liking myself, because that feeling is extremely unpleasant. But when I repress or deny the conflict, I distort the way I see the world. My lens goes out of focus. I misinterpret what people say, get angry for no obvious reason, or see people as hostile. But if I can push the conflict into my unconscious, one way I can deal with it is by using defense, or coping, mechanisms.

The ultimate method for dealing directly with these defenses begins with an awareness of their presence.[6] If they are brought out into the open—that is, made conscious—I can understand them, see that we all use them, realize that it is unnecessary to exert all the energy I put into them, and acknowledge my shared humanity. When you and I are no longer wasting energy on unproductive behavior and feelings, we can work together better to achieve our common goals.

The following descriptions show the behavior and beliefs involved in several kinds of defense mechanisms. The Pause for Reflection at the end of this section allows the actual charting of defense mechanisms.

Clues to Defensive Behavior

I am probably using defense mechanisms when I do the following things:[7]

- Hold to my position rigidly, no matter what
- Do not listen to people
- Misinterpret what other people say to me
- Stop talking and begin withholding
- Feel that no one understands me
- Do not want to negotiate
- Am easily irritated
- Do not want to talk about "certain things"
- Do not want to probe or look for causes
- Become indignant when challenged

- Anger easily
- Become confused
- Lose my sense of humor

Now let's move on to six specific defense mechanisms. Each is presented in terms of a person using that defense mechanism: *denier, victim, critic, self-blamer, helper,* and *demander.*

Denier (Denial)

What I say: For me, there are no problems. I will find a way to diminish or dismiss any concerns that anyone has about anything. My motto: "No problem."

What I believe unconsciously: By denying there are any problems, I can avoid having to deal with my feelings of inadequacy.

Example   A top executive of a computer hardware company was warned that the company's mainframe business was in danger of becoming obsolete because of growth in the use of work stations and personal computers. He called a meeting of the engineering department, to allay fears and assure everyone that there was no problem. Despite his assurances, the threat continued, and his superiors decided that they could not afford to keep him in such a key position. What emerged, as they were able to speak candidly with him and as he became willing to look at himself honestly, was that he had spent his whole career becoming an expert in the mainframe business, and he knew virtually nothing about work stations and personal computers. He was also unsure of his ability to learn at this late date. Rather than acknowledge his insecurity, even to himself, he denied the threat and seriously imperiled the future of his company.

Victim (Projection)

What I say: If anyone says anything that I can interpret as an attack or a criticism, even if I have to stretch to interpret it that way, I become offended and hurt. I become offended at every opportunity. If I am clever, I can even become a martyr. My motto: "Poor me."

What I believe unconsciously: Being a victim allows me to be the object of pity, get support from others, and not have to deal with my own feelings of inadequacy. (I am not distorting entirely when I feel that I am a victim; there is some reality to my perception, but how much reality depends on my self-awareness.)

Example   Pat, passed over for a first-line manager's job, cried, "Discrimination! That's why I wasn't promoted. They've always favored other groups. People my age always have a disadvantage." Pat's colleagues were puzzled by that reaction, since someone of exactly the same age was ultimately selected for the job. Pat found it easier to play the victim than to deal with personal feelings of inadequacy.

Critic (Displacement)

What I say: I comment on everything that is not perfect. I correct everyone's grammar, point out when people are wrong, call attention to all stupid remarks, and criticize all ideas that are not mine. My motto: "You dummy, I know better than you."

What I believe unconsciously: If I make sure that other people don't look any better than I do, my own inadequacies will be easier to deal with.

Example   Periodically, Kris became critical of her assistant, Josh. Everything he did was wrong; no matter how trivial the task, Josh botched it up. Kris and Josh started to explore what was happening. Josh was irritated, and he could not understand why Kris would become so critical, so suddenly. As they reviewed his faults, Kris was struck with an insight: she was feeling very bad about herself, but by criticizing Josh, she could avoid her own self-critical feeling. She could also reduce the difference between them, since if he were flawed, too, then her own flaws were not so glaring. From then on, whenever Kris became excessively critical she realized that she was displacing her own negative feelings toward herself onto someone else.

Self-Blamer (Masochism)

What I say: I know that everything that happens is my fault. I take full responsibility and blame for everything. I do not let people placate me or talk me out of it. My motto: "I am a wretched creature."

What I believe unconsciously: If I blame myself first, I may avoid other people's accusations, and then I will not have to deal with my own inadequacies.

Example   Maria was regarded as one of the most able employees in her company, except that she required extraordinarily careful handling: whenever anything went wrong, she was sure she was responsible for it, and her anguish went far beyond anyone else's. Reassurances came from all sides, with people telling Maria that many others had contributed to the problem, and that it certainly was not all her fault. In time, people began tiring of Maria's reactions: reassuring her took valuable time and diverted attention from what really had happened and how to fix it. In a workshop, Maria had the insight that she had been blamed often as a child. She decided that she had learned that if she blamed herself first, she would avoid other people's criticism. That unconscious ploy worked very well. Even when Maria was indeed to blame, people were hesitant to bring it up. Her self-blame let her deal with her insecurity about her competence by exaggerating her responsibility.

Helper (Identification)

What I say: I look for anyone I think needs help. Whether others know it or want it or not, I "help" them in every way I can, regardless of their reactions. My motto: "There, there."

What I believe unconsciously: If I focus on other people's problems, I will not have to deal with my own inadequacies.

Example   Everyone was amazed when Henry, a fatherly, work-aholic colleague, was suddenly on the verge of divorce, with his elder son in trouble with the law. The astonishment occurred because Henry was the first one anyone would go to with a personal problem. Henry was caring and wise. He constantly stressed the importance of balance between work life and home life. Apparently, however, he found it more comfortable to deal with other people's problems than with his own; he would often stay late to hear someone else's difficulties instead of going home. Counseling revealed that Henry felt inadequate as a husband and father because he did not feel basically lovable.

Demander (Compensation)

What I say: Tell me I am okay. That's not enough. Tell me again. Convince me. My motto: "More, more."

What I believe unconsciously: By demanding, I may get someone to compensate for my inadequacies, and I will not have to deal with them.

Example   Carmine had just been promoted to line manager. The people who reported to him thought he was doing a good job, and so did his boss, Sophia. But in every meeting, Carmine asked Sophia how he was doing. If Sophia was not effusive, Carmine felt bad. He drooped, or he became unaccountably angry and stomped out. Sometimes Carmine even went to his staff and asked for "feedback." If he heard anything but the highest praise, he seemed not to listen. He was so insecure about his competence in his new position that neither his staff nor his boss could ever say enough to make him feel that he was really doing a good job.

I trained some San Luis Obispo prison personnel who were leading groups of inmates. There were two types of trainers: the "old bulls," who were tough and experienced, went into cells, and took knives away from tough cons; and the social workers from the University of

California. To my surprise, the "old bulls" were more effective group therapy leaders, although intellectually they knew less about group therapy than the social workers did.

Interviews revealed that most of the inmates were in prison because they could not control their violent impulses. Unconsciously, they saw the "old bulls" as capable of compensating for their uncontrolled aggressive impulses, by restraining them. Therefore, they could relax and attend to the group sessions. The social workers could not compensate for them in the same way. The inmates saw them as too permissive, unwilling or incapable of being external enforcers. The inmates were so anxious with the social workers that they could not focus on the group therapy.

Perception and Self-Concept

Every human relationship is partly realistic and partly distortion. Since all defense mechanisms are based on distorted perception, my awareness of my feelings about myself plays a major role in the accuracy of my perceptions. If I am not aware of my self-concept, I tend to distort how others see me. If I am totally aware of my own self-concept, I am more likely to see myself and other people as we really are.

Figure 2.1 illustrates this important point. According to my awareness of my own feelings about myself, I see you (*perception*) as you are (*reality*). To some degree, I also project unconscious feelings

Figure 2.1. Perceptual Accuracy.

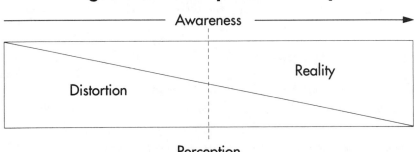

onto you (*distortion*). Even when I distort, I am somewhat accurate because I am particularly sensitive to your actions or feelings, which I am interpreting (this is expressed in Figure 2.1 by the vertical dotted line representing perception, which falls partly into the *reality* section). For example, I may project my dislike of myself onto you (*distortion*); and even if you generally like me, you probably have some dislike for me (*reality*).

Every perception is partly accurate, or realistic, and partly a distortion, given the defensive aspects of my perception. The more self-aware I am, the less I use defenses, and the more accurately I can perceive. If my perceptions are completely realistic, I have "immaculate perception"—all reality, no distortions or defensiveness.

The 1 Percent Rule

What about when you want to give me feedback on my behavior? How do I know to what extent you are projecting from your own defensive behavior? I may say, "Feedback varies from person to person, and so it is definitely in the eye of the beholder, especially if the beholder doesn't know me well enough to be accurate. You generalize too much from one incident. You are just trying to get even with me." I may be right, but I will probably learn more if I assume that at least 1 percent of what you say is accurate. The 1 percent rule allows me to listen and learn more about myself than if I dismissed your feedback completely because I was clever enough to think of reasons for dismissing it. Receiving, filtering, and accepting feedback, even if it is delivered with some distortion, is part of the process of enhancing self-awareness and developing a clearer self-concept.

Gain with No Pain?

During my time at Esalen, I sometimes wearied of my quest for enlightenment, and I longed for a period of utter debauchery. I liked the idea so much that I presented a workshop on "endarkenment," the opposite of enlightenment, in which each person was to decide what he or she did worst and then teach the rest of the workshop group how to do it really well.

Many of the selected frailties turned out to be related to defenses. To our delight and my great surprise, this exercise led to less use of defenses. When the participants caught themselves being victims or critics or helpers or whatever, they found it very amusing and easy to laugh at themselves.

We found that we might not have to go through pain in order to gain. There was something about letting ourselves be thoroughly defensive, without criticism—in fact, with great support and approbation—that suddenly reduced the negative charge around defensive behavior and made it just a human response, not horrid but simply ineffective and unnecessary. Having the whole group of twelve to thirty-five people on the same quest underlined the humanness of it all and allowed each of us to examine, without judgment, when and why we were defensive, and this allowed us to choose to replace the defensive behavior.

Why not try it? Next time you begin to condemn yourself for being defensive, enjoy it. Wallow in it. Exaggerate it. Think of all the times you defend, and of the events leading you to defend. Think of all the ingenious ways you defend. For example, if your defensive style tends to be that of a victim, make sure to take every ambiguous comment in the worst possible way. Turn it into an unfair and unwarranted attack. Once you allow yourself to examine your defensive terrain, you may come to understand it better, see what function it is serving, and find some more satisfactory way to take care of yourself.

Pause for Reflection: Coping Mechanisms

This Pause allows me to look at my defensive patterns and coping mechanisms. I choose whether I want to change them; but, in any case, the more I know about what they are, the more I can do what I want with them. And the more awareness I acquire, the better a problem solver I become.

Denier. Here, I look at the cells in the first and fifth columns of Table 2.1. I consider whether I have made any of these statements to someone at some time, when in fact I was fooling myself and, consciously or unconsciously, knew that this was not how I felt. I circle one number (0–9) for each item that applies. How often have I said these things and not meant them (deceptive)?

Cell 11. **I include you.**
accurate 0 1 2 3 4 5 6 7 8 9 deceptive

Cell 21. **I control (or don't control) you.**
accurate 0 1 2 3 4 5 6 7 8 9 deceptive

Cell 31. **I am open with you.**
accurate 0 1 2 3 4 5 6 7 8 9 deceptive

Cell 41. **I feel you are significant.**
accurate 0 1 2 3 4 5 6 7 8 9 deceptive

Cell 51. **I feel you are competent.**
accurate 0 1 2 3 4 5 6 7 8 9 deceptive

Cell 61. **I like (love) you.**
accurate 0 1 2 3 4 5 6 7 8 9 deceptive

Cell 15. **I am fully alive.**
accurate 0 1 2 3 4 5 6 7 8 9 deceptive

Cell 25. **I determine my own life.**
accurate 0 1 2 3 4 5 6 7 8 9 deceptive

Cell 35. **I am aware of myself.**
accurate 0 1 2 3 4 5 6 7 8 9 deceptive

Cell 45. **I feel significant.**
accurate 0 1 2 3 4 5 6 7 8 9 deceptive

Cell 55. **I feel competent.**
accurate 0 1 2 3 4 5 6 7 8 9 deceptive

Cell 65. **I like myself.**
accurate 0 1 2 3 4 5 6 7 8 9 deceptive

Victim. Here, I make the statements in the third column negative. When have I said these things? In what circumstances? Was I being a victim? I circle one number (0–9) for each item that applies.

Cell 13. You exclude me.
I seldom complain   I often complain
of this 0   1   2   3   4   5   6   7   8   9   of this

Cell 23. You control me too much.
I seldom complain   I often complain
of this 0   1   2   3   4   5   6   7   8   9   of this

Cell 33. You are not open with me.
I seldom complain   I often complain
of this 0   1   2   3   4   5   6   7   8   9   of this

Cell 43. You feel I am insignificant.
I seldom complain   I often complain
of this 0   1   2   3   4   5   6   7   8   9   of this

Cell 53. You feel I am incompetent.
I seldom complain   I often complain
of this 0   1   2   3   4   5   6   7   8   9   of this

Cell 63. You don't like (love) me.
I seldom complain   I often complain
of this 0   1   2   3   4   5   6   7   8   9   of this

Critic. Here, I make the last three statements in the first column negative. How often do I react to people with these feelings? How do I feel about myself at those times? I circle one number (0–9) for each item that applies.

Cell 41. You are insignificant.
I seldom say or   I often say or
feel this   0   1   2   3   4   5   6   7   8   9   feel this

Cell 51. You are incompetent.
I seldom say or   I often say or
feel this   0   1   2   3   4   5   6   7   8   9   feel this

Cell 61. **I don't like (love) you.**

I seldom say or   I often say or
feel this   0   1   2   3   4   5   6   7   8   9   feel this

Self-Blamer. This defense uses the negative of the statements in the nine cells listed here. Do I have a tendency to blame myself excessively in any of these areas? I circle one number (0–9) for each item that applies.

Cell 11. **I exclude you.**

I seldom blame   I often blame
myself   0   1   2   3   4   5   6   7   8   9   myself

Cell 21. **I don't control you.**

I seldom blame   I often blame
myself   0   1   2   3   4   5   6   7   8   9   myself

Cell 31. **I'm not open with you.**

I seldom blame   I often blame
myself   0   1   2   3   4   5   6   7   8   9   myself

Cell 15. **I'm not fully alive.**

I seldom blame   I often blame
myself   0   1   2   3   4   5   6   7   8   9   myself

Cell 25. **I don't determine my own life.**

I seldom blame   I often blame
myself   0   1   2   3   4   5   6   7   8   9   myself

Cell 35. **I'm not aware of myself.**

I seldom blame   I often blame
myself   0   1   2   3   4   5   6   7   8   9   myself

Cell 45. **I feel insignificant.**

I seldom blame   I often blame
myself   0   1   2   3   4   5   6   7   8   9   myself

Cell 55. **I feel incompetent.**

I seldom blame   I often blame
myself   0   1   2   3   4   5   6   7   8   9   myself

Cell 65. I don't like myself.

I seldom blame   I often blame

myself   0   1   2   3   4   5   6   7   8   9   myself

Helper. With this defense, I say or feel the things listed in the six cells of the eighth column. I can better understand myself by using each cell to think about the *defensive* part of my being a helper. When am I being helpful so that I can feel good about being a helper? Do I fail to notice whether the person wants to be helped, or whether what I am doing is in fact helpful? Of course, there are aspects of what I do that other people find truly helpful; the defensive aspect is the one I identify here. How often do I say or feel the following things? I circle one number (0–9) for each item that applies.

Cell 18. I want you to be fully alive.

I seldom say or   I often say or

feel this   0   1   2   3   4   5   6   7   8   9   feel this

Cell 28. I want you to determine your own life.

I seldom say or   I often say or

feel this   0   1   2   3   4   5   6   7   8   9   feel this

Cell 38. I want you to be aware of yourself.

I seldom say or   I often say or

feel this   0   1   2   3   4   5   6   7   8   9   feel this

Cell 48. I want you to feel significant.

I seldom say or   I often say or

feel this   0   1   2   3   4   5   6   7   8   9   feel this

Cell 58. I want you to feel competent.

I seldom say or   I often say or

feel this   0   1   2   3   4   5   6   7   8   9   feel this

Cell 68. I want you to like yourself.

I seldom say or   I often say or

feel this   0   1   2   3   4   5   6   7   8   9   feel this

Demander. This defense uses the statements found in the cells of the fourth column. Excess is what makes this behavior defensive. I look at each cell and think about whether I make excessive demands on anyone in order to compensate for my own inability to fulfill my desires in that area. I circle one number (0–9) for each item that applies.

Cell 14. I want you to include me.

| I seldom say or feel this | 0 | 1 | 2 | 3 | 4 | 5 | 6 | 7 | 8 | 9 | I often say or feel this |

Cell 24. I want you to control me.

| I seldom say or feel this | 0 | 1 | 2 | 3 | 4 | 5 | 6 | 7 | 8 | 9 | I often say or feel this |

Cell 34. I want you to be open with me.

| I seldom say or feel this | 0 | 1 | 2 | 3 | 4 | 5 | 6 | 7 | 8 | 9 | I often say or feel this |

Cell 44. I want you to feel I am significant.

| I seldom say or feel this | 0 | 1 | 2 | 3 | 4 | 5 | 6 | 7 | 8 | 9 | I often say or feel this |

Cell 54. I want you to feel I am competent.

| I seldom say or feel this | 0 | 1 | 2 | 3 | 4 | 5 | 6 | 7 | 8 | 9 | I often say or feel this |

Cell 64. I want you to like (love) me.

| I seldom say or feel this | 0 | 1 | 2 | 3 | 4 | 5 | 6 | 7 | 8 | 9 | I often say or feel this |

Now I go back and review the patterns in my answers, remembering that this is not an evaluation; it is an attempt to gain an accurate self-picture, a part of my self-concept. I recall the clues to defensive behavior given on pages 86–87. If I decide to eliminate some of my defensive behavior, it's important for me first to recognize when I am being defensive. Using the concepts presented in this chapter, I can begin to figure out why.

What do I think of this statement? "I am most satisfied when my behavior and feelings are flexible, not rigid; when I am comfortable with how alive I feel; when I determine my life as much as I want to and can vary my actions at will; when I am as aware as I want to be at any given time; and when I feel as significant, competent, and likable as I wish to. As my self-concept approaches these ideals, my self-esteem rises."

Self-Esteem: Building a Positive Self-Concept

The realization that a positive self-concept is the bottom line for the human side of organizations led me to reflect on the ambivalence that this notion causes in the general culture. For example, critics of the "me generation," like Tom Wolfe, called members of this generation narcissistic, conceited, self-absorbed, selfish, prideful.[8] *To me, these descriptions were bewildering. With few exceptions, the people I knew who were pursuing greater self-knowledge had none of these traits. As they came to know and like themselves better, they seemed to become calmer, stronger, more real, more honest, more successful in their relationships, and more genuinely caring and helpful people. I was equally puzzled by the cascade of invective against California assemblyman John Vasconcellos,*[9] *Gloria Steinem,*[10] *and other champions of self-esteem. From my vantage point, the self-esteem advocates were and are exactly right: self-esteem is indeed the bottom line for human relations and the key to solving our social problems.*

The irony, of course, is that the critics of self-esteem are focusing on something else entirely: an inordinate or exaggerated fondness for oneself. What I am talking about is respect and objective liking for oneself. Another irony is that someone who has self-respect does not have an exaggerated sense of self and is not arrogant. In fact, low self-respect is what leads me to arrogance and bragging, as a way of convincing you (basically myself) that I am all right. It is impossible to have high self-respect and self-liking without great self-awareness. Greater self-awareness leads to better relations in general.

Self-esteem is the feeling I have about my self-concept. When what I want for myself matches what I perceive myself to be, I have a positive self-concept, which in turn helps me feel as alive, self-determining, self-aware, significant, competent, and likable as I want to be. Self-esteem comes from choosing to be the type of person I want to be: I'm aware of what that means, and I behave accordingly.

Self-esteem is both conscious and unconscious. It begins in childhood, and it is developed as I create my self-concept through internalizing (or rejecting) messages about me that I get from my parents and others, and from my own experiences of what I can and cannot do and what I am and am not. I compare myself to others, or to an ideal of the type of person I want to be, or to others' definitions of an ideal.

I am not aware of some parts of my self-concept. They are unconscious because I was uncomfortable with them, or I felt I could not or did not want to deal with them. For example, I may have assumed that I was basically a bad boy. I made this feeling of being unlovable, as well as my feelings of being insignificant or incompetent, unconscious: they were too painful to acknowledge.

When I hide these feelings, or when I defend myself against having to experience them, I become arrogant; that is, I exaggerate my own importance, or I brag about my accomplishments, or I act too ingratiating. This behavior arises out of unconsciously low self-esteem and low self-respect. I demonstrate high self-esteem, by contrast, by being flexible, being able to express myself fully, and being in charge of myself. My perceptions are accurate, and I have learned to make all my reactions conscious.

At the height of the House Un-American Activities Committee's anticommunist witchhunt, in the 1950s, I was a graduate student at the University of California at Los Angeles, supporting myself through the G.I. Bill and my salary as a teaching assistant. As a university employee, I was required to sign a loyalty oath in order to retain my job. I took the position that I would not sign, for reasons of principle, because I thought that people should be judged on their job performance, not on the basis of their political beliefs.

I became very active in opposition to the loyalty oath. My father heard of what I was doing and flew out from the Midwest. He spent three days with me, discussing the situation and the position I was taking. His attitude was, as usual, very logical: "Of course you are right in principle, but you will jeopardize your future. You are just an untested teaching assistant. No one knows you, and once you graduate, others will be hired first. They're less risky for an employer."

His arguments persuaded me. I went to lunch with my fellow nonsigners and told them that I had decided to sign and "fight from within"—a euphemism we used for dropping the fight. When I left the restaurant and walked into the bright sunlight of Los Angeles, I felt as if I weighed three tons. My muscles were stiff and heavy, and I felt totally dark.

At that point, a little voice whispered in my ear: "What kind of person do you want to be?"

"Be quiet," I said. "Can't you see I'm miserable?"

But the voice persisted, and I finally got the point: signing or not signing was not a matter of logic; most people could think of many excellent reasons for taking either position. It was a matter of what kind of person I wanted to be.

I decided not to sign the loyalty oath. My body lightened. I felt as if I weighed three ounces. I felt wonderful. My body was telling me what kind of person I wanted to be. When I followed that picture, I felt good. Looking back, I can see that this was my first experience of realizing that my self-esteem depends on how close I am to being the kind of person I want to be.

To the degree that I experience myself as being like my ideal, and as being unlike the self I want to avoid, I have positive self-esteem. Similarly, the more I fall short of my ideal, the more disappointed I am in myself, the more anger I feel toward myself. Feelings of disappointment in and anger with myself reduce my self-esteem. Why do I feel these inadequacies in my self-concept? How can I heighten my self-esteem? The answer to that question lies in the concept of choice: I choose feelings and behavior because, ineffective as they may seem, they are associated with a payoff. When I choose low self-esteem, it is because I get a payoff for it.

For example, suppose I want to be funny but am not. I am dour and ponderous. What do I get out of being humorless? On reflection, I find that it feels safer to me. I suspect that people are laughing at me anyway, and I fear that if I take something as a joke when it is meant to be serious, I will be caught off guard and feel hurt. Therefore, I assume that everything is serious, so that I can avoid painful surprises. My fear prevents me from being the person I want to be, and that lowers my self-esteem.

When I am not feeling good about myself, I notice that compliments and support from other people are pleasant to hear but do not make me feel better for very long, if at all. I dismiss compliments because I believe that people do not know me as well as I know myself. They like what they see, but they do not know all my faults, all the thoughts and feelings I have, and all the things I have done. If they did know, they would not feel the same way about me. I may even perceive other people's praise or liking for me as a threat: What if I do something to disappoint them? They may withdraw their liking, and so it is risky for me to feel good when they say good things about me. And there are other payoffs for choosing not to like myself more: "It is arrogant to like myself. If I appear modest people will like me better." "People will not expect much of me if I appear unsure of myself." "I will not be impertinent enough to think that I am better than my parents or siblings." "I would be ridiculous to like myself if no one else did."

Improving Self-Esteem in Organizations

Here is a new twist on an old saying: *If I give a hungry woman a fish, she won't be hungry. If I teach her how to fish, she'll never be hungry. But, if I create conditions within which she teaches herself how to fish, she'll never be hungry and she'll have enhanced self-esteem.* Self-esteem, then, is at the heart of all human relations in organizations. Exhibit 2.1 shows the general characteristics of low and high self-esteem. Teamwork difficulties arise from rigidities and defenses, which come from low self-esteem and fear of exposure, not from differences among members. Likewise, conflict resolution depends on dissolving rigidities and getting people to see conflict as a logical puzzle for team members to solve together. Problem solving is blocked when a person is anxious about being exposed, or is determined to be right, or shows other kinds of defensive behavior that come from low self-esteem. Leadership, too, relies centrally on self-awareness, which in turn requires sufficiently strong self-esteem for looking clearly at oneself and feeling comfortable about being known to others. Performance appraisal is successful to the extent that each person feels acknowledged for his or her strengths and weaknesses and for who he or she is and, through healthy self-esteem, is willing to give up blame in favor of mutual problem solving. Healthy, injury-free workplaces are also attained through self-awareness. Quality programs succeed when personal agendas based on low self-esteem are handled effectively. Diversity can be celebrated when threats to self-concept from "different" groups are alleviated.

My relationships with others depend largely on how I feel about myself. Problems arise because I believe that you create conditions that cause me to doubt myself. For example, if I don't feel significant and you ignore me, I may work only hard enough to keep my job. If I feel important, however, I may tell you what I would like from you (such as your giving me feedback about my work). If you present me with a situation I don't feel capable of handling, I may become very angry with you and resist doing what you want me to do. If I feel competent, however, I welcome the challenge. If I feel that you don't like me, I may try to get even with you or try to "get" you. If I feel likable, however, I may use the negative feelings you have about me as valuable tools for learning about myself.

I can use these insights into self-concept and self-esteem to understand why I feel as I do about myself. I may then choose to

Exhibit 2.1. Characteristics of Self-Esteem.

Low Self-Esteem

I feel dull, bored, tired, and lifeless.

I lack stamina and the ability to stay the course and finish a job.

I lack motivation and am often tempted to give up and say, "What's the use?"

I feel helpless, at the whim of forces in the universe beyond me; I am the victim of luck, coincidence, the environment, the economy, the changing business climate, and other people.

I am unaware and don't really know who I am or what I am doing.

I don't know why I do some things that get me into trouble and that seem not to be what I really want.

I feel insignificant, like a nobody, a person no one would be interested in: if I didn't go out of my way to call attention to myself, no one would notice me, and if I didn't show up for work, nobody would miss me.

I feel incompetent. I don't know what I am doing and am not a responsible person. I cannot be relied on to do a good job or make good decisions.

I am not a nice person. If people really knew me well, they would reject me immediately. Anyone who knows me very long will dislike me.

I blame other people and circumstances for my bad feelings. I am harsh and demanding, so that I can attribute my lack of popularity to my "dedication" to the job.

I act furious with myself when I miss a shot on the handball or tennis court, as if to tell observers, "I usually hit shots like that," but in fact I have never hit a shot like that in my life.

High Self-Esteem

I feel alive to the degree I wish to.

I have control over myself and make optimal use of my capacities to think, feel, sense, and move.

I'm not a helpless victim. I don't blame. I influence my life in the direction I want.

I feel the joy that comes from realizing my potential.

I am aware of my thoughts and feelings and know what's going on with me.

I'm not afraid to see myself clearly. I don't deceive myself.

I speak directly to others instead of talking behind their backs.

I feel significant and important, and so I do not have to demand attention. I understand the impact I have on other people.

I feel competent to deal with any situation confronting me.

I feel free to admit it when I don't know something, and I can ask for help when it is appropriate.

I feel likable and lovable.

I'm comfortable letting people know me well, since I'm confident they will like me and I will gain friends.

I feel good when I help people. I take risks with confidence. I'm neither foolhardy nor overcautious.

I'm not shattered by lack of support or not being liked. I prefer being liked, but if I am not, I know I am still likable.

I can follow directions without resentment and give directions without guilt or fear of punishment.

I accept criticism and make positive use of it.

increase my self-esteem. By bringing some of my unconscious feelings about myself into my awareness, I may discover that I have not appreciated some of the positive feelings I have about myself. I may also find that some negative ideas I have about myself are not accurate anymore.

There are three major avenues to improving self-esteem. First, I can practice new behavior while I seek causes for my old behavior. The new behavior will not in itself cause changes in my self-concept, but it may simplify the process of change and, in the meantime, bring about some temporary improvements. Second, I can find the unsatisfactory aspects of myself and discover what payoff I get for maintaining them. Third, I can find out where in my history and origins I acquired my idea of an ideal self (or a self to be avoided) and revisit those decisions. The following Pause for Reflection provides activities that may help me begin moving in these three directions.

Pause for Reflection: Self-Esteem

This Pause begins with several exercises for helping me start a process of improving my self-esteem. These exercises are even more valuable if I can find another person or even a group of friends who will complete them with me and participate in a discussion after we have finished.

Behavior: I start with my behavior, which may not get at the root of my low self-esteem but will lead me to more positive action while I look for causes. Changing my behavior is in itself often helpful in training myself for new, more constructive ways of being. I rate myself on each item[11]:

Not true   Especially true
of me   0   1   2   3   4   5   6   7   8   9   of me

_____ Telling my truth; letting myself and others know what my
       truth is

_____ Being aware that I am always choosing; accepting responsibility, without blame, for everything happening in my life

_____ Seeking deeper self-awareness; reading, discussing, pondering; improving my awareness of old unexamined beliefs and deeper levels of being

_____ Giving up blame, postponing judgment, and listening and understanding before defending or attacking or making others wrong

_____ Envisioning my ideal self; keeping in mind that I am choosing the way I want to be

_____ Giving up withholding from myself and deceiving myself

_____ Questioning my limiting beliefs

_____ Being in touch with my body and listening to it as a source of cues to my feelings

_____ Treating my growth and myself with respect and patience, rather than irritation and judgment; maintaining the larger perspective that I am developing enhanced self-esteem

Unsatisfactory aspects: This exercise is designed to pinpoint the unsatisfactory aspects of myself that prevent me from feeling better about myself. Once I find these unsatisfactory aspects, I can discover the payoffs I receive for not being more the way I want to be. The exercise helps me describe the specifics of how I fall short of my ideal self (or, just as potent, how I am being what I don't want to be). By analyzing the difference between what I am and what I want to be, I get a measure of my self-esteem.[12]

The following questionnaire (Exhibit 2.2) represents all the dissatisfactions that I may have with interpersonal relations and with my self-concept. They do not necessarily match how other people see me or how I "really" am (as if there were some objective way of measuring that).

Exhibit 2.2. Dissatisfaction Questionnaire.

	I include people too much.
	I don't include people enough.
	I allow people to include me too much.
	I don't let people include me enough.
	I don't feel alive enough.
	I get too involved.
	I don't feel enough that people are significant.
	I feel people are more significant than I want to.
	I prevent people from feeling I am as significant as I am.
	I care too much whether people feel I am significant.
	I act more significant than I really feel.
	I care too much about being significant.
	I control people too much.
	I don't control people enough.
	I allow people to control me too much.
	I don't let people control me enough.
	I don't have enough control over my life.
	I don't seek help enough.
	I don't feel enough that people are competent.
	I feel people are more competent than I want to.
	I prevent people from feeling I am as competent as I am.
	I care too much whether people feel I am competent.
	I act more competent than I really feel.
	I care too much about being competent.
	I am too open with people.
	I am not open enough with people.
	I allow people to be too open with me.
	I don't let people be open enough with me.

	I don't know myself well enough.
	I analyze myself too much.
	I don't like people enough.
	I like people more than I want to.
	I prevent people from liking me as much as I want them to.
	I care too much whether people like me.
	I care too much about being liked.
	I like myself too much.

Score	Item	Payoff

I indicate the degree to which I agree with each item by placing a number in the box to the left of the item. The numbers range from 0 (disagree) to 9 (agree). I realize that this is not an evaluation. It is an opportunity for me to be more aware of myself and see more clearly the directions I can take to strengthen my self-esteem, if I choose to. Next, I circle the boxes with the largest numbers. These represent behavior that blocks me from feeling better about myself. Then, using the concept of choice, or responsibility for myself, I take the next step: rather than simply promising to change, I assume that I choose these deficiencies because I get a payoff for them. Setting aside judgments of whether the behavior is right or wrong, good or bad, I look for the payoffs in a spirit of exploration and self-understanding.

I have now chosen to be more aware and am in a position to make a conscious decision about what I want to do. On the grid that follows the questionnaire, for each of the boxes with the largest circled numbers I write down the payoff. The payoff must be stated positively, not flippantly; the payoff is rewarding enough to prevent me from gaining higher self-esteem, and so it must be potent.

Origins: I now explore the origins of the feelings and opinions I've identified about myself. Where did I get my ideas about who I am? Knowing the sources won't necessarily increase my self-esteem, but it may point me in directions that will enhance my self-awareness. For each of the items on the grid, I ask myself:

- When was the first time I acted or felt this way?
- Did I ever act this way toward a parent or close relative?
- Did any close relative act or feel this way toward me during my childhood?
- Did any close relative behave in this way toward another close relative during my childhood?
- Is this what I really want?
- What am I willing to do about it?

Now I take the next step (even if it is a leap of the imagination) and answer the following questions:

- What influence does my self-esteem, or lack of it, have on my effectiveness?
- What would a workplace made up of people with low self-esteem look like?
- What would a workplace made up of people with high self-esteem look like?
- Which workplace would have higher productivity? Why?
- What is the overall level of self-esteem in my organization? In my group or team? How could it be improved?

PART TWO

The Human Element at Work

Part One explored the basic dimensions of self-concept and self-esteem; Part Two takes up the task of applying those concepts to organizational goals and problems. Chapter Three discusses practical methods for increasing compatibility within teams, forming teams, enhancing team relations with outside forces and groups, and using the Open Teamwork approach to elicit superb performance. Chapter Four examines the enhancement of individual performance through a new approach to performance appraisal, job fit (and satisfaction), and individual decision making, paying particular attention to creative and logical problem-solving processes. Chapter Five discusses *concordance*, a new approach to group decision making that provides a method for groups to work together and make efficient and satisfying decisions. Chapter Six concludes the discussion of applications with a focus on leadership and the creation of an organization that reflects the concepts and practices of the Human Element model. The Conclusion offers a few final thoughts on the difficulty and necessity of change.

3

Open Teamwork: Building Compatible and Productive Teams

An industrial crisis . . . comes from being between paradigms. The old way to win the game of commerce was to have smart *individuals* manage organizations that turned high profits by producing products in large batches at low cost. The new way to win the game is to build *teams* that design and continuously improve the function of organizational processes in order to satisfy customers.

—*R. Redenbaugh and C. Bell*[1]

Starting in the 1950s, with my earliest research on internal group relations, I had been trying to get to the bottom of why teams do or do not work well together.[2] As I tried different approaches to improving team performance, I found that none of my assumptions was right. At first I had thought that harmonious groups would be more efficient, while conflicted groups would be inefficient. But that didn't hold up. Raucous groups and quiet groups alike sometimes excelled and sometimes failed. Then I thought that group success depended on how the members dealt with disagreement. That proved to be a bit closer. Effective groups tended to bounce back from conflict, while ineffective groups disintegrated after they disagreed.

Next, I looked into the notion that teams must have common goals to work well together. But I worked with a computer group that had just spent three years developing a new machine, only to be told that there was no market for it. The members were crushed, and they struggled to recover. Many, ready to quit, were already looking for other jobs, but suddenly the team members realized that they really wanted to work together. Their relationships within the group, not the common goal of building a computer, held them together. Once they realized that, they were confident that they could create another product to build together.

So much for the "common goal" assumption. I asked myself, "What about the belief that a team needs someone of each psychological type in order to function?" That one didn't match my observations of a self-directed team at a large manufacturing plant. When that team lost a member, the others would replace the person, shift roles to cover the lost member's specific function, or reorganize.

Effective teams seemed to have great flexibility, which made the need for specific people in specific roles secondary. As I kept looking for the ingredients of successful teams, I examined the idea that a strong authoritarian leader or a life-threatening situation could force team-work. Research, however, showed that coercion sometimes worked in the short term but not over a long time. Later I saw confirmation of the research experiments, when several new computer companies worked feverishly and successfully to turn out new products, succeeded, and then almost folded because so many of their people no longer wanted to work for them. Was it the crisis, the pressure, that had dissolved the teams? I still didn't have a clear answer.

Then I became interested in the possibility that self-esteem might be a key to good teamwork. I recalled a common situation, in which a lengthy labor-management dispute is eventually settled on almost the same terms the two sides fought over in the beginning. I had already seen how rigidity leads to defensive, unproductive individual behavior. Connecting that work to my thinking about teamwork suggested that good teamwork occurred when team members (1) were open enough to one another and to themselves to recognize when they were personally threatened and (2) were willing to acknowledge those feelings to the whole team. Team members who feel threatened but who are not aware of it become rigid—and that stops teamwork.

In other words, teams do not fail because they disagree, or because they do not have common goals, or because their members' approaches to solving problems differ, or because they do not include certain personality types. They don't work because one or more people are rigid, and a person is rigid because his or her self-concept is threatened.

What a wonderful irony. If we want to improve team performance, we must work on individuals.

This chapter examines the relationships between individual self-esteem and group compatibility. It explores how groups develop and how rigidity depresses compatibility and effective group functioning. It also looks at how team members can use their insights about their relationships to create more effective relations with external forces, such as other departments or a headquarters management staff. The chapter concludes with a discussion of two practical applications, the Open Teamwork model and the Team Compatibility Index.

Teamwork and Productivity

The term *team*, as used in this book, means all the people in an organization, or the people who belong to any unit within it, ostensibly working toward a common goal. Units may include work teams, panels, administrative staffs, matrix organizations, investigative teams, committees, special-project groups—in short, any group of people who produce a better product or service if they are successful working together.

Few managers would say that teamwork is unimportant. In fact, most leaders spend a good deal of their time worrying about and trying to improve teamwork, as part of the overall drive toward greater efficiency and productivity. Nevertheless, it's important to clarify a misconception about teamwork that often leads to disappointing results. That misconception results from the failure to see the close relationship between team compatibility and productivity. Most real interpersonal struggles—peace negotiations, labor issues, divorces—have to do mainly with feelings, fears, insecurities, and rigidities, not primarily with the logic of a situation. Understanding the connection between compatibility and productivity is crucial to understanding the vital role of good teamwork.[3]

Compatibility—the ability of people to work well together—is positively related to productivity. A common organizational myth is that there is no time to deal with personal relationships; there are deadlines, bottom lines, and payrolls to meet, and they take priority. But ignoring teamwork problems in favor of "practical" matters is the expression of a massive organizational self-deception. It is more true to say that an organization cannot afford *not* to take the time to deal with relations between people; otherwise, those relations inevitably affect productivity, often in a devastating way.

Example   A marketing team in a Fortune 500 company proudly proposed to management a plan for marketing a "family" of personal grooming products. Management turned the proposal down flat as a poorly thought-out plan.

The marketing team was dismayed. Investigation revealed that in the marketing team's planning meetings the concept of a "family" of products had arisen as a solution to the group's interpersonal problems, not to the marketing problem. Group members had great difficulty saying *no* to one person's idea and *yes* to another person's idea. The "family" of products proposal rescued them by allowing all ideas to be accepted, regardless of who had presented them. No one had to face having an idea rejected or rejecting someone else's idea.

As a marketing idea, the "family" of products was indeed inadequate. When the concept had been adopted, no one really knew why. Everyone was convinced that it had been adopted for marketing reasons.

When interpersonal problems exist but are not dealt with, the organization's productivity inevitably diminishes; how much depends on the task. Some tasks require cooperation in order to be done well. Other jobs can be done by one person just as well as (and sometimes better than) by a group. Many jobs can be organized either to require cooperation or to be accomplished independently. The effect of compatibility on productivity is greatest for tasks in which cooperation is necessary to the achievement of results. Experiments[4] have demonstrated that compatible groups perform even better under time pressure than they do without pressure, while incompatible groups become less effective.

Approaches to Teamwork

The most traditional and perhaps the oldest approach to teamwork is *coercion*, which works on the principle that people are hired and paid to work together. If they don't, fire them and hire people who will. As a British stage director put it, "A team effort is a lot of people doing what I say." Fear of discipline, dismissal, or punishment is assumed to motivate team members to do a good job.

Example   Colonel Wayne addressed his eight-man team at an outpost in the Persian Gulf: "Men, this is a highly classified mission and is of great importance to the defense of the United States. You have been selected to carry out this mission. You are expected to work well together for at least a year. If there is any trouble, I'll find the guilty party, put it in his record, and transfer him—and you all know what that means for your careers. Good luck."

Despite these stern instructions, the team performed poorly. Follow-up interviews revealed the reasons. As one of the men said, "At first I was anxious and made certain everything I did was beyond criticism. In the army, 'to err is terminal.' I realized that since one of us would be blamed if we didn't produce, I would make sure it wasn't me. I backed away from making suggestions for fear they would fail, though I'm sure some of them would have been valuable. If anyone else made a suggestion I knew was bad, I didn't say a word. If it didn't work, it wasn't my fault. I was just being a good soldier and following orders. I did just what I had to do to stay out of trouble. We all did. That's why we produced so little."

Coercion sometimes leads to the accomplishment of short-term goals, but its drawbacks far outweigh its advantages. Rather than empowering team members, it encourages self-protection and limits creativity and productivity. But it is often the method that new managers reach for: they may not know what else to do, they think it's what they're supposed to do, or they don't know of other ways to be a manager.

By contrast, *compromise* as an approach to teamwork assumes that it is inevitable for people to disagree. Team members are supposed to forget about their disagreements, respect each other, appreciate diversity, and resolve their differences for the good of the team.

Example Professor Clay, department chair, gave instructions to her faculty committee at the state university: "Your mission is to produce a curriculum that covers all your areas of interest. You are all professionals, and so I expect you to work together harmoniously. Any bickering, hostility, or injection of personal feelings into discussions can only deter you from your goal. You are all experienced committee members and know the art of compromise. Good luck."

The curriculum that this team produced was highly unsatisfactory. Many students complained of the enormous number of requirements. An insightful committee member talked about what had happened: "For some reason, I had several illnesses during the time the committee was meeting. I found the group very frustrating. There were many ideas I thought were absurd, but since we had implicitly agreed not to express any negativity, I held back in the interest of harmony. Everyone did—and that put us in a box. We had no way of expressing a preference for one person's ideas over another's. As a result, we accepted everyone's pet ideas and overloaded the curriculum."

Compromise may not produce the overtly negative behavior that coercion does, but it falls far short of creating effective teams. Everyone superficially "gets along" while hidden agendas rule the day.

Complementarity in teamwork divides tasks so that people individually do the things they are good at and thus complement other team members. The sum of members' diverse skills and personalities creates the wherewithal to accomplish a task successfully. For example, team members can be classified according to their cognitive and decision-making styles (authoritarians, thinkers, feelers, intuiters, extroverts, left-brainers, high controllers, and so on). In a complementary approach, the leaders try to compose a team from the right mix of individuals. This approach may help make a team more efficient, but complementarity will not ultimately get to the heart of the matter when the team runs into real difficulties that have to do with anxiety and with members' other feelings about themselves and their interpersonal relations.

Example   Ms. Myers addressed her training group at a major manufacturing company: "The exercise we are about to do requires at least two different skills: thinking through some mathematical calculations, and being sensitive to human feelings. We have already administered a test that indicates which type you lean toward. Your work teams have been set up so that you have both logical and feeling types represented. Good luck."

One of the participants explained the lackluster results that the teams achieved: "The first thing I did was carve out an important niche for myself. I was the group 'sensitive.' I represented feelings. I noticed the group 'logician' starting to dominate the meetings, and so I slowly began making slightly barbed comments about how mechanistic and unfeeling it was to concentrate only on numbers and not on the flesh-and-blood reality of actual people. I may have overdone it a bit, but I didn't like being shoved aside."

With the *open teamwork* method, group members understand that problems arise from rigid adherence to positions, not from differences of opinion or differences between cognitive and personality styles. We agree to openly discuss our personal feelings and the fears behind our rigidities (which stem from issues of low self-esteem; see

Chapter Two). Moreover, those feelings are accounted for in the solutions to problems. Teamwork results from using openness as a method for solving any problem.

The complementarity approach solves some team problems by making sure that all personal requirements for a task are in place. The team's behavior is thus efficient at first. It weakens, however, when someone is threatened and becomes defensive and rigid. Complementarity, which does not entail any explicit method for dealing with this behavior, may therefore founder. A more adequate solution to this problem is open teamwork, with its concept of compatibility.

Pause for Reflection: Teamwork

1. How do I function as a team player? What are my strengths and weaknesses? Do I prefer to work alone or in groups? Why? What's the payoff for my preferences?

2. In what areas of team interaction do I hold to my position rigidly, even when it is not in the best interest of the team? In a group or on a team, what experiences make me anxious or leave me feeling threatened? What is an example?

3. Am I as open as I want to be in team interactions?

4. What is my opinion about honesty in teamwork? Are honesty and openness of equal importance in teamwork?

5. How important is it to hold people responsible (accountable) for the team's effectiveness? Can I think of times when it helped and times when it interfered?

6. In my organization, when might the coercive approach to teamwork be appropriate? Why?

7. In my organization, when might compromise be an effective approach to teamwork? Why?

8. What is my initial reaction to the complementarity approach to teamwork? What are its strengths and weaknesses?

9. What approach to teamwork best describes what happens in my organization?

10. How have I seen rigidity hurt teamwork in my organization? in my own participation in a team?

Compatibility: The Human Element Approach to Complementarity

Lack of rigidity is basic to good teamwork, but my ability to work with others depends to a large extent on our compatibility and complementarity—that is, on the ability of our personalities or styles to enhance each other, supply each other's missing traits, and support each other. The phrases "birds of a feather flock together" and "opposites attract," apparently contradictory, can thus be reconciled. The "birds of a feather" maxim is related to *atmosphere compatibility*—that is, the climate, ground rules, or stage setting within which we interact. The "opposites attract" maxim has to do with *role compatibility*—that is, the parts we wish to play. When our preference for how we want to work as team members is primarily rational, complementarity may well be enough to handle any issues that arise, but that is often not the case. How do I come to prefer a particular working atmosphere and certain roles? The bases of my preferences tell me a great deal about why and how my team and I do or do not resolve our differences.

Atmosphere Compatibility

In an organization, I may prefer different types of atmospheres that can be located along the Human Element dimensions of inclusion, control, and openness. The term *atmosphere* refers to the working environment and approaches to decision making. The atmosphere is composed of shared behavior, beliefs, values, and settings and may incorporate different levels and types of inclusion, control, and openness. No one type of atmosphere is necessarily good or bad. Each type has advantages and disadvantages, which depend on the organization, the people, and the tasks. Brainstorming is usually best in a high-inclusion, low-control atmosphere. Getting work done in a short time is more efficient in a high-control, low-openness (that is, structured and businesslike) atmosphere, where everything is planned and well organized.

An atmosphere can be described in high-low terms, as in the following schema:

Dimension	Atmosphere
High inclusion	Together, interactive
Low inclusion	Alone, individual
High control	Hierarchical, structured
Low control	Flowing, spontaneous
High openness	Open, candid
Low openness	Businesslike, impersonal

If the atmosphere for inclusion is high, we communicate often, meet and interact with one another, and rely on interaction to solve problems. Work teams or people who must work closely together and reach decisions jointly are in high-inclusion atmospheres. In an atmosphere of low inclusion, we seldom meet, communicate, or even see one another. Jobs in which we each have our own tasks and work at them alone in private offices are jobs in a low-inclusion atmosphere. In such an atmosphere, I rely on myself to solve problems.

Incompatibility in inclusion occurs when some of us like a high-inclusion atmosphere while others prefer a low-inclusion atmosphere. I may want to get together and interact with you, while you want to be left alone. The difference is similar to that between extroverts and introverts. In marriage, an example of inclusion incompatibility would be the wife's wanting her husband to go out at night with her and friends (high inclusion) and the husband's wanting to stay home and watch television alone (low inclusion). In organizations, the use and planning of work and office space often bring inclusion issues to the surface. I may want a nest of offices where we all have easy access to one another, or at least an open-door policy (high-inclusion atmosphere). You may prefer a private office with a lock on the door (low-inclusion atmosphere).

Control preferences can likewise affect compatibility within teams. A high-control atmosphere entails a strict hierarchy, a structure, clear lines of authority, and definite rules for giving and taking orders. Plans typically are made far ahead of time, and the person with the most power resolves conflicts. The military is an excellent example of an organization with a high-control atmosphere. By contrast, in a low-control atmosphere there is little hierarchy. We all have equal decision-making power, and power shifts between us as necessary. I prefer to "go with the flow" and make up my plans as I go along, resolving conflicts by mutual negotiation. A democratic or laissez-faire organization (such as the leadership council of a commune) typically has an atmosphere of low control. Incompatibility can arise when some members want a clear power structure, with everything planned out ahead of time, and others want an egalitarian structure, with everyone participating in decisions. *Disciplinary* versus *permissive*, and *hierarchical* versus *democratic*, are contrasting adjectives that express control incompatibility. The incompatibility may arise in the first place because I do not agree with you on how conflicts are to be resolved. I want the person with the most power to make the decisions that resolve conflicts, and you want everyone to resolve conflicts jointly. Our difficulty persists when you or I hold rigidly to our position.

Openness in atmosphere has to do with preferences about the expression of feelings. In an atmosphere of high openness, I am candid about my feelings, and I resolve differences through considering feelings. In a low-openness atmosphere, personality issues and personal relations on or off the job are discouraged, and I am businesslike or impersonal. Incompatibility arises when you want an emotionally open atmosphere and I want to stick to business. You want to consider the feelings of the people involved in a problem, while I want a resolution that is based on "the facts." The issue is not so much our disagreement itself as our lack of agreement over how to resolve our differences.

Example   Bob, the department head of a research laboratory, was aware of serious problems in the department and scheduled a meeting to lay everything on the table. He knew people distrusted him, and he was critical of the way certain people were doing their jobs. He wanted to air all these grievances and clear things up.

At the meeting, Bob ran into strong opposition. Fred, a key section leader, didn't want to discuss these matters, and he simply would not express his opinions. The meeting failed.

Later, Fred told a consultant that he had not felt it was safe to say what he was really feeling, for fear of being fired (that is, making a "career-limiting move"). The problem was one of disagreement about openness.

Role Compatibility

Role compatibility involves the parts we play with respect to each other as we interact in the work atmosphere. There are two types of role incompatibility: you and I are *confrontive* (that is, we both want to initiate behavior, but neither of us wants to be the recipient); or we are *apathetic* (that is, we both want to be on the receiving end of behavior, but neither of us wants to initiate it).

Confrontive incompatibility is usually overt and obvious. It leads to open confrontation, power struggles, and turf wars. Apathetic incompatibility is covert and difficult to identify. Its most noticeable symptom is that nothing happens when it should. Nobody does anything, because someone else is supposed to do it. Table 3.1 represents role incompatibility in terms of the Human Element dimensions of inclusion, control, and openness.

Where inclusion is concerned, compatibility means that I like to initiate being together to the same degree that you like to be asked to get together. For example, if I like to be the host (that is, I like to invite you, or initiate the contact) and you like to be the guest (that

Table 3.1. Role Incompatibility.

	Confrontive	Apathetic
Dimension	Both sides say:	Both sides say:
Inclusion	"Don't call me, I'll call you."	"I'm waiting for your call."
Control	"I'm in charge here. Don't tell me what to do."	"Tell me what to do. I won't tell you what to do."
Openness	"I want you to know about me, but I don't want to know about you."	"Tell me all about yourself. I won't tell you about me."

is, you like to receive my invitation), then in that regard we get along well. Confrontive incompatibility arises when we both strongly want to *initiate* inclusion, but neither of us wants to *be included*; we both want to choose our own company. Apathetic incompatibility arises when we both want to be included, but we both hang back, waiting for an invitation, without offering one ourselves.

Where control is concerned, role compatibility means that each of us likes to give orders to the same degree that the other likes to take them. If you like to take charge of the situation, and I like someone to take over to the same extent, then in this regard we are compatible. Confrontive incompatibility arises when we both like to be in charge, and neither of us likes to take orders. We then enter a power struggle. We may be so intent on winning or on being right that we do not appreciate or even listen to each other's position. Apathetic incompatibility arises when we are both submissive and want to be told what to do. If you as my boss have trouble making decisions, and if I as your employee have no initiative, then together we are ineffective. Ultimately, we seek other people to work with.

In the openness dimension, role compatibility means that each of us likes to initiate openness to the same degree that the other likes to have it initiated. For example, I may like to confide my deepest thoughts, fears, and ideas to people, and you are highly receptive to hearing them, but you may prefer to keep your own feelings to yourself, and I may prefer not to hear others' confidences and feelings. Regardless of our other differences, we have role compatibility because we each receive what the other wants to give. Confrontive incompatibility arises when we both want to initiate openness, but neither of us wants to have it initiated toward us. We are both saying, "When I want to be open, I will decide with whom." Apathetic incompatibility arises when we both want to have a more open relationship, but neither of us will risk initiating it. For example, we may be attracted to each other, but neither of us makes the first move.

Pause for Reflection: Atmosphere and Role Compatibility

On the basis of the dynamics of inclusion, control, and openness within roles and atmosphere, it is possible to assess a group of individuals' preferences and determine how well we are likely to work together. Such an evaluation is especially useful in situations where we have not worked together before or don't know each other, such as on work teams in new organizations.

To assess their role compatibility, all team members rate themselves on initiating and receiving for inclusion, control, and openness. Then we compare our initiating ratings with our receiving ratings for all three areas. The closer these scores are on a particular dimension, the more likely we are to be compatible on that dimension. For example, if we both rate ourselves low on "I am open with you" (cell 31), it may help to explain why our communication is superficial and why we think we've agreed on an issue but it turns out later that we haven't. The Periodic Table of the Human Elements for atmosphere and role preferences shows the twelve cells (concerning behavior) that determine complementarity in teamwork.

	Interpersonal: Do Self (I) to Other (You)		Interpersonal: Get Other (You) to Self (I)		Individual Self (I) to Self (I)		Other Other (O) to Other (O)	
	See	Want	See	Want	See	Want	See	Want
Inclusion	I include you.	I want to include you.	You include me.	I want you to include me.				
	11	12	13	14	15	16	17	18
Control	I control you.	I want to control you.	You control me.	I want you to control me.				
	21	22	23	24	25	26	27	28
Openness	I am open with you.	I want to be open with you.	You are open with me.	I want you to be open with me.				
	31	32	33	34	35	36	37	38
Significance								
	41	42	43	44	45	46	47	48
Competence								
	51	52	53	54	55	56	57	58
Likability								
	61	62	63	64	65	66	67	68

Role Compatibility

Compare:

Cells 11, 21, 31. How I behave toward you (*I include you, I control you, I am open with you*)

with

Cells 14, 24, 34. How you want me to behave toward you (*you want me to include you, you want me to control you, you want me to be open with you*)

We will be compatible on control, for example, if you want to be controlled to the same degree that I want to control you.

Atmosphere Compatibility

Use the following items to get a numerical score on all four aspects of each dimension.

Cells 11, 12, 13, 14. **This is my atmosphere preference in inclusion.**
Alone   0   1   2   3   4   5   6   7   8   9   Together

Cells 21, 22, 23, 24. **This is my atmosphere preference in control.**
Flowing 0   1   2   3   4   5   6   7   8   9   Hierarchical

Cells 31, 32, 33, 34. **This is my atmosphere preference in openness.**
Impersonal   0   1   2   3   4   5   6   7   8   9   Open

Which are my high scores? In which of these preferences might I be somewhat rigid? If I prefer a high level of inclusion on all four dimensions, and you prefer a low-inclusion atmosphere, we will be atmosphere-incompatible with respect to inclusion. The closer our preferences on each dimension, the higher our atmosphere compatibility.

Rigidity: The Enemy of Teamwork

As already mentioned, teams become frustrated and ineffective not because of differences among group members but because of the rigidity with which members hold to their positions. Rigidity, as we have seen, is part of the defensive aspect of behavior. Its presence or absence depends significantly on my self-esteem. When my self-esteem is high, self-awareness leads me to recognize when I'm being defensive. Without self-awareness, my defense mechanisms are likely to dominate my perceptions. When I allow my defenses to harden, my behavior, feelings, and perceptions may very well become rigid.

Rigidities result directly from my personal fears (mostly unconscious) of being ignored, humiliated, or rejected. These fears stem from my feelings (also mostly unconscious) of being insignificant, incompetent, or unlikable. If we all have high self-esteem—that is, if we feel both consciously and unconsciously significant, competent, and likable—then differences among us (intellectual, ethnic, stylistic, gender-related), although they may be difficult, are all conscious and are puzzles to be solved. Team members who are aware of their fears and feelings can acknowledge their differences and integrate them creatively in order to enrich the solutions to problems.

I develop certain preferences related to atmosphere and roles. Like my behavior and feelings with respect to inclusion, control, and openness, my role and atmosphere preferences have rational and defensive aspects. The rational aspect is a result of my conscious choices. Self-awareness allows me to be flexible enough to operate in any atmosphere and occupy any role as the need arises. The defensive aspect indicates personal insecurities that can lead to rigidity. I may cling to a particular preference beyond the point where it is rational because I sense unconsciously that I need to protect myself from experiencing unwanted, painful feelings.

Atmosphere Preferences

When I rationally choose a particular atmosphere, I prefer it because I find it useful and enjoyable. I am still flexible enough that if a situation calls for me to work in a different atmosphere, I can do so comfortably. For example, I may prefer to work alone (low-inclusion atmosphere), but if a problem can be solved best by my being part of a team, I can do so comfortably. By contrast, if I choose an atmosphere out of anxiety, because it is less threatening to me, then I have difficulty adapting. Because of weakness in my self-esteem, I have certain fears about myself of which I am unaware. I show excessive zeal for a particular atmosphere because I anticipate that it will be less threatening. For instance, I may avoid working with a group and insist on working alone in order to alleviate my unconscious expectation of feeling insignificant in the group and my fear of being ignored, even though the task could be performed much better cooperatively. If I do not feel competent, I may imagine or hope that an atmosphere of high control will provide a structure that will prevent my incompetence from being revealed. Table 3.2 shows how my defensive personal beliefs can lead to my preference for a type of atmosphere that will relieve my anxiety, reduce threats, and alleviate my fears and negative feelings.

Table 3.2. Bases of Rigid Atmosphere Preferences.

Since...	I hope that in an atmosphere of...	...my anxiety will be relieved because...
Inclusion		
I'm not fully alive, I won't feel anything.	High inclusion	You will stimulate me, and I will feel more alive.
I'm not fully alive, I won't feel anything.	Low inclusion	Without other people to consider, I can do what stimulates me.
Significance		
I'm not significant, I'm afraid I'll be ignored.	High inclusion	You will have to pay attention to me.
I'm not significant, I'm afraid I'll be ignored.	Low inclusion	I will ignore you before you ignore me.
Control		
I don't control myself enough, I fear getting out of control.	High control	You will control me from outside myself.
I control myself too much, I fear being too controlled.	Low control	At least *you* will not control me, too.

Competence

I'm not competent, I am afraid of humiliation.	High control	I can prepare and avoid surprises that reveal my incompetence.
I'm not competent, I am afraid of humiliation.	Low control	Little will be expected of me, and people won't notice my incompetence.

Openness

I'm not aware, I don't know why I do what I do.	High openness	You will help me find myself.
I'm not aware, I don't know why I do what I do.	Low openness	You will not find out how unaware I am.

Likability

I'm not likable, I'm afraid I'll be rejected.	High openness	You will tell me right away if you don't like me (no unexpected rejection).
I'm not likable, I'm afraid I'll be rejected.	Low openness	I'll never know if you don't like me.

If I have an unsatisfactory self-concept in any area, I may choose an atmosphere accordingly. I may withdraw (low atmosphere), which is an unconscious way of saying, "I know you will ignore or abandon me (*inclusion*), humiliate or embarrass me (*control*), or reject or despise me (*openness*), and so I won't give you a chance." Or I may dive into the atmosphere and try to make people treat me as I don't treat myself—that is, make them heed, respect, or like me. Unconsciously, I am saying, "I know I'm not significant (*inclusion*) or competent (*control*) or likable (*openness*), but I'm going to do everything I can to get you to feel that I am significant, competent, or likable."

When team members hold rigidly to preferences for particular kinds of atmosphere, that rigidity can be resolved only if the members become aware of it and deal with it directly. A team atmosphere in which my fears are accepted usually enhances my willingness and ability to cope with them. I can then use the self-esteem—building methods to reduce them further (see Chapter Two).

Pause for Reflection: Rigidity and Atmosphere Preference

1. Have I ever wanted to be with people in order to feel more alive? When?

2. Have I ever been alone in order to avoid being ignored? When?

3. Have I ever sought to be controlled because I didn't trust what I would do on my own? When?

4. Have I ever avoided responsibility so that I would not be exposed as incompetent? When?

5. Have I ever tried to stick to business partly to prevent people from expressing dislike for me? When?

Role Preferences

I may simply like one role better. I am more used to it, I have a talent for it, and it makes me feel more comfortable, but I can easily adapt if I need or want to. For example, if I prefer to be in charge, but the situation calls for me to become a follower rather than a leader, I'm comfortable following.

When, as team members, one or more of us adhere rigidly to our particular roles, that can also create incompatibility. For example, if you and I both want to be leaders, but neither of us wants to be led, we may have a power struggle. Our roles are not complementary. Whether the power struggle leads to an impasse or to a stimulating interchange and a creative solution depends on the rigidity with which we hold to our roles.

I may also play a particular role because I feel very uncomfortable in any other role. For example, if I prefer low inclusion, I may like the role of guest (that is, I like to be invited), but if anyone asks me to be a host, I feel nervous because I am uncomfortable being the one who invites. To the extent that anxiety is the basis for my choice of roles, I will be rigid and try to stay in my preferred role—by force, anger, refusal, intellectual argument, false promises, or whatever other means are available to me. I am rigid because I am afraid of being exposed—that is, of being ignored, humiliated, or rejected—and I will cling to my preferred role regardless of how inefficient it is in solving our problem.

Role rigidity exists regardless of the type of incompatibility. In confrontive incompatibility, we both insist on having things our way and refuse to back down or compromise on any point. Labor-management strikes, marital discord, and ethnic enmities often follow this pattern. In apathetic incompatibility, we are paralyzed. Neither of us is willing to initiate, for fear of a devastating outcome to our self-concept. We remain inert, unable to move forward. This too has a disastrous effect on our productivity. I avoid meetings where you are present. I fail to confront you about an important decision on which we disagree. As a result, we miss our deadlines, people waiting for our decisions are delayed, and our efficiency suffers.

Table 3.3 delineates many possible reasons for my becoming rigidly fixed in a role. The only way I can dissolve my rigidity is to become aware of and face my fears, my feelings, and my anxieties, then choose whether to change my behavior.

Table 3.3. Bases of Rigid Role Preferences.

Since...	I hope that if I take this role, I will be...	...my anxiety will be relieved because...
Inclusion		
I'm not fully alive, I will not feel anything.	Host (initiator)	I will be stimulated by you.
I'm not fully alive, I will not feel anything.	Guest (receiver)	You will stimulate me.
Significance		
I'm not significant, I'm afraid I will be ignored.	Host (initiator)	You can't ignore me, your host.
I'm not significant, I'm afraid I will be ignored.	Guest (receiver)	You must pay me attention—I'm your guest.
Control		
I don't control myself enough, I fear getting out of control.	Leader (initiator)	Responsibility as a leader requires self-control.
I don't control myself enough, I fear getting out of control.	Follower (receiver)	You will control me from outside.

I control myself too much, I fear being too controlled.	Leader (initiator)	Since I'm in charge, I won't let you control me.
I control myself too much, I fear being too controlled.	Follower (receiver)	Having no responsibility may allow me to be less controlled.

Competence

I'm not competent, I'm afraid I'll be humiliated.	Leader (initiator)	I set the agenda, and so I am prepared for anything.
I'm not competent, I'm afraid I'll be humiliated.	Follower (receiver)	I'll do just exactly as I'm told, so I will not be responsible.

Openness

I'm not aware, I'm afraid I don't know why I do what I do.	Discloser (initiator)	I will initiate only things I'm already familiar with.
I'm not aware, I'm afraid I don't know why I do what I do.	Receiver	I rely on you to tell me what's happening.

Likability

I'm not likable, I'm afraid I will be rejected.	Discloser (initiator)	If you're going to reject me, you'll get it over with quickly.
I'm not likable, I'm afraid I will be rejected.	Receiver	I'm less likely to be rejected if I let you make the first move.

Pause for Reflection:
Rigidity and Role Preference

1. Have I ever invited people over partly because I was afraid that no one would invite me? When?

2. Have I ever taken a leadership role in order to avoid being told what to do? When?

3. Have I ever taken a subordinate role so that I would not have to think for myself? When?

4. Have I ever become quiet so that I would not offend anyone? When?

5. Have I ever wanted to deny any of the behavior I have just acknowledged? Why?

6. What do these insights tell me about any rigidity that I may want to change?

Issues in Group Development

Groups evolve through particular stages along the dimensions of inclusion, control, and openness.[5] Compatibility issues are also involved in group development. The importance of understanding these issues, which come up in particular stages, is that by doing so we all can become more tolerant of what is happening in a group and deal more skillfully with the group's evolution.

Example   A number of university students in a dormitory were each asked to select one person they would (1) want for president of the dorm, (2) want to hitchhike with across the country for two weeks, and (3) want as a roommate (one person was to be selected for each situation). The situations were selected because they differ in terms of the length and the depth of the relationship. The students were also given a test that measured their atmosphere and role preferences, and then atmosphere compatibility for each pair of students was calculated.

The results confirmed the hypothesis: the best predictor of selection for the shortest relationship, dorm president, was inclusion compatibility; the best predictor for selection of the moderately long relationship, hitchhiking partner, was control compatibility; and the best predictor for selection of the long-term relationship, roommate, was openness compatibility.

Stage 1: Inclusion

In the early period of team development, inclusion compatibility is most important. The inclusion phase begins with the formation of the group.

When I am confronted with other people, I look for where I fit in this group. Am I in or out? Am I going to be paid attention to or be left out and ignored? If the answers make me anxious, I may start talking excessively, withdrawing, becoming exhibitionistic, or telling personal stories—presenting my cards of identity. At the same time, I am deciding how committed I will become to this group.

My assessment of how I believe I'll be treated determines how much time and energy I devote to this group, in light of my other relationships and commitments. If I anticipate that I will not have the role I like and am comfortable with, I will probably find that my other commitments make it "impossible" for me to devote much time to this group. If I expect my role to be desirable—I will be the leader, or the joker, or the idea person, or whatever I like to be—I "miraculously" rearrange my schedule to give a great deal of time and energy to this new group.

"Goblet issues"[6] are characteristic of groups in stage 1. The term suggests a cocktail party where we pick up our glasses, or goblets, and figuratively peer through them to size each other up. My real purpose is to see what I think and feel about the people I'm with. "Goblet issues" in themselves are typically of minor importance, but they perform the crucial function of helping me get to know you. Discussions of goblet issues often seem inane—arguing about the shape of the table or seating arrangements—but they usually allow me to get to know you much better, even if I don't remember what we have said. Most groups have such discussions. If they don't, they will find another vehicle (such as a crucial first decision) to serve the same purpose. In our first decision as a group, we use our discussions to compete, impress one another, ingratiate ourselves, excel, and pursue other personal agendas.

In the inclusion phase, I watch the leaders' commitment to the group, their attendance, their interest, their preparation, and their punctuality. If they falter, I may feel, "If you don't care, why should I?" If the leaders are not committed, then the group is of less interest to me.

After I feel confident enough in the leaders, I shift my concern to the other members. I am alert to their absences, lateness, and amount of participation, and to the importance they give to outside activities relative to the priority they give to this group. The withdrawal of any member is usually an occasion for lengthy discussion: "Is it something I did? Was she right to leave? Should I leave, too?" At this stage, I am initially most compatible with those who share my atmosphere preferences (being alone, or being with people) and who complement my preferred role.

Stage 2: Control

Once we have resolved inclusion issues (at least temporarily), we turn to compatibility in control issues, which is characteristic of groups in mid-development. Behavior at this stage includes competition for leadership, determination of procedures and methods of decision making, and distribution of power. My concerns center on whether I have as much or as little power, responsibility, and influence as I am comfortable with.

I again focus my attention first on my control relationships with the group leaders. I want to have a special relationship with them. Typically, I am ambivalent toward authority, but I usually lean in one direction. On the one hand, I may want to replace the leaders and have all their power; on the other hand, I want them to take care of me, tell me what to do, and protect me.

I often express criticism and dissatisfaction because I believe nothing is happening the way I want it to—but I don't know what I want. At this point, I almost leave the group, but I rarely do leave.

When I turn my focus to competition with my peers—"sibling rivalry"—I compete for leaders' and peers' approval and admiration. At this stage, I often preen and show off, sometimes overtly and sometimes more subtly. One particularly devious method is the "Olympic games" approach, telling heroic stories in which I ostensibly reveal something weak about myself while subtly slipping in my other glowing characteristics: "I am so clumsy! I bump into things, I drop things, I trip over things. Why, just the other day, I tripped on the hose in the infield on the way to getting my Olympic gold medal. I dropped my Phi Beta Kappa key and my Nobel Prize medal. I'm so *very* clumsy!"

At this stage, I am most compatible with people who have the same atmosphere preferences, whether hierarchical or flowing, and who complement me in my role preferences (for example, if you prefer to control people, and I want to be controlled).

Stage 3: Openness

By the third stage of group evolution, crucial for any team that is going to work over the long term, I now have an idea of our boundaries and of our commitment and methods for distributing power. Now I turn to other questions: How close shall I get? Shall I be completely open and express all my feelings honestly? Or shall I keep my relationships superficial and task-oriented? Shall I find some middle ground?

At this stage, I am ambivalent about openness with group leaders. On the one hand, I am afraid of the leaders' power. I would be vulnerable if I told them my secrets. On the other hand, perhaps in this way I can truly grow. Can I trust them? Similarly, hearing them be open makes them more human, but do I want that?

Openness with my peers presents similar problems. Do I want to be close to them and confide in them? Or should I play it safe and not let other team members get any information they can use against me? Common at this phase is the "porcupine phenomenon,"[7] as illustrated by this fable: One cold night, some porcupines huddled together for warmth, but their spines pricked each other, and so they all backed away. Then they were too cold, and so they moved toward each other. All night they went toward and away from each other, trying to feel warmth without feeling pain, until they reached a comfortable balance.

In groups, I often go through this process in a subtle fashion, testing how close I can get without risking rejection or other kinds of pain, and how far away I can go without feeling cold and alone. At this stage, my compatibility is greatest with people who share my preference in atmosphere, whether open or businesslike.

Group Relations with the Outside

Apart from their internal dynamics, groups can also behave as single units, especially in their responses to external influences and forces (vendors, customers, other departments, the general public, stockholders, consultants, government agencies, top management). Incompatibility can develop between a group and the outside world, just as it can among the group's members.

External incompatibilities develop, just as internal ones do, from conflicts over inclusion, control, and openness. A team may want more or less inclusion, control, or openness than the outside world provides. This dissonance can result in several types of incompatibility, combinations of atmosphere and role incompatibility.

Inclusion Problems with Outside Relations

Intrusion   If my team members and I feel that outside organizations and individuals are intruding—that is, including us too much—it is difficult for us to maintain sufficient privacy. Outer reality becomes incompatible with our team, since there is not enough distance between team members and the environment. For example, my boss may require me to entertain and escort visitors around the plant, to the point where my work is disrupted.

Isolation   We may feel that we are insufficiently included in the activities of outside organizations and individuals and are not informed about what is going on. When I belong to a sales staff with territories spread out across the country, I may feel isolated. I can go for weeks without seeing a fellow employee. Without enough communication from sales managers and the main office, I can come to feel isolated.

Control Problems with Outside Relations

Burnout   Our team may burn out if we are given too much responsibility for events, visitors, projects, and activities outside our main work: too few people are trying to do too much more. I have more than I can handle, and I am not aware of my ability to change things, and so I experience burnout.

This can happen, for example, if a parent company with several smaller divisions insists on completely revamping its management information and computer hardware systems, so that they will be consistent across all divisions. The company appoints a task force of middle managers from around the divisions, who set to work but find the parameters and demands of the assignment growing at each meeting. They soon have to admit that they cannot finish the task in the time assigned. They simply burn out as further demands are heaped on them, and they feel that they have no way of communicating their feelings to distant upper management.

Subjugation   If I as a team member feel that I am subject to too many outside restrictions and limits, I may feel helpless to do my job well. For example, if headquarters dictates how a certain type of work is to be done, without consulting those of us who know best how to do it, we may feel that we are being controlled too much from the outside.

Confrontation   When we want to set the agenda and give orders, and another group wants to do the same, we have a power struggle. Labor-management negotiations can become confrontations when neither side will accept the other's offer.

Apathy   When two of our teams must conduct a project together, and neither of our teams will take responsibility for creating the plan for accomplishing the task, our work grinds to a halt. Each of our teams wants the other to take charge and get things done, and neither will do it.

Openness Problems with Outside Relations

Lack of Privacy   The team must accommodate more openness than it wants in order to deal with other people's problems and behavior. For example, a gossip column in the company newsletter may reveal more about my feelings toward my leader than my leader wants to know—or than I want him or her to know.

Being Out of the Loop   I feel that we are not told the truth about outside events and cannot trust others to tell the truth and not to withhold. For example, managers in some organizations take a "need to know" approach to informing their employees about policies, changes, and so on. I may feel that we are the last to know, and I often do not trust my leaders.

Pause for Reflection: Outside Relations

It is my job, as team leader, to ensure that we balance external relations with regard to inclusion (to avoid both isolation and intrusion), control (to avoid both subjugation and burnout), and openness (to avoid both lack of privacy and being "out of the loop"). This version of the Periodic Table of the Human Elements shows group relations with the outside in terms of what is happening to the team (first and third columns) and what the team wants to have happen (second and fourth columns). The behavior that the team expresses toward outside units is shown in cells 11, 21, and 31. The behavior that the team receives from outside units is shown in cells 13, 23, and 33. (*Others* or *you* means vendors, customers, other departments, the general public, consultants, and any other external group or force.) Team leaders can use this portion of the Periodic Table in an internal process to clarify what they want to express and how they want to relate to outside entities (cells 12, 22, 32) and what they want to receive from other entities (14, 24, 34).

	Interpersonal: Do Self (I) to Other (You)		Interpersonal: Get Other (You) to Self (I)		Individual Self (I) to Self (I)		Other Other (O) to Other (O)	
	See	Want	See	Want	See	Want	See	Want
Inclusion	The team includes others. 11	The team wants to include others. 12	Others include the team. 13	The team wants to be included. 14	15	16	17	18
Control	The team controls others. 21	The team wants to control others. 22	Others control the team. 23	The team wants to be controlled. 24	25	26	27	28
Openness	The team is open with others. 31	The team wants to be open with others. 32	Others are open with the team. 33	The team wants others to be open. 34	35	36	37	38
Significance	41	42	43	44	45	46	47	48
Competence	51	52	53	54	55	56	57	58
Likability	61	62	63	64	65	66	67	68

These statements can be used to comment on my strengths and areas for improvement as a leader in group relations with the outside. (I think of a present or past team in answering these questions.)

Cells 11, 12. **I protect the privacy of my workers from outside intrusion.**
Disagree   0   1   2   3   4   5   6   7   8   9   Agree

Cells 21, 22. I say *no* to people who want to give my team more work than it can handle.
Disagree   0   1   2   3   4   5   6   7   8   9   Agree

Cells 31, 32. I make sure our team is "in the loop" (that is, gets told the truth about outside events), and I see that important information is given to us.
Disagree   0   1   2   3   4   5   6   7   8   9   Agree

Cells 13, 14. I get my team included with outside groups (put on routing lists, invited to relevant meetings).
Disagree   0   1   2   3   4   5   6   7   8   9   Agree

Cells 23, 24. I prevent outside authorities from putting restrictions on my team members that make it more difficult for them to do their work well.
Disagree   0   1   2   3   4   5   6   7   8   9   Agree

Cells 33, 34. I prevent personal issues with people outside the team (personal relationships, marital difficulties) from interfering with our effectiveness.
Disagree   0   1   2   3   4   5   6   7   8   9   Agree

This is what I want to do about any of the difficulties I have revealed:

Open Teamwork

Case Example   Scott was frustrated with Bill, who would not commit himself to a deadline. Bill claimed he was working well without a deadline, but Scott persisted and finally prevailed.

The deadline came, and Bill didn't meet it. Scott was right! Bill did not keep his word. Productivity bottomed out.

The team recognized that the tension between Scott and Bill was a serious, almost lethal, block to productivity. They were the two most experienced and knowledgeable people on the project. Everyone relied on them, but they continued to have a destructively competitive relationship. Scott could not fire Bill without seriously impairing the project, and his attempts at asserting authority led to more resistance. Bill felt that Scott did not appreciate him. Other team members felt that they had to choose one over the other and were paralyzed. What were they to do?

If blocks to teamwork are due to individual rigidities and unresolved issues between people, how can these difficulties be overcome to create highly productive teams? Traditional approaches—coercion, compromise, and complementarity—try to solve the problems of teamwork through logic or power. But trying to solve them by deciding whose argument is more logical does not always yield the best solution.

The Open Teamwork method relies on a new level of consciousness to break through conflicts and stalemates. If all parties to a disagreement become more self-aware, we have an entirely new basis for resolving our differences. Our adversaries' feelings and fears are vital parts of our disagreement, which must be factored into the solution, or else the solution won't be adequate. Accounting for our feelings and fears requires us to identify them and their sources, be self-aware, and be willing to communicate about them (see Chapter Two).

Case Example   In their frustration at not being able to get past being stuck, Scott and Bill and the other team members agreed to go to a Human Element workshop. As they examined their situation, it became clear that they were battling one another, rather than cooperating to get the job done.

Scott realized that, for him, being right was of paramount importance because of his uncertainty about his own competence. Being wrong even once about anything at all was very threatening; it called his total competence into question, and that kept him from seeing Bill clearly. If Scott had been less preoccupied with himself, he would have been more aware of Bill's body language, and he would have realized that Bill had no intention of meeting the deadline. But by overlooking Bill's obvious signs, Scott once again got to be right when Bill did not keep his agreement, and the project suffered.

Bill resented Scott but was only vaguely aware of that feeling and was unwilling to confront Scott. He found it easier to fend Scott off with promises that he unconsciously knew he was not going to keep.

When they both allowed themselves to be aware of the feelings they had been denying, they talked about Bill's resentment and cleared that up. Bill got some insights into his lifelong pattern of making false promises as a way of avoiding directness, and he talked with Scott about how it had got him in trouble before. That successful discussion emboldened Bill to begin expressing his thoughts and feelings directly, instead of making phony agreements, as a way to deal with interpersonal difficulties as they arose. Scott saw how he had developed a long-standing pattern of being so preoccupied with being right that he cut himself off from seeing what was happening with other people. That had earned him a reputation for being insensitive and, occasionally, a bully. When he realized this pattern, he chose to reduce his desire to be right all the time, and he felt more relaxed and able to understand what other people were feeling.

Armed with these insights, Scott and Bill looked at their work issue from the standpoint of how to get the job done best, so that they both would be working toward the same goal. The new mutuality was very different from saying, as they had before the workshop, that they would ignore personal feelings and just get the job done. They now recognized that sort of truce as self-deception. With these insights, they set the stage for a higher quality and quantity of work, for themselves and for their team.

Bill and Scott came to understand how and why they were using defense mechanisms to the detriment of their team. They were willing to look at their own behavior and feelings, discuss what they had discovered, and use their heightened self-awareness to be more open with each other. That helped put them into a problem-solving mode, rather than a defending mode.

To foster productive teams, the larger organization establishes an atmosphere of understanding and acceptance of whole individuals— our feelings, behavior, and other traits. Acceptance doesn't mean that the organization legislates tolerance of weakness or foibles. Instead, the organization can create an atmosphere where it is expected that we will all be pursuing greater self-awareness in order to make the enterprise run more smoothly, productively, and humanely. If we all see that expressing feelings and fears and acknowledging weakness are part of the process of uncovering problems that are getting in the way, we will feel safe in doing so. Personal revelation then becomes an honored act, rather than a cause for ridicule. An organization gets to this point more readily to the degree that it dedicates itself to establishing an atmosphere of openness, where truth, honesty, and self-awareness are not only tolerated but also encouraged and rewarded. Such an atmosphere frees us all to explore issues at the level where they truly exist, a level deeper than the conscious bickering where so many problems seem to get stuck.

Once this open atmosphere is established, I will choose to be tolerant because I have a full and realistic picture of how people (including myself) really are. I feel a shared humanity that leads me to drop my defensiveness. True teamwork is achieved to the extent that team members are self-aware and willing to be truthful and open with one another, and to the extent that the organization creates and nurtures an atmosphere that supports self-awareness. Good teamwork does not require us to solve all problems, but rather to have openness available as a method for solving any problem.

Openness as a model for teamwork is a radical notion. Typical organizations do not often reward openness and self-insight. They are more likely to foster such behavior as denial and "spin control," as well as a general strategy of my getting what I want from people without their knowing what I have done. To reveal a weakness, or to tell you directly how I feel about you, is a rare and often risky act.

Yet it does work, often magically. If I want to improve teamwork,

I must know all the human factors blocking it and then remove them by getting them out in the open for the whole team to see and deal with. I can then enlist the abilities of the entire team to create a solution that incorporates all these factors, including satisfying the feelings that created them.

Open teamwork has proved to be the key that unlocks a great productivity surge. It has resulted in decreased time to market, greatly reduced time required for meetings, more efficient and satisfying working conditions resulting in higher motivation, greater union-management cooperation, and increased profitability. For example, the "traditional packing start-up curve—the time between the concept and full production—is about 22 months.... The incase fill start-up at Baltimore [using the Human Element approach] took about 4 months. This saved the company...$9 million compared to the average start-up." Or, as another client reported, "Union and plant leadership attended the [Human Element] workshop in the fall of 1985. Two weeks after the workshop, in November 1985, the union and the company signed an unprecedented amendment to the current contract.... Both the union and plant leadership attribute the success of the negotiations... to the workshop. Headquarters was prepared to shut down the plant if there was no signed agreement."[8]

Using Open Teamwork for Top Performance

The Human Element assumption is that it's not a company's specific behaviors that determine its success in the long run. Success depends on team members' ability to deal effectively with one another and adapt to changing conditions. If people in our group are compatible, we can devote all our abilities to solving our work problems. We can be flexible enough to adapt our behavior to changing situations. Compatibility is highly correlated with productivity, and so if relations among the leaders of a company are not open and well developed, employees will stick with the same behaviors that worked once, even when the business environment has been radically altered.

How can these ideas be put into a practical framework? The Team Compatibility Experience (TCE) is designed to establish and capitalize on an atmosphere of openness, self-awareness, and self-responsibility. It provides a framework for the open, honest, aware exchange of feelings and thoughts between every pair of team members, to improve present relationships and build better ones for the future. It can pinpoint the trouble spots in a team, particularly people in key positions who are not working together as effectively as they might, and members who are underutilized and ready to handle new positions. The objective of the TCE is to help each of us on the team emerge from the interaction capable of expressing and willing to express, *at the time we experience it*, any thought or feeling that may interfere with our combined success, and work through to a mutually satisfactory solution.

The TCE improves teamwork by using a method based on openness. Team members exchange honest opinions and feelings, face to face, about how well each of us is working with each of the other people on the team. Each of us takes full responsibility for having brought about the present situation of our team, and each of us is self-aware.

It is important that the TCE be used with the team as a whole, rather than with subgroups. Problems between two people almost inevitably affect other team members anyway, and several perceptions of a situation can provide more accurate information. There is also greater impact when several people give the same feedback to a person than when only one person gives feedback; we can stay more honest and avoid colluding with one another to avoid issues. Moreover, one principle of group life states that the first unit a person becomes attached to receives that person's basic commitment. For example, if I want to establish people's commitment to a ten-person team, it would be unwise for me to begin the team's activities in pairs and then bring the pairs together; it would be much more effective to start with the group of ten. Once commitment to the whole team is established, smaller units can be used effectively, as appropriate.

CASE: The Boss and the Bright Young Guy

Here is a firsthand account of a TCE event from the vice president for engineering of a large computer company:

I am in charge of developing and managing the company's most important line of products. Jack is my bright young subordinate, also a vice president, who oversees the business management of the products. The rest of the people in the group are my direct staff—ten people, mostly directors of engineering organizations.

Before we used the TCE, I had a problem with Jack. Our private discussions were satisfactory, but in my weekly staff meetings things were different. I found myself getting angry at Jack. It seemed that we were usually on opposite sides of issues. Jack would say, "What you really want to say is. . . ." And I would think, No, damn it, that's not what I want to say. I often opposed Jack's ideas simply because they came from him. I didn't confront the problem directly with Jack. I rationalized: Jack is a pain, but he's worth it.

While we were using the TCE, I was able to admit to myself and to the group that I had been competing with Jack for leadership of the group. I was in awe of his youth, his charisma, and, most of all, his mental quickness. From his side, I discovered that, wonder of wonders, Jack had fears and insecurities, too. Behind the fast thinking and fast talking was a warm, likable person who in turn liked and respected me.

Afterward, Jack still did many of the same things, but I saw them differently. I spent less time being angry, and I was able to consider Jack's ideas on their own merits. When the old feelings of competition came up, I found myself thinking, You can't fool me, you smooth talker; I know who you are, and I'm really glad you're here. A critically important relationship between two people was cleaned up. Staff meetings were a lot more fun for me, and my staff and I had more time and energy to work on technical and business problems.

The TCE is more effective the more open our group is, but it still works well (usually not as well) when we are less open. Before beginning to use the TCE, if we wish to focus on establishing an atmosphere of openness, we can best do this in a workshop setting, where we explore the material (from Chapter Two) on self-concept.

We begin by exploring the ideas of truth and choice. Then we look at our preferences for behavior, in terms of inclusion, control, and openness. We discuss these preferences, express how we feel about them, and give feedback on how we perceive one another. We follow this activity with a similar mutual exploration of our preferences in terms of the interpersonal feelings of significance, competence, and likability. Finally, we assess our self-concepts and self-esteem and the defenses we tend to use in particular circumstances. The impact of candid mutual exploration gradually creates an atmosphere of trust and closeness in the group. Any fears of vulnerability, exploitation, and embarrassment that I may have experienced when I thought of revealing myself in front of others are transformed in this supportive climate, where each of us is revealed as dealing with essentially the same issues in our own unique ways. Our connection as human beings supersedes our fear.

Use of the TCE differs from the traditional method of gathering feedback from co-workers and presenting it anonymously. The TCE assumes that some work has already been done to open the atmosphere—primarily work to increase self-awareness for each of us on the team, so that honest, direct, face-to-face communication, which is much more effective and complete, can replace indirect, anonymous feedback. Here's how it works.

Using the Team Compatibility Index

All the members of a work team (usually six to twelve) sit in a circle in a private room. We use the following steps to get started.

1. *Inclusion (Operating Pattern):* We consensually identify our team goals and describe the actual operating pattern of team members. This pattern is often similar to the one on an organizational chart, except that the lines connecting me with you represent interdependence.

2. *Control (Centrality):* We consensually rate the centrality of the relationship of each pair of team members (that is, how important it is to team effectiveness for the people in each pair to work well together). If you are the manager and I am the assistant manager, then the quality of our working relationship is crucial to the team's effectiveness and is therefore rated high on centrality. My ability to work with a technician three levels down, in another department, is not so crucial, since we do different types of work and don't work together very much, and so our centrality is low.

3. *Openness (Compatibility):* We consensually rate the compatibility—the ability to work well together—of the members of each pair. This key step is performed by designating two chairs for each pair to sit in, surrounded by the other members of our team. You and I, for example, openly discuss (as much as we are currently willing and able to do) our perceptions of each other and of our relationship. Then the other team members give their perceptions of how we generally operate and of our current interaction as we speak to each other. They point out when they feel that we are not being totally open and honest, either consciously or unconsciously. When the groundwork for this type of communication has been laid, this activity becomes a cooperative search for truth, not a vehicle for attacking others.

There are many advantages to discussing our pair relationships with the full team rather than taking the more typical approach of going into an office, closing the door, and talking privately. As already noted, any trouble between you and me inevitably affects most or all of our teammates. Reducing the number of secrets on our team also brings us closer, since every secret creates distance among members and is therefore toxic. Knowing the background of the relationships between the others typically brings understanding in situations that used to be puzzling and helps the rest of us know how to behave more appropriately toward others. Exchanging feelings at this level is the fastest way to bring the members of a group truly close. Closeness typically leads to caring, mutual assistance, and cooperation.

Behavior That Enhances Teamwork

1. I am open at all times about my feelings and my ideas. I keep no secrets from myself or others.

2. I say what I feel about whatever is relevant at the moment when I feel it.

3. I stay aware of myself—of what is motivating me and of what I am feeling at every moment. I am aware of the deepest levels of truth. I do not deceive myself.

4. I assume that all team members are on the same side, trying to produce the best solutions to the team's problems, and not trying to protect themselves or blame others.

5. I make sure that each person fully agrees—with head, heart, and feelings—on each decision.

6. I listen to others' thoughts and feelings. I empathize with each person's point of view, acknowledge it, and state my honest reaction to it.

7. When I understand each person's point of view and feelings, I begin to seek a solution that integrates all the ideas and feelings of all team members.

8. I am aware of differences in atmosphere preference and am sure to say, in a timely fashion, how I feel. I stay in touch with my deepest levels of truth.

9. I make sure that we agree on our mission, vision, and goals. I am aware that these often change as we get farther into a task. I do not hesitate to change them if we all agree that change would be appropriate.

10. I participate in meetings to decide specifically how decisions will be made. These meetings are about the *process of our decision making*, not about any of our specific decisions.

No list of rules or guidelines for behavior can affect my behavior unless I am aware of the underlying reason for why I do what I do. But the preceding list can be used with the understanding that it will become more and more helpful as I attain more self-awareness. Then I can deal with the causes of my behavior, rather than simply changing my behavior.

Pause for Reflection: Open Teamwork

Open Teamwork uses all forty-eight cells of the Periodic Table of the Human Elements, printed on the endsheets of this book.

1. In my organization, is it realistic for team members to be totally open and honest with one another? Is it desirable?

2. Would I feel comfortable as the leader of such a team? What fears do I have about open teamwork?

3. What role does openness play in communication? Truth?

4. What is the relationship between trust and truth?

5. In my organization, what would be the advantages and drawbacks of leaders' being totally open with the people who work with them?

6. How important is self-awareness to a successful team? What are the obstacles to its achievement?

7. What is the relationship between open teamwork and productivity in my organization?

8. How could I help my organization get ready for open teamwork?

9. Can I envision myself in a TCE session? If not, what are my anxieties or concerns?

10. What do I think of this statement? "The reward for my winning all the time is that I get to live with losers."

4

Optimal Individual Performance: Enhancing Performance and Unblocking Creativity

If you're not thinking all the time about making each person more valuable, you don't have a chance. What's the alternative? Wasted minds? Uninvolved people? A labor force that's angry or bored? That doesn't make sense.
—*Jack Welch, CEO, General Electric*[1]

Maintaining healthy dynamics in groups and effective individual functioning, and keeping both in balance, are two of the challenges of leadership. In my experience with American and Japanese organizations, I see both countries moving toward each other in the effort to find and keep this team-individual balance. American companies have traditionally had teamwork difficulties, especially as compared to the efficient Japanese companies, and only relatively recently have begun to focus on teamwork. The Japanese, for their part, are realizing that effective teamwork is sometimes undermined by the relative neglect of individuals. One of the reasons why the Japanese have imported the Human Element approach and why it is popular there is that it allows them to focus on themselves as individuals, often for the first time. Obviously, individuals and groups alike must work well for top performance. In modern organizations, there are numerous sensitive, thoughtful, effective ways to deal with individual workers so that they come close to reaching their full potential, as workers and as human beings. Unfortunately, other practices, similarly widespread, may lead to lesser human achievement.

Chapter Three explored how organizations can nurture superb teamwork by creating an open atmosphere that encourages each of us to be aware of and express feelings in our interpersonal relations. As a result, we can focus our energy on solving problems and doing our work, rather than on diversionary power struggles, turf wars, hidden agendas, or the myriad other conflicts that may come up when we have not truthfully addressed the rigidities that block our performance. To use open teamwork effectively, I must have strengthened my own self-esteem, and I must feel that my organization values me. To make sure that I feel treated fairly and well—which is a big part of creating an open atmosphere—my organization must also pay particular attention to its handling of individual performance. A primary tenet of the Human Element model is that productivity and performance improve when relationships between individuals (especially between employees and managers) are consciously improved.

This chapter looks more closely at employee-manager relationships, specifically in terms of performance appraisal, job satisfaction and fit, and individual decision making. These dynamic relationships, which involve the interpersonal, job, and intellectual aspects of performance, are fundamental to the organization's efforts to enhance self-esteem—and thus productivity and the bottom line.

Sometimes the notion of openness throughout an organization seems highly unrealistic and impractical. Indeed, there is some justification for this objection, since Human Element workshops and consulting have shown that there are precious few organizations where an honest atmosphere is consistently present. But why dismiss the possibility of openness without a thorough investigation, since it has so much potential for solving so many organizational problems? The Human Element model can be seen as an ideal toward which any organization can strive. The model works best when you and I are open and honest with each other. I may feel cautious the first time

I try the Human Element approach, but if management is consistently trustworthy, the atmosphere of truth grows very rapidly. Then the excitement of the new way of relating, as well as the effectiveness of the new methods, will become the main responses.

Another Look at Individual Performance Appraisal

It is ironic that performance appraisal is so unsatisfactory in so many modern organizations, despite the enormous amounts of time and energy devoted to it. Many managers and employees find performance appraisal a frustrating process, one that not only creates conflict at times but also doesn't achieve its own purposes. Some new approaches, based on research and experiments,[2] to performance appraisal have improved the situation. Nevertheless, it never seems quite right for many organizations. Management and human resource leaders are constantly revising appraisal forms and standards. The reasons for the general dissatisfaction with performance appraisal have to do with the assumptions behind it. Performance appraisal is most commonly supposed to improve worker performance by doing the following things:

- Providing a fair basis for rewarding excellence
- Serving as a monitoring system for keeping workers on their toes, since not everyone is self-motivating
- Defining work roles
- Aiding the development of each worker

The typical performance appraisal follows a particular procedure in industrial, government, and military institutions. You, the supervisor, rate me, the employee. The rating determines my raises, bonuses, and promotions. I am allowed to see your written evaluation and respond to it. Together, we choose goals for me to accomplish during the next appraisal period, and we agree on the criteria to be used for evaluating my success. In the overall system, ratings are supposed to take the form of a bell-shaped curve, which produces a kind of quota and limits the number of us who get top ratings. The assumption is that not everyone can or will turn in a superb performance, and so the rankings will be distributed along the curve.

In the worst case, performance appraisal assumes that my performance is an individual matter. It minimizes my interaction with my supervisor, as well as his or her opportunity to receive feedback from me. It encourages competition among employees for limited rewards, and it invites defensiveness by encouraging my supervisor and me to take adversarial roles. It also diminishes the value that I derive from listening to and reflecting on feedback, since I may feel in danger of losing my job. The fact that feedback is infrequent and in one direction makes the process more likely to elicit my defensiveness and rigidity. Moreover, the worst kind of performance appraisal breeds anxiety, repression, fear, and suspicion—all factors that lead to antagonism with my manager, or that may mean I will work only as much as necessary for me to keep my job. If my manager "accuses" me of inadequacy, I am prepared to say, "She didn't give me clear directions. She didn't give me enough people to do the job. I didn't have enough time. I wasn't supervised properly." And so on.

No wonder performance appraisal is often a destructive process! Creativity and risk taking are discouraged. Alternative viewpoints are dangerous. The specter of blame looms heavily, and self-protection predominates, especially in civil service or military organizations, where one negative evaluation can threaten an entire career.

Obviously, performance appraisal doesn't always work in such a negative way, but it could be much better for organizations if one principle were implemented: *separate the two functions of performance appraisal—improvement of performance, and allocation of rewards—and use a distinct procedure for each one.* That approach seems unusual, but think about how difficult it is to hear feedback about performance when dollar value is attached to it. All I listen for is the bottom line. Then I get defensive, and we are no longer talking about my performance. We're arguing about my raise. What if performance appraisal offered an opportunity for the open exchange of our ideas and feelings, an exchange aimed at improving our work and our work situation? If it were carried out differently, performance appraisal could incorporate and expand such powerful ideas as quality circles (used with such success by the Japanese) because it would include exploration of feelings as well as of ideas.

The Human Element Approach

This section compares Human Element assumptions about performance appraisal with those of a generalized traditional system. The comparisons may seem a bit too striking, but there are dramatic differences between traditional performance appraisal and the Human Element approach.

Common assumption: I am motivated primarily by the promise of rewards and the threat of punishment.
Human Element assumption: I am motivated primarily, but not only, by work consistent with my self-concept.

Common assumption: I will not work to my potential without rewards and punishments.
Human Element assumption: I work to my full potential to satisfy myself. What I want from other people is honest feedback.

Common assumption: The organization must set up procedures to make sure I work optimally.
Human Element assumption: The organization creates conditions within which I will choose to work optimally.

Common assumption: My performance is a function of how competent I am.
Human Element assumption: My performance is a function of my competence and of my interaction with my co-workers, especially my supervisor.

Common assumption: You, my supervisor, should maintain your role as supervisor and not tolerate insubordination.

Human Element assumption: You profit from hearing honest feedback about yourself from me, your employee.

Common assumption: Competition between me and other employees is healthy and leads to increased productivity.
Human Element assumption: Competition is healthy when I feel stimulated and motivated by it. Competition is unhealthy when I react to it by undermining colleagues, blaming, and sabotaging others' efforts.

How can I put the Human Element assumptions into practice? The first thing that you (my manager) and I must do is compare our individual perceptions of what is happening between us and of how we each feel about it. This discussion will allow us to explore our relationship fully.

1. *Do we, as employee and manager, see our situation the same way?* Do you and I see what is happening between us in the same way? Do we agree about what is happening to each of us as individuals? When our perceptions of our work situation differ, confusion enters our relationship, since we are not seeing the same world. We must clear up that difference before we can proceed.

2. *Are our goals the same?* Do you and I have the same objectives? Do we want the same things for ourselves as individuals? Our personal goals play a large role in how we operate. If we are striving for different goals and achieve them, we will end up very far from each other. If each of us sees my task differently, we had better align our views quickly, or else what would be success for me may look like failure in your eyes.

3. *How satisfied are we with our situation?* Do we like the way we act and feel toward each other? Do I like my own actions? Do I like yours? If we do not feel good about ourselves and each other, our jobs inevitably suffer. Our dissatisfaction provides us a springboard for deciding what we must work on to improve our relationship and our productivity.

Here is a procedure for devising a method of performance appraisal that capitalizes on the Human Element assumptions:

1. *We establish honest feedback between me as the employee and you as my supervisor.* We make this a symmetrical, two-way exploration—that is, we give feedback to each other on the same issues. This removes threat, partly because I can tell you first what I felt was unsatisfactory about my performance over the last rating period. I am usually well aware of my shortcomings; with the threat removed, I will acknowledge them (in most cases, I don't need someone else to tell me). If I don't acknowledge my shortcomings, then you can. Since I also tell you my perceptions of how you are functioning, this typically becomes a discussion of how we are working *together*, rather than a blaming session.

2. *We each respond independently, expressing our perceptions of, goals for, and level of satisfaction with our relationship.* Then we can compare our reactions as the basis for a comprehensive discussion of our relationship.

3. *We realize that both you and I are on the same side.* We are exploring how to improve our work relationship, rather than blaming each other for what has gone wrong, or setting up a pattern whereby you simply tell me how I should improve. The traditional one-way evaluation implies that whatever did not go right was my fault, and I become defensive.

4. *You and I explore all aspects of our relationship.* The Human Element model ensures that we cover all relevant interpersonal and personal areas. We pinpoint our difficult areas and devote as much time as necessary to resolving our specific differences.

The Work Relations Experience

One tool for using the Human Element approach in performance appraisal is called the *Work Relations Experience (WRE)*.[3] It's not necessary to use the WRE in its written form; people can use it simply by talking about each area. It has proven simpler and more comprehensive, however, to provide a structure for this activity, by means of a written list of issues for exploration. The structure does not have to be strictly adhered to, but its use can ensure that all relevant aspects are covered. This approach may seem to require a large investment of time and energy; in practice, however, many of the dimensions are not problematic and take little time to discuss, while the relevant ones emerge and can be discussed throroughly. The average time for completing a Human Element performance appraisal discussion is one to two hours.

Troubles that stem from incompetence are relatively infrequent by comparison with those that originate in personal relationships. Experience indicates that problems stemming from the personal and relational aspects of jobs account for as many as 90 percent of cases in which people are fired or quit. Both you and I need to try to improve our ability to recognize difficulties as they occur and increase our willingness to tell each other about problems. It should not be necessary for us to wait for a formal, biannual administration of the WRE before we tell each other how we feel about what is happening. Ideally, we express ourselves at the time we experience the need to do so, deal with any blocks to our working well together, and become as productive as possible.

The dimensions to be explored with the WRE correspond to follow the three behavioral (inclusion, control, and openness) and three feeling (significance, competence, likability) components that are the basis of the Human Element model. Each of us answers the questions on our own. Our independent responses become the basis for a discussion covering the following areas.

Inclusion

Discussions cover inclusion at meetings, being on lists for routing of memos, and being kept informed about what is happening. Sometimes people who are affected by various activities are not being informed about them, so that resentment grows and efficiency suffers. Often you as a supervisor express a desire to be more included in our (your employees') activities, often to our surprise.

- How much do I include you in my work activities? How much do you think I include you? Do I want to include you more? Do I feel you want to include me more? Do you want me to include you more? How much do you include me in your activities?

- Is each of us satisfied, or does either of us want more or less inclusion? Is each of us satisfied with the amount we include or are included by the other? Should it be more or less?

Control

Control discussions often unearth power struggles, issues of discipline and conformity, differing philosophies of leadership (authoritarian versus cooperative), and techniques for rebelling or not conforming (such as promising to do something and then "forgetting").

- How much do I control you? How much do you think I control you? Do we agree on how much you control me?

- Are we both satisfied with the control relations between us? How much do we want to control each other? How much do we think the other wants to control and be controlled?

- Do I want to be controlled more by you (that is, given more direction)?

Openness

Issues of how open the relationship is and how much openness we both desire can get a thorough airing, as can issues concerning the extent of separation between what is business-related and what is personal, especially when the personal issues may affect the work situation. The issues that often surface in this discussion have to do with honesty and trust.

- How open am I with you? How open are you with me? How open do we want to be with each other? How satisfied are we with our openness? How open do I think you want to be with me? How open do you think I want to be with you?

- Do I trust that what you tell me is the truth, or do I think you are trying not to hurt my feelings? Do I think you are telling me only what you want me to know or what you believe will motivate me to work harder?

Significance

These questions apply both to you as supervisor and to me as employee.

- How significant are you to me? How significant do I think I am to you? Do I have any significance in your life? If I were not to show up to work tomorrow, would you notice? Would you care? Or would I simply be replaced and forgotten? Am I simply a cog in this corporate machine, valued only for what I can produce? Or am I treated like a human being with feelings? Do I want to be treated that way? Do you want to treat me that way?

- Are we both satisfied with the amount of significance we have for each other? Is it too little or too much? Do you really care about me?

Competence

I have an opportunity first to state how I feel about my past performance. When I feel I am more competent than you feel I am, our discussion becomes very much like a traditional performance appraisal. You bring up instances where you feel I did not do a good job, and I may explain why. I am free to say where I feel you did not do a good job, and then we can mutually explore what improvements can be made. Because of the symmetry of the discussion, defensiveness is often reduced. We are seeing the situation as a mutual problem to be solved, rather than as an occasion for assigning blame.

- How competent do you think I am?
- How competent do I feel you are?
- Do you want to feel I am more competent, or would you prefer me to be only moderately competent?

Likability

In this discussion, we can discover—and often change—what you do not like about me and what I do not like about you. I may have a personal habit I am unaware of that annoys you, and vice versa. In many cases, the habit is very easy to alter.

- How much do I like you? How much do you like me? Do I think you like me? Do you think I like you? Do we want to like each other? Is it important?
- Are we satisfied with our liking of each other? How do we both feel about the importance of personal liking in the workplace? Should personal feelings of this type be left out of workplace relationships? Or do these feelings create a climate of friendship and make work a more enjoyable place to be?

Aliveness

Perhaps I feel low energy when I am at work, or I feel that you are burned out and that your job has become boring to you. We can discuss what each of us could do to feel more alive at work, use more of ourselves, and not shut down. We can also ask ourselves whether we feel more alive in some other part of our lives and, if so, what makes the difference between the two environments. If we differ in our perceptions, we can explore what is behind them. Perhaps you feel that I am not putting everything into my job.

- How much of ourselves do we want to give to our work?
- How alive do I feel at work? How alive do you feel at work? How alive do we each want to feel? How alive do you feel I am?

Self-Determination

You may feel that I do not use my own initiative enough, and that I wait to be told what to do. You may feel that I do not take enough responsibility for what I do, and that I act like a victim too often. You may also feel that I am too independent and do not call on other people to help me, even when I should. I may feel that you do not stand up to your superiors sufficiently, with the result that I do not feel protected from being given more work than I can reasonably handle.

- How much do I feel I determine my own life? How much do you feel I determine my own life?
- How satisfied are you with how much you control your own life?

Self-Awareness

Discussions of self-awareness cover self-deception, one of the most insidious problems. Since you and I are both exploring the issue, we can help each other reduce self-deception, rather than attack each other with accusations.

- How much do I feel I am aware of myself, by comparison with how much you think I am? (A discrepancy means that you feel I deceive myself sometimes.)
- Are you satisfied with how self-aware you are?

Self-Significance

If I sense that you do not feel significant, I may feel that this accounts for some areas of your behavior (such as your *insisting on being in-*

cluded, even when we both acknowledge that your inclusion is not relevant). Similarly, if you feel that I do not feel significant, you may believe that this keeps me from asserting myself and thus from producing as much as I could. If I feel that you do not feel significant as a boss, you may tend to be reluctant to tell me what you want from me, which leaves me confused.

- How significant do I feel? How significant do you feel? How significant do I think you feel?
- Are we satisfied with our own feelings of significance?

Self-Competence

If I am insecure about my competence, I may be reluctant to tell you my ideas, especially if they are original or creative. If you reject them, I will feel foolish and humiliated. Feelings of low self-competence can also lead to anxiety and concern about my being exposed as a phony. By contrast, if you think you are more competent than I think you are, I may see you as making decisions without consulting people who know more than you do about an issue.

- How competent do I feel in my job? How competent do you feel in your job?
- How competent do I think you feel in your job? How competent do you think I feel?

Self-Liking

Lack of self-liking may lead me to withdraw, be angry, criticize others, be sensitive to anything that could be interpreted as critical, or act in a foolhardy or dangerous manner. If I am not likable anyway, what does it matter if I do something that people will not like? With this attitude, I am less likely to be affected by your reactions.

- How much do I like myself? How much do you think I like myself?
- How much do you like yourself?

This process may seem rather extensive, but it saves much time and energy in the long run. If it's conducted thoroughly and openly, neither employees nor supervisors have to spend time on withholding, deceiving, complaining, backbiting, in-fights, turf battles, power struggles—all the unproductive activities that flourish in an organization that doesn't promote openness and self-awareness, especially in relationships between managers and employees.

Example   Susan and Beth, good friends, were department heads in a midwestern hospital. During a Team Compatibility Experience, they agreed that they got along very well together. Their only regret was that they didn't see each other enough, given their "very heavy workloads."

The other group members were skeptical and felt that there was something not quite right about Susan and Beth's relationship. Using the WRE, Susan and Beth realized that they had some unfinished resentment over a ten-year-old event, which they had unconsciously colluded to forget. Both realized that not speaking about this event made their relationship fragile, since bringing it up would have been threatening. As a result they had kept their contact relatively superficial, to preserve their relationship. Thus their workloads were not the only reason why they seldom met; they had an unconscious agreement not to meet too often.

With the WRE, they saw how each of them avoided going to meetings where the other would be, and how they delayed getting together to make decisions. As a result, many times their subordinates were also delayed and had to wait a long time for instructions.

As these insights emerged, everyone else was amazed at the inefficiency that had resulted from their being "professional" about their difficulties—which had meant ignoring them. As is typical, after Susan and Beth aired the problem and worked it through, they became much better friends. Their work efficiency—and that of those around them—increased dramatically.

The WRE can be used to resolve difficulties between departments, or between branches and headquarters, or between any two groups. For example, the members of one branch come together and respond as *I* (using consensus to frame their answers), while headquarters becomes *you*. The people at headquarters complete the form as *I*, using the branch as *you*. At a joint meeting, the two groups discuss their responses just as if they were two individuals.

To illustrate this approach to supporting people in reaching their full potential—through honesty, self-awareness, and feedback—the following case recounts one way of beginning the transition from traditional methods to the use of the Human Element tools, especially the Team Compatibility Experience and the Work Relations Experience. The report is in the words of a computer services department chairperson at a Big Ten university.

CASE: The Human Element at Work

I get so tired of the word *empowerment*. It's sounding really trite to me these days, but I'm not sure I have another word that reflects our experiences with the Human Element approach to performance review.

Our campus computer services organization, about fifty full-time employees, worked with the Human Element (HE) folks about two years ago. We provided HE training to all staff members who were interested in participating.

We did some follow-up work with a member of the HE organization after the intensive training program for the staff. Our commitment to truth, as a powerful tool in our work-related relationships, is now part of our organizational culture and is accepted by most of us as an important part of how we are with each other and how we do our work. But not all fifty of us accept it. There are some folks who would prefer that the organization be less open in its approach to issues, problems, interpersonal relationships, and group processes.

During the first performance review cycle after our Human

Element training, three of the work groups elected to implement a public performance review process. Each of the groups defined its process and the criteria (technical skills, quality and quantity of work, and interpersonal work relationships) it would use in evaluations. Each group also scheduled a review for every member, to which all the other group members would be invited. In some cases, other members of the larger organization would also be invited. In a meeting, staff members provided the person being evaluated with their assessment of his or her performance. Then a member of the group recorded and wrote up the assessment and submitted it as the staff member's formal performance review.

The first year yielded mixed results. Two of the groups provided good, tough feedback to their members. The third group was very careful about feedback and did not deal with the tougher issues around staff performance, issues on which people would have been much more critical of one another.

We have just finished our second annual review process. This time, all seven of our groups chose the public review process. (Each group member chose whether to participate in the public review process. Some opted to have individual reviews by their supervisors.) Since reviews took three or more hours of group time, they represented a major organizational commitment. In each instance, the individual groups again determined the categories that they would use to review their members. Some groups asked a member of the organization's leadership (not a part of the group) to sit in and facilitate the review process. Other groups managed the process themselves. Some of the people being evaluated invited specific people outside their groups, from whom they wanted feedback.

The individual being reviewed began his or her session by giving an assessment of his or her own performance in one of the specified categories. Then each member of the reviewing team had an opportunity to assess the person's performance. It was clear that everyone, including the person's direct supervisor, had thought about his or her performance before the session, and that many members of the group had also given it serious thought.

The second-year reviews were more open than those in the first year. Staff members were willing and ready to confront one another on tough performance and interpersonal issues. Leaders and staff members differed in their opinions about individual reviews. In several instances, organizational leaders reevaluated their assessments of selected staff members, always toward the more positive side. In one case, an entire group took on the organization's director and the associate director about their unfair assessment of the performance of the group's manager. It is interesting to note that this group had assessed the same manager more negatively the year before. The manager, taking the group's assessment to heart, had addressed many of his weaknesses during the year, and so his group actually knew more about his performance than his own managers did.

After group members finished discussing a specific category of performance, they voted on the "grade" they would assign, as follows: *outstanding, exceeds expectations, meets expectations, needs improvement,* and *unacceptable.* There were no quotas for any of these grades. The group members (including the person being evaluated) assigned numbers to these categories (one to five or, in some groups, one to ten, so that they could consider more points on the scale). Then all the members voted at the same time by holding up the appropriate number of fingers so that the group facilitator could record the scores. If all group members, including the reviewee, did not agree on the performance, the group members resumed discussion of that category and continued until agreement was reached. As is usual in such discussions, issues that seemed far removed from the performance of the reviewee were brought to the table. Some of these issues were resolved. The group simply recognized others and tabled them for the time being.

Once they had discussed all the categories, the group members assigned an overall performance rating to the person being evaluated. The overall "grade" was not necessarily an average of all the categorical scores. In one instance, all the categorical scores were lower than the overall grade: the group was trying to give this person a message about areas for improvement but also wanted to recognize that his performance, by and large, exceeded expectations.

In each instance, the direct supervisor formally wrote up the outcome of the performance review process. The written review reflected the group's assessment. The distribution of scores, in terms of the percentage placed in each "grade" category, was just about the same as in previous years (that is, ratings were not higher than usual).

The Human Element approach was exciting but not uniformly successful. All the staff members welcomed the positive feedback they received, and some received much more positive feedback than they had expected. Most staff members were also able to welcome the criticism they received, and many identified their own weaknesses in assessing themselves. But some staff members received critical feedback only with great difficulty, even when their reviews were overwhelmingly positive. Other staff members were surprised that their peers and supervisors had assessed their performance as less than adequate. A few folks were surprised at how positively their performance had been assessed, both by their peers and by their supervisors.

A major benefit to everyone was what I began by talking about—empowerment. The groups chose to adopt the public review process. They chose the criteria and the categories. Individuals chose whether to participate. Everyone had an equal opportunity to provide performance input to the folks they worked with and to their managers.

And so what? This organization spent a lot of time providing performance feedback to its staff. Did it make a difference? Will it make a difference? Recall the story about the manager whose staff judged his performance as having improved significantly over the preceding year, thanks to the feedback he had received in the first year. As a result of the second-year assessments, some staff members are being offered new and more challenging assignments because their supervisors have new information about their performance and abilities. Others, taking to heart information about where they need to improve, are deliberately seeking professional development opportunities in those areas. Some folks who were having difficulty working with one another have taken the initiative to improve their relationships, so that they can get on with the work.

Our organization, because of its function, must constantly change its priorities on the basis of new technologies and the university's evolving strategy and needs. We do not walk on stable ground, and so it is imperative that we deal effectively with change. The work we did in performance assessment, as well as our ongoing commitment to truth and choice, put us in a position to accommodate rapid change. Two years ago, minor organizational changes would have caused major disruption in our ability to do our work. Now, however, folks know what is expected of them. They also know what to expect in terms of information and feedback from their managers, and so fear is not an integral part of the work environment. We look at what has to be done next, we talk about it, and then we get on with it.

Most of our staff members look on this as a particularly good place to work. The rest of the university respects us and sees us as a little unusual but productive and responsive. Our organization remains productive because communication is open and expectations are clear.

Pause for Reflection: Work Relations

1. What are the advantages and limitations of taking a subordinate into my office, shutting the door, and telling him or her a difficulty that I am having with him or her, as opposed to giving feedback in a group?

2. In my organization, is there a problem between two team members that is causing trouble for the rest of the team? How could the WRE help?

3. What advantage do I see for my organization in having feedback that goes in all directions, not just from supervisor to subordinate?

4. How would use of the levels of truth be especially helpful in the WRE process?

5. What are the advantages and disadvantages of anonymous feedback? In my experience, how well has it worked?

6. How comfortable am I personally with the process of honest feedback in all directions? What do I fear?

7. Do I agree or disagree with this statement? "By giving honest feedback, I run the risk of damaging a person."

8. When a team opts for total, honest feedback, what underlying assumption about the nature of people is conveyed?

9. What are the reasons why the WRE process could not possibly work in my organization?

10. Now I imagine that I have chosen to make the WRE process work in my organization. Looking at my answer to the previous question, I write what I would do to overcome my objections to the WRE process.

Getting the Right Person for the Right Job

Just as my work relationships can be improved through the WRE process, so can the relationship—that is, the "fit"—between me and my job. There is every reason for work to be a source of great pleasure, but it often is not. The Human Element approach to the fit between me and a job may improve my job performance by helping me make better vocational decisions.

The wrong fit can lead to loss of energy and loss of my desire to do the job. Going to work may feel like such an ordeal that I long to escape. I lack a feeling of aliveness, vitality, and excitement. Solving the problem of fit goes a long way toward awakening an alive, vital, excited feeling in me, which will lead to higher levels of performance in my job.

Some organizations still hold to the "bad apple" concept: certain people are simply troublemakers, incompetents, or malingerers, to be rooted out and fired. Firing is at best a short-range solution, however. The time, energy, and resources required for recruiting and training replacements, along with the lack of guarantees that the new hires will be better than the people they replace, make firing less than desirable or cost-effective. But interviewers who fear lawsuits, or who simply lack awareness, often avoid systematic probes of job candidates' typical job behavior and ignore the potential interpersonal characteristics of jobs, for fear of censure. Organizations therefore end up with typical job-fit problems:

- "The job requirements aren't clear to me. I'm not sure what I should be doing."
- "Requirements appeared later that were not part of my original understanding of the job."
- "I thought I would have more autonomy than I do."
- "I thought I would get more direction than I do."
- "I thought I would get more support or recognition than I do."
- "My duties overlap with those of other jobs, and so it's not clear who is supposed to do what."
- "I'm not included in making decisions that affect my job."
- "I'd like to do more, but I'm not sure that is allowed."
- "I wonder if this is the best job for me. Perhaps I have more talent for something else."
- "I'm bored with my work. It's no longer challenging."

Obviously, when my mind and heart are preoccupied with such concerns, I don't give my all to my job.

The Human Element approach to job fit assumes that if I specify the interpersonal and personal aspects of a job along behavioral (inclusion, control, and openness) and feeling (significance, competence, and likability) dimensions, I can better match myself to the appropriate job. Job descriptions and candidate profiles can be created to identify the criteria for a match more precisely. That would help in hiring and in avoiding the job dissatisfaction and high turn-over that so often plague organizations.[4] For example, if my desire to include people is low, it would not be sensible for me to be a travel-ing sales representative, in a job that required a great deal of time and effort devoted to including people. It would not be wise for me to be a highway patrol officer if I wanted to be liked.

Behavioral Aspects

I can define the behavioral aspects of a job by using the dimensions of inclusion, control, and openness (the *I* in the following descrip-tions represents the successful jobholder). If I agree with the itali-cized statement, this means that in my job I exhibit the behavior being described. If I disagree, this means that I might be happier in another field, such as the ones suggested here. (These examples are only illustrations, of course; there are exceptions to each one.)

To do this job best, it is desirable that I include people.
Agree: Traveling sales representative, fundraiser
Disagree: Bridge toll taker, bank teller

To do this job best, it is desirable that I control people.
Agree: Military officer, supervisor
Disagree: Laborer, waiter

To do this job best, it is desirable that I be open with people.
Agree: Nursery school teacher, priest
Disagree: CIA agent, professional poker player

To do this job best, it is desirable that people include me.
Agree: Complaint department employee, therapist
Disagree: Lumberjack, farmer

To do this job best, it is desirable that people control me.
Agree: Secretary, army private
Disagree: Artist, consultant

To do this job best, it is desirable that people be open with me.
Agree: Mother, rabbi
Disagree: Lie-detector operator, professional poker player

Feeling Aspects

Feelings of significance, competence, and likability (from me to others, and from others to me) can also be used to define job requirements. For example, if I want people to like me, it will be unwise for me to spend my working life serving people with subpoenas. If I desire fame, being a ghostwriter will be unsatisfactory.

To do this job best, it is desirable that I feel people are significant.
Agree: Nurse, judge
Disagree: Bank examiner, efficiency expert

To do this job best, it is desirable that I feel people are competent.
Agree: Parachute jumper, flight attendant
Disagree: Job inspector, driving-test examiner

To do this job best, it is desirable that I like people.
Agree: Poverty worker, teacher of retarded children
Disagree: Customs inspector, loan officer

To do this job best, it is desirable that people feel I am significant.
Agree: Building inspector, governor
Disagree: Custodian, assembly-line worker

To do this job best, it is desirable that people feel I am competent.
Agree: Computer programmer, mechanic
Disagree: Messenger, unskilled laborer

To do this job best, it is desirable that people like me.
Agree: Fundraiser, minister
Disagree: Bill collector, bouncer

Job fit certainly determines my job satisfaction and thus affects my productivity. When I feel good about myself and my work, I am highly motivated to do an excellent job. But I may not be aware of how I feel about my job: I have resigned myself to working for a living, or I have assumed that I do not deserve more than I have, or I may feel self-righteous about sacrificing pleasure for practicality, or I may feel that I have no choice. When I allow myself to know how I really feel, I can make a conscious choice about my job.

Example   John worked as a manager of training in a government agency. He felt that he had a good job, but he also felt a vague uneasiness when he thought about it.

He filled out a Human Element questionnaire designed to help him measure his job satisfaction. The first thing he learned was that he did not know which part of his job to describe.

John decided to complete one form for the administrative aspect of his job and another form for the training aspect. The results were dramatic and clarifying. He now knew what his vague uneasiness was about: his satisfaction score on administration was dismally low, while his satisfaction score on training was extremely high.

This insight felt so important to him that he went to his boss and asked to have his job shifted in the direction of more training. His boss complied, and John was happier. But he decided to go even farther. He quit his job and became a full-time training consultant.

Pause for Reflection: Job Fit

Job fit and job satisfaction involve relationships between the employee and superiors, the employee and subordinates, the employee and peers, and the employee and clients. A complete assessment includes the twenty-four cells dealing with relationships. My satisfaction is indicated by how well the way I want to be on the job matches how I really am, including my behavior and feelings toward other people and their behavior and feelings toward me in the areas relevant to my job. Dissatisfaction may arise in my relations with my co-workers, or in a discrepancy between my preferred behavior and what I am required to do.

	Interpersonal: Do Self (I) to Other (You)		Interpersonal: Get Other (You) to Self (I)		Individual Self (I) to Self (I)		Other Other (O) to Other (O)	
	See	Want	See	Want	See	Want	See	Want
Inclusion	I include you.	I want to include you.	You include me.	I want you to include me.				
	11	12	13	14	15	16	17	18
Control	I control you.	I want to control you.	You control me.	I want you to control me.				
	21	22	23	24	25	26	27	28
Openness	I am open with you.	I want to be open with you.	You are open with me.	I want you to be open with me.				
	31	32	33	34	35	36	37	38
Significance	I feel you are significant.	I want to feel you are significant.	You feel I am significant.	I want you to feel I am significant.				
	41	42	43	44	45	46	47	48
Competence	I feel you are competent.	I want to feel you are competent.	You feel I am competent.	I want you to feel I am competent.				
	51	52	53	54	55	56	57	58
Likability	I like you.	I want to like you.	You like me.	I want you to like me.				
	61	62	63	64	65	66	67	68

On my job:

Cells 11, 12. **Am I required to include others too much, too little, or just enough?**

−4	−3	−2	−1	0	+1	+2	+3	+4
Too little				Just enough				Too much

Cells 21, 22. **Am I required to control others too much, too little, or just enough?**

−4	−3	−2	−1	0	+1	+2	+3	+4
Too little				Just enough				Too much

Cells 31, 32. Am I open with people more than I want to be, less than I want to be, or just enough?

−4	−3	−2	−1	0	+1	+2	+3	+4
Too much less				Just enough			Too much more	

Cells 13, 14. Am I included too much, too little, or just enough?

−4	−3	−2	−1	0	+1	+2	+3	+4
Too little				Just enough			Too much	

Cells 23, 24. Am I controlled too much, too little, or just enough?

−4	−3	−2	−1	0	+1	+2	+3	+4
Too little				Just enough			Too much	

Cells 33, 34. Are people too open with me, not open enough, or open just enough?

−4	−3	−2	−1	0	+1	+2	+3	+4
Not open enough			Open just enough				Too open	

Cells 43, 44. Do people feel I am as significant as I want them to feel?

−4	−3	−2	−1	0	+1	+2	+3	+4
Not as much				Just enough			Too much	

Cells 41, 42. Do I feel people are as significant as I want to feel?

−4	−3	−2	−1	0	+1	+2	+3	+4
Not as much				Just enough			Too much	

Cells 53, 54. Do people feel I am as competent as I want them to feel?

−4	−3	−2	−1	0	+1	+2	+3	+4
Not as much				Just enough			Too much	

Cells 51, 52. Do I feel people are as competent as I want to feel?

−4	−3	−2	−1	0	+1	+2	+3	+4
Not as much				Just enough			Too much	

Cells 63, 64. Do people like me as much as I want them to?

−4	−3	−2	−1	0	+1	+2	+3	+4
Not as much				Just enough			Too much	

Cells 61, 62. Do I like people as much as I want to?

−4	−3	−2	−1	0	+1	+2	+3	+4
Not as much				Just enough			Too much	

Which of these answers do I find most disturbing? Do I want to do anything to change it? Which answer may reveal an obstacle to my fit with my job?

Improving Individual Decision Making

Individual decision making is the final component of individual performance to which the Human Element will be applied in this chapter. Once performance appraisal has been made an open, honest process and the best fit between person and job has been ensured, the next step is to maximize creative and logical thinking by uncovering psychological blocks. Technical expertise plays an important role in decision making, but it will not be considered here (apart from the statement that the team must determine who has the technical expertise for a task, identify where gaps exist, and figure out how to fill those gaps). The focus here is on practical steps for identifying and removing blocks to creativity and logical thinking, for the sake of better individual decisions.

Creativity

Creativity in thinking and solving problems is universally admired and (in the abstract, at least) generally encouraged in organizations. Putting aside interpersonal and organizational effects on creativity, I can do much to enhance my thinking by being fully aware of the stages of the creative process[5] and knowing about the psychological blocks that can arise at each stage. The Human Element approach helps leaders and individuals use self-awareness to diminish and remove those blocks.[6]

Blocks in the Creative Process

Stage 1: Experience   Before I can discover a creative solution, I must acquire a repertoire of experiences. I must be open to experience, able to perceive and sense my environment, and be aware of my own feelings. It is no accident that physicists make the most creative discoveries in physics, or that basketball players invent most of the new ways of shooting a basket. A strong background and information allow for more possibilities for new solutions. Experience-related blocks include the following:

- *Fear of not learning:* If I feel I cannot learn or retain information, I feel anxious about new experiences. If I feel I will be tested on what I learn, I may also shut down. If my self-concept is that I am not intelligent (that is, not competent), I do not put myself in a position where I will be humiliated. If I am regarded as phenomenally smart, I may not learn because I am afraid I will drive other people away. As a result, I limit my experiences.

- *Fear of violating secrecy:* I may have been brought up to believe that certain areas are not to be known. They are "naughty" or "none of my business" or "evil" or "sick" or "impertinent," and so forth. If I accept these evaluations, I keep myself from investigating a wider range of phenomena because they make me anxious—I'm out of bounds. In particular, I am not open to my unconscious and all the creative potential within it. Self-censoring may seriously limit my ability to know my experiences.

Stage 2: Association   After I acquire experience, I must have the ability to associate two or more experiences that, when put together, create a useful product. Much poetry is made up of such remote associations, or metaphors ("The fog comes/on little cat feet," in Carl Sandburg's "The Fog"). Association-related blocks include the following:

- *Fear of self-awareness:* Allowing association means that I will be open to knowing the relationship between my actions and their consequences. This does not allow me much room for self-deception. For example, association may reveal to me that every time someone does not follow my orders, my back hurts. If I don't want to recognize the negative consequences of lying or withholding, I will not allow myself to explore possible connections. My fear of self-awareness will keep me from being able to associate freely. Thus I will avoid exploring imagery, using drugs or alcohol, keeping late hours, becoming fully relaxed, blindly following orders, or doing anything else that may pull down my guard.

- *Overvaluing rationality:* If I stay in control by being utterly rational, I must reject nonlinear or associative thinking. If I reject any reasoning that is not immediately logical, I don't develop my intuition, or hunches. Many extremely creative people have said that intuition is what brought them to their discoveries. I greatly curtail my creativity when I fear the consequences of being "flaky" or unacceptable to the establishment.

Stage 3: Expression   Once I have associated diverse experiences or information, I must express them in spoken or written words or in other physical form. A creative association is of little social value unless I communicate it adequately. Sometimes the expression is the creative product itself (as in the arts of painting, sculpting, dancing, or acting). Sometimes the expression is the vehicle for a creative accomplishment, such as a scientific paper or an innovative marketing plan. Expression-related blocks include the following:

- *Fear of embarrassment:* If I am uncertain about my abilities, I have difficulty exposing my ideas to public view. For example, I may have writer's block because I am afraid that readers will criticize or ridicule my work and I will be exposed as not very bright or talented (that is, incompetent). As a result, I tend not to tell people my ideas. The ideas are therefore not exposed to feedback, and so they may remain underdeveloped.

- *Bodily inhibition:* I have learned to distance myself from my body, perhaps because I feel that it is ugly or sinful or clumsy. I am reluctant to express (that is, be open about) my ideas or creations through singing, dancing, drawing, acting, or even speaking in public. I am afraid of being embarrassed, of making a fool of myself.

- *Fear of assertion:* If I express what I feel, people may not like me. Whatever I have to express may get me in trouble, and so I had better not say anything. My parents may have conveyed that notion to me. If I accept it, I inhibit myself from expressing any idea whatsoever and therefore limit my creativity.

Stage 4: Evaluation   At this stage, the worth of a creative solution must be evaluated. This phase distinguishes the creative from the bizarre, the productive from the mundane. Evaluation-related blocks include the following:

- *Fear of humiliation:* If I evaluate my own product or solution highly, but other people think it is no good, I will look like a fool, and so I tend to undervalue what I do, and I do not follow through on what I start. I may either fall into false modesty or actually convince myself that my creations are unworthy. In either case, I do not put my full energy into completing my works.

- *Conflict over being ignored and being rejected:* If I evaluate my own solution or product negatively, people may tend to ignore it (that is, not include it and therefore not include me, which will make me feel insignificant). If I do not think highly of my work, why should others? But if I evaluate it positively, people may think that I am boastful and reject me (not like me). This dilemma clouds my ability to evaluate my work accurately. The possible outcomes are that I will proceed on an unpromising project or prematurely drop a potentially valuable one.

Stage 5: Perseverance   After generating an original idea or product, I must persevere to completion, or an end state. Most authors revise their manuscripts many times. Artists redo paintings and sculptures until they "work," or provide their creators with the right feeling. An innovative scientific discovery typically requires a great deal of detailed effort after an initial breakthrough. The concept of continuous improvement implies that any process or product must be endlessly improved through constant revision. Perseverance-related blocks include the following:

- *Fear of failure:* What if I carry my idea to completion and find that it is not nearly as good as I thought it was (that is, I'm not competent)? If my idea is a scientific one, perhaps I have overlooked some factors. It may turn out that my artistic product or performance does not get any better as I work on it; perhaps it even deteriorates. As a result, I don't develop my product to the point of being a truly creative work.

- *Lack of rewards:* Much of my creative activity is motivated by the admiration I receive for my creations. The perseverance required to turn an initial creative impulse into a more developed work is often not as immediately rewarding as the original impulse was. Or I may regard myself as an "idea" person, not as one who works out the details. This attitude may come from the fear that I am not very good at following through, and so my impulse will come to naught anyway.

Pause for Reflection: Creativity

The following items can help me assess my strengths and current limitations in the realm of creativity.

1. For each stage of the creative process, which blocks sound familiar to me? Are there any I want to remove?

2. Do I have any blocks to acquiring knowledge? Do I fear that I won't remember information? Am I reluctant to explore secret areas?

3. Have I developed the ability to make creative associations? Am I reluctant to let my mind go wherever it wants to, without controlling it? Why?

4. Am I inhibited in writing, speaking, moving? Am I afraid of ridicule? of making a fool of myself? What are my fears?

5. Do I trust myself to judge my own creative efforts?

6. Do I have any trouble staying with something until it is complete? Am I afraid of failure? Of being disappointed when I have completed something? Why? What are my fears?

Logical Thinking and Problem Solving

Creative thinking, of course, is not the only mode of thought needed for effective individual decision making. Rational, linear, logical thinking is also important in evaluating, testing, and justifying plans and ideas. This kind of thinking is subject to its own brand of psychological blocks, which often arise from feelings, self-deception, and lack of awareness (I may believe that logical reasoning has nothing to do with feelings, but that is usually little more than self-deception). This section of the chapter looks at blocks (which stem from weaknesses in self-esteem) to the logical process of problem solving, especially as they apply to the leader's role.

Example   *Two mathematics instructors at Stanford University were teaching a summer course that I took in mathematics for social scientists. They had a long-running argument. Pat felt that problems could best be solved with continuous distributions, which assume that between any two numbers there is another number, with no gaps. Bob was equally convinced that problems could best be solved with discrete distributions, which assume that any separate measurement is represented by one whole number or another.*

We students were puzzled. Both Pat and Bob were brilliant mathematicians, capable of solving virtually any problem with their favorite distributions. It finally dawned on us that their preferences were expressions of their life-styles.

After class, Pat would play softball with us, have dinner with us, and spend time talking with us. He was "continuous" with the class. Bob left immediately after class and went home. He would reappear the next morning when classes began. His life-style was "discrete." His work life and his home life were separate, even though he lived close to campus.

There was apparently no mathematical way to establish the superiority of either Pat's or Bob's preference. Their logical differences were not logical at all. Both of them were unwittingly trying to justify their life-style preferences mathematically. Logical statements are often not completely logical at all but actually have a feeling component.

The Logical Problem-Solving Process and What Blocks It

Stage 1: Anticipation I, the leader, anticipate problems, plan for the future, and organize my staff and resources to meet future events effectively. One block at this point is *lack of foresight:* I fail to anticipate and plan because I'm afraid I'm not good at long-range planning. I have trouble foreseeing future issues, and so I will be revealed as incompetent.

Stage 2: Recognition I recognize problems when they occur, see them clearly, and can present them clearly to others. A block that may occur here is *denial:* I'm afraid I won't see problems until it is too late. Sometimes I don't want problems to exist, and so I overlook them. I use the defense of denial to avoid feeling incompetent.

Stage 3: Data Collection When a problem arises, I gather all the available information relevant to solving the problem. I hear all sides before deciding. At this point, *confusion* may block my logical thinking: I am afraid I will get confused by too much data. I feel more se-cure if there is one simple source of information. Besides, I don't want to appear indecisive.

Stage 4: Complaints   When confronted with a complaint, I check into its source, to determine its reliability. Here, my logical thinking may be blocked by *threat:* I just want to comply with the complainer, so that there will not be any trouble with the law, customer rela-tions, or my reputation. My competence and my likability must be protected.

Stage 5: Causes   I am creative and imaginative in determining causes and getting to the source, the reason behind a problem. I can sense things going on that most people miss. At this point, I may be blocked by fears of *superficiality:* I'm afraid I'm too shallow (that is, incompetent) to see underlying causes. I feel more comfortable just solving immediate problems.

Stage 6: Alternatives   In addition to employing the usual methods, which I know well, I am creative in thinking of and considering many other approaches to solving a problem. When deciding what action to take, rather than doing the first thing that occurs to me, I avoid rigidity and consider all the possibilities before choosing one. What can block me here is my concern for *safety:* I will be safer if I stick with what I know than if I risk doing something unfamiliar. Even if my method is not as good as established ones, it's safe.

Stage 7: Effects   I am aware of the possible effects of my actions on others. I can anticipate people's reactions accurately. Here, fear of *weakness* may block my logical thinking: I do not want to look at ef-fects that I would not like.

Stage 8: Organization   I am well enough informed about my entire organization to be aware of all the implications of my actions. What may block me here is fear of *deprivation:* I avoid learning about the problems of other people in the organization, for fear that I will have to be more considerate, take less for myself and my people, and be deprived of what I have.

Stage 9: Goals   I know the goals of my unit. I have a clear idea of which goals are more important than others, and I can communicate the goals and objectives of the organization to my staff, so that there is no ambiguity about what the organization is trying to achieve. A potential block at this stage is concern for *deniability:* If I do not agree with the corporate goals, I make little effort to learn more about them and can therefore plead ignorance (that is, deny what I don't know). That makes it convenient for me not to keep people informed of everything that is happening.

Stage 10: Pressures   I am not easily swayed by pressures that would interfere with accomplishing the goals of my unit. I stick with my convictions. Here, though, fear of *disapproval* may block me: I am afraid that I will lose my job or that people will not like me if I do not comply with their personal requests, even if these requests are somewhat opposed to our goals.

Stage 11: Reasonableness   My decisions are reasonable, not unjustifiably wild or bizarre. What may block my logical thinking here is fear of *ordinariness:* I want to distinguish myself, not simply be ordinary (that is, insignificant) and just do what I am told. If I conform, I feel weak.

Stage 12: Imagination   My decisions are not excessively conservative, safe, or unimaginative. I may find my logical thinking blocked at this stage by my fear of *risk:* I think it is better not to take risks and be sorry later.

Stage 13: Decisiveness   When the time is right, I move decisively and clearly. But I may encounter a block in the form of my fears about *humiliation:* I am afraid of being authoritarian because that could be wrong, and I would be humiliated to be wrong.

Stage 14: Evaluation   I follow up my solutions to see if they have worked and produced good results. I can profit from this knowledge, but I may be blocked by fear of *exposure:* I hate being evaluated. I resent it when other people, no more capable than I am, rate me. They may discover my inadequacies.

Dissolving Blocks to Creativity and Logical Thinking

I will never forget Mrs. McIlvain, my high school geometry teacher. I did well in geometry and was proud of my ability to solve the tough problems "correctly."

One day, I handed her an extra-credit problem—done "correctly," of course.

"Very good," she said. "Now do it another way."

"What do you mean?" I almost screamed. "The book says to do it this way. I did, and I got it right."

She agreed but quietly persisted. I went home and stared blankly for what seemed like hours. Then I looked at the problem again. Sure enough, there was another way to solve it. In fact, there were three other ways.

Until that moment, it had never even occurred to me that I could be creative in geometry; I was anxiously, desperately, focused on doing things the "right" way. Later, as a teacher myself, I found that simply telling people it is all right for them to be creative is one of the most potent ways of helping them break out of their self-made limits.

The key to dissolving our blocks to creativity and logical thinking lies in self-esteem that is allowed to thrive in an open and truthful organizational atmosphere. When we can focus on problems rather than on our defenses, and when it is safe for all of us to express our feelings and acknowledge our fears, the organization constitutes a community that can help us identify and remove these blocks.

The Human Element methods for this area are similar to those for performance appraisal. They are designed to create an atmosphere dedicated to helping me and all my colleagues be more creative and more logical. Here are some guidelines:

1. All of us read the material in this section about blocks to creativity and logical thinking, and then we all think about where each of us is blocked.

2. We establish that since each of us has barriers, it is all right for us to talk about them. The best way for us to overcome them is to get them out in the open and explore them.

3. We hold a meeting for the sole purpose of talking about creativity and logic and about the personal blocks we all have to using ourselves to the fullest. This is not a meeting for criticism or comparisons but rather for acknowledgment of how each person could be functioning even better.

4. We go over the creativity blocks one at a time, asking one another to say how we feel about each particular block. In as much detail as we can recall, we give examples from our personal experiences. When any of us recounts a very meaningful block experience, we all try to remember the first time we experienced the same block or were told about it. For example, maybe my father told me I was clumsy ("You dance like a baby elephant") and that I couldn't sing; I believed him, and since then I have been very reluctant to sing or dance when I can be seen.

5. We give feedback to one another on how we feel about the same issue and how we see one another in this regard. And we create ways to set up situations where our inhibitions can be transcended with group support.

6. We think of creative ways to overcome our blocks by creating opportunities to do the things we fear most, preferably in front

of the group. When each of us has finished doing the thing we feared, we tell the group how it felt, and we each receive feedback.

7. We form circles of about five people each. Each person turns to the person on the left and asks, "How do you block yourself from being more creative?" The second person answers, and the first person says, "Thank you." Then the second person turns to the person on the left, asks the same question, and follows the same procedure. We continue around the circle for about eight to ten minutes. When we have finished, we all shut our eyes and silently answer three questions: *What was the most meaningful thing I said? What was the most meaningful thing anyone else said? Was there anything I thought of and didn't say?* Now we open our eyes and discuss these answers, as well as anything else that emerges.

8. We agree that whenever any feeling of being blocked arises in the future, the person who feels it will express the feeling, in a group meeting or wherever else he or she is. Co-workers will be supportive without being excessively "helpful."

9. Now we go through steps 4 to 8 again, this time with reference to problem solving. (In step 7, the question becomes "How do you block yourself from thinking more logically?") The key to this exercise, again, is to keep going around the circle for at least eight to ten minutes.

Pause for Reflection: Individual Decision Making

Creativity

1. I limit my awareness because I believe that certain things should not be known or talked about.

disagree   0   1   2   3   4   5   6   7   8   9   agree

2. I fear letting my guard down and letting my associations run free.

disagree   0   1   2   3   4   5   6   7   8   9   agree

3. I fear humiliation when I express my thoughts or feelings publicly.

disagree   0   1   2   3   4   5   6   7   8   9   agree

4. I fear not being liked if I am better than other people.

disagree   0   1   2   3   4   5   6   7   8   9   agree

5. I fear being unappreciated if I do not tell people of my abilities.

disagree   0   1   2   3   4   5   6   7   8   9   agree

Other comments:

Logical Problem Solving

6. I deny that problems exist, and so I don't plan very well.

disagree   0   1   2   3   4   5   6   7   8   9   agree

7. I am afraid that I will be confused by too much information, and so I don't have the patience to gather enough.

disagree   0   1   2   3   4   5   6   7   8   9   agree

8. I am too influenced by criticism, and I acquiesce too quickly.

disagree   0   1   2   3   4   5   6   7   8   9   agree

9. If I don't agree with the organization's goals, I ignore them.

disagree   0   1   2   3   4   5   6   7   8   9   agree

10. I sometimes do something different, even if it is not as good, just to be noticed.

disagree   0   1   2   3   4   5   6   7   8   9   agree

Other comments:

People I have known who show some of these behaviors:

5

Concordance Decision Making: Developing Better Decisions That Everyone Supports

The demise of the old authoritarian structures, from the USSR to General Motors, is a global historical phenomenon that none can evade. Like it or not, everyone who works for a living is helping create a new relationship between individual and corporation and a new sense of self for employer and employee alike.... The result promises to be worth some suffering. The workplace will be healthier, saner, more creative, and yet more chaotic— like nature itself.   —*Stratford Sherman*[1]

At the heart of this transition is a radical change in the way organizational decisions are made, a change from authoritarian decisions to decisions contributed to by all appropriate persons. Organizations, teams, and individuals all spend much of their time making (or not making) decisions, or complaining about those that others make. Yet few groups or teams discuss *how* decisions in general will be made, apart from any particular decision. Decision-making methods are adopted by default, or by custom, or by adherence to the boss's idea of how decisions should be made, or by a show of behavior that gives the public impression of a strong and assertive decision-making process. Making decisions without a conscious process can cause problems instead of solving them.

Managers often complain that they have made excellent decisions but they have no "buy-in" from employees (for example, in creating corporate values); the CEO proudly presents his or her well-thought-out and noble-sounding values, but few people seem to care about or follow them. It takes a while for management to see the reason: the CEO is not presenting *corporate* values but the values of top management.

Many companies talk about participative management and empowerment as goals, yet too few employees in those organizations feel empowered. Top management is reluctant to really give up power (that is, final decision-making ability). Without a commitment to self-determination for everyone, an organization cannot create an empowered environment—no one, in fact, can empower anyone else. And the irony is that when leaders use more participative methods and increase productivity, their superiors often rate them low on leadership because they do not fit the "strong leader" model and do not look decisive.

As I observe the imbalance in the decision-making process—with most decisions made by a few people, and many other people making very few decisions—I see a parallel with how we use our bodies. In far too many organizations, a small number of people at the top make a huge proportion of all decisions, and the huge number of employees at the bottom make relatively few final decisions. The results are burnout at the top and loss of interest and loss of involvement at the bottom. The way we typically use our bodies is to forgo the very efficient small muscles (employees) attached to the bones, which can move the bones a long distance with little effort, in favor of the very large muscles (top management) on the outside, which must move a long distance and use more effort to move the bones the same distance. Just as in the organization, in the body the large muscles wear out and get pulled (burnout), while the small muscles atrophy (low morale) and, after a while, are not of much use. A method is needed that uses every muscle within its zone of comfort and harmonizes all the muscles so that the integrated sum of them all provides strength, stamina, and grace without strain. So may it be with the organization.

The Human Element Approach

Most of what work groups or teams do is make decisions about how and when they will do what they are supposed to do. Earlier chapters (especially Chapter Three, on teamwork) have demonstrated that groups are more productive if organizations create an open and truthful atmosphere for them to function in, and if members learn to achieve compatibility and use open teamwork. Even when these interpersonal dynamics are working well, however, teams need methods for making decisions. Decision making depends on open teamwork but does not necessarily grow out of it automatically. This chapter looks at an approach to group decision making—concordance—that takes full advantage of the Human Element model and, if used in a supportive atmosphere, can improve the quality of decisions and thus lead to correspondingly excellent results.

Of the most commonly used approaches to organizational decision making, by far the most widespread is the *authoritarian* approach, where one vote—the boss's—determines decisions. The preferred method for many boards, committees, and democratic bodies is *majority rule*, where a decision is determined by which position receives more than half the votes. In *participative management*, which has become popular in the past few decades, all are invited to give input to one person or to a group, and that person or group makes the final decision. The method of *consensus* usually requires everyone to agree before a decision is final. All these methods have their advantages and their limits, which is why concordance was developed as part of the Human Element.

Applying the basic principles of the Human Element to group decision making brings in inclusion, control, and openness as part of the process. Doing so provides a structure for the full use of all team members' creativity and logical capacities by capitalizing on members' ability to speak honestly to one another. This method is called *concordance* in decision making. (We use the term *concordance* rather than *consensus*, which is similar, because it is more precise, clearly includes the Human Element components, and goes somewhat beyond consensus. *Concordance* is defined in the dictionary as "agreement, concord, harmony." *Concord* is defined as "agreement among persons; concurrence in attitudes, feelings, etc." It derives from the Latin word *cors*, meaning heart.) Concordance occurs when all members of the decision-making team are in agreement with their attitudes, feelings, and hearts, not just with their intellects. More precisely, a decision is concordant to the degree that it fulfills specific criteria on inclusion, control, and openness. The next section describes those criteria.[2]

Concordance in Decision Making: Inclusion, Control, and Openness Criteria

The *inclusion* criterion states that the decision-making team consists of those who know the most about the content of the decision and those who are the most affected by it. Including the most knowledgeable people ensures the highest-quality decision, while including those most affected is the best way to guarantee buy-in for the decision—that is, swift and unconflicted implementation.[3]

The following report describes one result of omitting the people affected by the decision from the decision-making team:

Example   Caterpillar chairman Donald Fites may have proved he was tough, but he didn't demonstrate that he was smart when he forced striking and locked-out workers back into the plants with the threat of hiring permanent replacements last spring. Now his tactics are hurting the company. After workers returned, union leaders urged them to do only what they were absolutely required to do, apparently with some effect. In an August 6 memo, Aurora, Illinois assembly plant manager Chuck Elwyn wrote that in July, "We had the worst month ever in terms of production ... the poorest performance in this plant's history... think it's the worst month by any plant in the entire corporation's history.... As far as whether the in-plant strategy is a factor or not, you be the judge. When the leadership of the UAW goes public with plans to slow down production, and then we have our worst month in history, what do you think?" Elwyn also noted that the average number of defects had risen from three per tractor before the lockout to seven per tractor, giving rise to customer complaints and a declining share of a tight market. "No doubt about it," he wrote. "Right now we're hurting our business."[4]

One assumption underlying concordance is that the group as a whole has more resources than any one individual or subgroup and is therefore in a better position to make creative, effective decisions. The team may designate different subgroups to make certain decisions. For example, an executive committee may decide to delegate the monthly financial statement to the accountant and the financial manager. That group of two is empowered by the team to make the team's financial report.

Example A computer company was planning a new building in California, to house a supercomputer. The Washington headquarters sent a plan for the interior design of the building. An uproar followed. The Washington plan would force people to work in spaces they felt were uncomfortable and inefficient. There was already plenty of animosity and anger. Headquarters had ignored the input of the people who would work in the new building and who knew most about how the space would be used. In a concordance-based solution, the Washington office would have provided the budget and let the future workers plan the space. Their creativity and experience would then have been utilized, and the design would have had immediate and widespread acceptance.

Inclusion, however, does not mean that everyone must participate in decisions. If I am qualified to be a team member and don't want to be included in the decision-making process, the team asks me to agree to carry out all decisions the group makes. If I agree, the team proceeds. The team retains concordance, and I may choose to rejoin the group at any time. For instance, a technician in a manufacturing plant objected to the use of concordance in her plant: "I work to make a living. I just want you to tell me what to do, and I will do it well. I don't want the responsibility of making decisions. I do that at home with my family." The group members then asked her if she was willing to go along with decisions they made. She had no objection: "I've been doing that all along. Why change now?" As time went on, she became curious about the group's activities and gradually began to participate, which she could do as part of the concordance team.

The *control* criterion for concordance states that every person on the decision-making team has equal control or power and that everyone has a veto. I cannot be overruled by the other members, as I could be in most of the other decision-making methods. I, or anyone else, can say *no* and prevent a decision. Sometimes, when I am the highest-ranking and most experienced member of the team and feel that a certain course of action would be foolhardy, I can prevent it simply by saying *no*. If, as the supervisor, I decide to use the concordance method for my decisions, I do not lose power (with the exception that I cannot make any decisions without the consent of the team). The group cannot force me to make decisions that I do not like, because no decision can be made until everyone, including me, says *yes*. The concordance method elevates others to my level of authority; it does not reduce my authority.

A key difference between the concordance method and most other methods, including participative management, is that *the whole team makes the final decision*. I, like any other member, have control—power—in the sense that the group cannot make a decision without my agreement. Everyone must agree with the decision before it becomes final. The decisions of the team are also the decisions of the highest-ranking member of the team. If the team wants to make a concordant decision at a still higher level, the team must *include the higher-level person in the concordance process.*

One of the first things that most concordance groups do is to decide which decisions will be made in what ways. It takes too much time away from individual work if we all have to contribute to every decision. Typically, we decide which people are best qualified to make which decisions, and then we deputize them to do it. Some decisions are best made through concordance. With others, the team advises one person, who is empowered by the group to decide. Some decisions, such as those about carrying out a policy, may best be made by one person. It takes experience to settle on the best way to allocate tasks. Varying the methods to fit the different conditions leads to the best solutions. The group is still the final decision maker, however, even about who is to make which decisions. We may agree concordantly to delegate one person to make certain decisions. I may choose at any time to surrender control over any or all decisions. I may decide that I am not knowledgeable in a given area, or I may simply not care and may hand my control over to others. In concordance, participation is a right, not an obligation.

I introduced the concordance method for decision making into a research project I was directing at Berkeley. The fifteen members of the project agreed to use this method, but the following week they complained: "How can we do our work when you interrupt us all day to make decisions?"

The group decided to deputize three statisticians to make all the final decisions on statistical issues. These decisions would stand as the decisions of the whole group. The group also decided that I would determine who would do which tasks, since I had the best overall view of the project.

The following week, Helen complained: "Will, you gave Albert the demographic job, and he kept asking me how to do it. You should have given it to me." She was right, and so the group continued to decide, as a whole, on the best person or persons to make each type of decision. Any method could be used if the group felt it was the most appropriate one. If that method did not work, the group could change it.

The *openness* criterion for concordance, the one that most distinguishes it from consensus, is the requirement that everyone be totally open and honest. We all openly express all relevant thoughts and feelings. I am willing to say to other people what I think and how I feel about an issue. I am aware of my real feelings about the issue, those of the other team members, and my relationship to each member. This total commitment to honesty and the unending quest for self-awareness take the form of increasing self-knowledge and using other members to determine when I am (or anyone else is) being self-deceptive. The "Yes Method," described as follows, illustrates a technique we can use to check to make sure all of us are expressing our full feelings. Deliberately not being honest is simply lying, even if euphemisms are used: "misleading," "shading the truth," being "less than candid" or "not forthcoming," telling "little white lies," or doing something "for your own good." Openness means not withholding; failing to say something relevant is as much a violation of the openness principle as intentionally lying is. It is a "withholding lie."

Concordance usually leads directly to mutual understanding and cooperation. If I am open with my feelings and take into account the feelings of the other members of my organization before decisions are made, cooperation typically follows. Conflict follows from lying, withholding, and lack of openness. Openness leads to the desire to cooperate. A tragic example of what can happen as a result of making a decision without openness has come to light in a recent book:[5]

Example   A nearby freighter failed to go to the rescue of the sinking *Titanic* partly because of an officer's neurotic fear of his domineering and overcautious captain. The *Californian's* second officer, Herbert Stone, realized that the rockets [from the *Titanic*] were distress signals. But Stone, who had fled a domineering father at age 16, was too afraid of the overbearing and aloof [Captain] Lord to go below to insist that action be taken.... More than 1500 men, women, and children drowned a few miles away the night of April 14–15, 1912.

The "Yes" Method

When a decision is about to be reached, if the leader says, "Does anyone disagree?" and no one responds, it doesn't necessarily mean we have concordance. It may be that I don't feel comfortable expressing my disagreement, especially if we do not yet have an open atmosphere. One technique for getting the most honest and open participation, therefore coming closer to creating true concordance, is the "Yes" method.

After discussion of the issue, when we seem to understand where everyone stands, we phrase the question—in written form—and ask everyone to say the word *yes* if they agree or the word *no* if they disagree. We go all the way around the circle in turn, even if there is a *no*. The rule is, if anyone says anything other than *yes*, we assume that he or she means *no*. If I feel reluctant to oppose the group, I often will not say *no* directly; I will express my lack of readiness implicitly, by saying *yeah, sure, okay, go ahead, uh-huh*, or something similar. Even a hesitant *yes* may mean no. Encouraging me to say how I really feel leads to true concordance.

If we have not all said the word *yes*, we continue the discussion until we either come to complete agreement or decide to postpone the decision. This does not mean that we resort to compromise or averaging. It means that we create a new formulation of the problem, so that the solution will satisfy everyone. One useful step is to ask dissenters, "What would it take for you to be satisfied?" Creativity often emerges at this point.

Table 5.1 compares concordance with other decision-making methods. When we as a team meet the inclusion and control criteria but are not open, we are like many consensus groups: the relevant people make the decisions, power is equal, and all have a veto, but I may be reluctant to speak out for fear of losing my job, not wanting to be disliked, or not wanting to be the one who holds up the group.

Table 5.1. Concordance and Other Decision-Making Methods.

	Inclusion Criterion Not Required	Inclusion Criterion Required
Control criterion and openness criterion not required	Authoritarian	Pseudodemocratic
Control criterion not required, and openness criterion required	Individual lobbying	Participative management
Control criterion required, and openness criterion not required	Pseudo– "New Age"	Consensus
Control criterion and openness criterion required	Paternalistic	Concordance

Quality circles and self-directed teams are also examples of groups that focus only on task behavior and do not require openness.

When we as a team meet the inclusion and openness criteria, but not the control criterion, we have successful participative management. We are all included, and we may express our feelings openly, but one person or subgroup makes the decision. This pattern could also apply when there is an authoritarian manager or a benevolent dictator who encourages input from team members but makes the final decisions. A majority group is another example of this configuration. If I am in the minority, I have equal power but not veto power, and so my opinion may be ignored.

If we as a group meet the control and openness criteria, but not the inclusion criterion, we may be paternalistic (that is, we make decisions for other people). A group made up of managers who decide bonuses for their employees by consensus does not meet the inclusion criterion, since the people for whom the decision is made do not participate in the final decision-making process.

Pause for Reflection: Group Decision Making

1. What are my experiences with authoritarian decision making?
2. What is my opinion of participative management? Has it worked for me?
3. What do I like about being the boss and giving orders? What do I dislike?
4. Would I feel comfortable in a true concordance situation? In what ways would I like it? In what ways would I dislike it?
5. Would I feel deprived of power if my team were to become concordant? How would I handle that?

	Interpersonal: Do Self (I) to Other (You)		Interpersonal: Get Other (You) to Self (I)		Individual Self (I) to Self (I)		Other Other (O) to Other (O)	
	See	Want	See	Want	See	Want	See	Want
Inclusion	I include you. 11	12	You include me. 13	14	15	16	17	18
Control	I control you. 21	22	You control me. 23	24	25	26	27	28
Openness	I am open with you. 31	32	You are open with me. 33	34	35	36	37	38
Significance	41	42	43	44	45	46	47	48
Competence	51	52	53	54	55	56	57	58
Likability	61	62	63	64	65	66	67	68

For decision making, *I* refers to the team authority (the rules of the leader), and *you* refers to other team members (including the leader). Six cells represent the criteria for concordance.

Cells 11, 13. The inclusion criterion applies to people who know the most and who are most affected by the decision. It also shows the leader's role in deciding which team members participate (are included) in making the decision (the leader includes members). Cell 13 shows rules for participation (members include members).

Cells 21, 23. The control criterion reflects equal control among all the included members. Cells 21 (the leader controls members) and 23 (members control members) indicate the procedure for deciding who makes the final decision.

Cells 31, 33. The openness criterion reflects that all members of the decision-making team are fully open. Cells 31 (the leader is open with members) and 33 (members are open with members) show the procedure for deciding how much of everyone's opinions and feelings will be expressed.

Characteristics of Concordance

There are several issues about concordance that must be dealt with to ease the transition from another decision-making method.

Acknowledgment of Feelings

An essential characteristic of the concordance process is that your feelings and mine are acknowledged. If I disagree with the majority and I feel they don't understand my position or how strongly I feel about it, I'm reluctant to go along. But if I express my opinion, describe the basis for it, and tell you how important it is to me, and if you still want to take another direction, then I am more likely to consider your position and how strongly you feel about it. We keep talking until we reach agreement. Suppose, for instance, that I am one of a minority opposing a merger. In the concordance decision-making method, we minority members express our feelings about the merger. Majority members acknowledge these feelings, express their own feelings, and have them acknowledged. Each side is aware of the vote of each member, of the reasons behind it, and of how strongly each person feels. If, after everyone's feelings have been heard and understood, the majority favors the merger, I may agree to the merger, for the sake of making a decision for the company. Or the majority may feel that since a few people feel so strongly against the merger, it would be prudent to postpone a decision. No matter what the outcome is, concordance allows feelings and thoughts to be considered.

Flexibility

A group may use any decision-making method within the concordance process. If we all agree to form an authoritarian structure, that is concordance. If we decide to solve certain issues by concordance and to delegate certain members to decide other decisions alone, that too is concordance. Anything we decide by concordance is concordance, even if we choose concordantly to abandon the concordance model. Concordance simplifies the process of achieving the ideal administrative goal. The organization functions so that each decision is made by those people best qualified to make it and by those who are most affected by it.

Size

Concordance may often seem to be realistic only in smaller organizations. Those in a large corporation may say, "We can't gather hundreds or thousands of employees together every time we want to make a decision." That is true, of course, but the members of the concordance group are aware of this. Therefore, they create a practical procedure to deal with the situation.

The most common technique is to divide the organization into tiers. Those on the bottom (the whole group) designate people to represent them at the next-highest level. That group selects people to represent them at the next-highest level, and so on. Concordance decisions are then made at the top level and passed down. At any time, the group as a whole may revise the system to fit changing circumstances or needs. One important assumption of concordance is that the group members as a whole, working well together, have more resources than any one individual and are therefore in a position to make more creative, effective decisions.

Speed

Concordance usually takes longer at the beginning than methods that demand less agreement, such as the authoritarian approach. As teams become accustomed to using the technique, however, discussions become briefer and more efficient. In an open atmosphere, for example, we may go straight to the question: "Does anyone disagree?" We are now certain that members feel free to object.

Even though concordance decisions sometimes take longer to make, they are almost always implemented more quickly, since they deal with blocks during the discussion phase rather than during implementation. Those who are to carry out the decisions have participated in the decision-making process and feel motivated to follow through.

Example Don, a Baltimore warehouse manager, wrote this account: "My first inclination was that concordance was fine for most decisions but probably not for the highly controversial issues where I'm certain not everyone would agree on any solution. What do we do about those who would block concordance in these situations? What has become clear to me is that it is precisely in these situations that concordance becomes especially appropriate. On the tough, conflicted issues, I now use concordance to deal directly with differences in facts, perceptions, opinions, and feelings. Before, all the blocking took place in the implementation phase, in the form of hard-to-identify sabotage. Now, the block is right in the middle of the group, to be stated, heard, internalized, and valued. No decision is implemented until all blocks have been incorporated into the solution. So, in a very real way, these stumbling blocks become building blocks. Overall time and effort, from problem identification to the implementation of a successful solution, are greatly reduced. In my opinion, most solutions arrived at by authoritarian decisions on conflicted issues are never fully implemented."

Empowerment

Concordance fosters a structure in which each person's full creativity and skill can best be used. Concordance allows an organization to capitalize on an atmosphere in which we employees are inspired and encouraged to express our ideas. It is well established that the more participatory and influential employees are, the more likely they are to be highly motivated.[6] If I am allowed to participate, but my suggestions are repeatedly turned down, after a while I lose my motivation to stay involved. In concordance, I participate equally in making the final decision. I cannot be ignored.

Creativity

Concordance decisions are almost invariably more creative because they elicit a wider variety of potential solutions through broader participation. Further, because group members hear and build on one another's ideas, the process stimulates new and more thoughtful decisions.

A hospital in Iowa was hit by an "economic downturn," and its filled beds were reduced from three hundred to two hundred. It appeared that the hospital would have to reduce its staff by one hundred employees by June 1.

Before that drastic step was taken, we consultants helped management to understand that creativity is stimulated most when a problem is stated most broadly. If, instead of saying that one hundred people would be fired, management said that everyone would have to live on a reduced budget, there would be more room for creativity.

Management then involved employees in a concordance process. Department heads divided the budget, and the members of each department decided how to allocate their departmental budgets. Creative ideas emerged immediately. In one department, two people wanted to job-share and spend more time at home. Several others wanted to take early retirement. Some had been wanting for a long time to be half-time consultants. The laboratory found a new supplier, who was less expensive, and used the savings for salaries. One group of seven wanted to quit, become outside consultants, and sell their services back to the hospital at a lower cost. After these ideas were explored, June 1 arrived—and no one had to be let go. The concordance process unleashed the employees' creativity and responsibility.

Win-Win Solutions

Discussions in concordance are aimed at having everyone win. During a concordance discussion, each person gets feedback. Feedback is best understood as a gift, not as being positive or negative. It tells me how others react to me, so that I learn more about myself, and the feedback process usually brings me closer to the other people in the group. In this sense, I win even if my specific solution isn't adopted. It is up to me to decide how I respond to the feedback. I can be hurt, angry, elated, grateful, suspicious, embarrassed, or however I choose to be.

If we as a group cannot decide, we don't decide. This nondecision often turns out to be the right decision: we do not have enough information, or we have not devoted enough time to satisfy everyone's concerns.

CASE: Concordance in a Hiring Decision

When a large paper manufacturer in Pennsylvania was about to hire a new industrial relations (IR) manager, management agreed to make the choice concordantly—but not without great trepidation and much curiosity. Ordinarily, the manager two levels above the open position did the hiring.

"About how many candidates will you have, and how many people will want to participate in the selection because they have significant work relations with the IR manager?" I asked, wanting to fulfill the inclusion criterion that those who know the most and those who are most affected should make the decision. I also wanted to make sure I could handle the size of the group.

"About ten candidates and about ten co-workers should show up," the division manager said.

"Fine," I said. "Twenty people will be a good number to work with."

When I returned to Pennsylvania in three weeks and opened the door of the meeting room, I saw sixty people, including some forty candidates for the job. Many in the group were skeptical that the process was really as advertised. In the past, they had been given various promises about their decision-making power, but the hierarchy always kept the final decision for themselves.

We began by discussing this skepticism. The division manager (the highest-ranking person present) and the plant manager assured everyone that they meant what they said: this group would make the final decision. The skeptics agreed that they would have to wait and see.

I then proposed that we break into smaller, more manageable groups—by which I meant groups that I could deal with better. The group members would not hear of it; they all wanted to experience the process together.

I started to worry. Then someone stood up and said, "I'm not a candidate, but I want to participate anyway. Would that be an acceptable role?" Others said they were in the same position.

This was our first opportunity for concordance. Several people said that if these observers had enough interest in the issue to appear, they should be allowed to stay and participate fully, like everyone else.

Next, I asked the group members if they were ready to try concordance. They indicated that they were, and I asked them to go around the room, in order, and say yes *if they agreed that observers should be regular members, or* no *if they didn't. I wrote the question on a flip chart.*

Everyone said yes *without hesitation. Success! Excitement and pride were rising.*

Someone suggested that each candidate stand and tell the group why he or she was the best person for the job. Everyone agreed. About forty candidates stood and talked about their qualifications and why they wanted the job. When that process was completed, about half of the candidates withdrew because, after hearing the others, they felt that they themselves were not best for the job, but all of them asked to remain and continue participating. In light of the first concordant decision, and hearing no objections, the group approved these requests.

Someone then suggested that we take a straw vote. Everyone agreed on the condition that each participant give each of the twenty remaining candidates the reasons for his or her vote. That was agreed to. The straw vote was taken.

The candidates who received no votes dropped out (except one, who felt misunderstood), and so we were down to nine. People then began to say why they had voted as they did, and lengthy discussions ensued about many topics only slightly related to the subject at hand—management versus workers, old-timers versus younger people, technical skill and knowledge versus vision, and several past events that had apparently never been resolved. This was the first real opportunity the participants had been given to express their feelings about those issues. Even though these discussions seemed to be a distraction, they did help clear the air, which is one reason why the first concordance meeting often takes a long time.

Someone suggested that the nine remaining candidates have a meeting in the center of the group and reduce their number to three. They agreed and had a lively exchange about whom each of them would choose and why they would not choose the others. This feedback, along with the feedback given to the original candidates during the earlier straw vote, made the session valuable for all the candidates: even if they were not to be selected, they would have the benefit of a great deal of information about themselves.

The candidates were only able to reduce their number to five. The rest of the group members objected because they liked one of the discarded candidates, and so that candidate was reinstated.

It was now about dinner time, but the energy in the room was so high that no one wanted to break for dinner. We sent out for pizza. Everyone ate in various groupings, with many discussions among subgroups. Part of the high energy was due to the growing realization that management was doing what it had promised. One original skeptic remarked that this was really different from past meetings.

After dinner, one person said, "Why can't two people do the job? Why don't we select two?"

Objections abounded: "We've never had two people in that job before."

"Well we've never used this process before, either."

The division manager agreed that it was within his power to allow two people in the job, and he said he would do it if that was the group's final decision.

"What about Herman and Tulio?" one member said. "Tulio is the assistant IR manager and knows the job well, and we've all been impressed with Herman's vision and creativity."

Immediately, someone else said something that is often heard when a concordant solution is found: "Of course."

The two-person proposal also satisfied all the other issues (management versus workers, old-timers versus newcomers, visionaries versus technicians, and so on). A pleasant calm settled over the group. It was about midnight, but we weren't done yet.

Someone objected that Herman was only a technician and was three grade levels below the job. But the feeling had begun to grow that the group had power and the creativity to come up with a solution to that problem, too.

At that point, one of the other candidates still felt that he was better qualified, and so the group spent some time giving him opinions. After much discussion, he still didn't agree; but, considering the sentiments being expressed, he felt that Herman and Tulio would work better with this group.

I put their names on the board, and someone said that we should allow Tulio and Herman to figure out together how they would divide the job. Everyone agreed. Now we were ready for the concordance vote. We went around the room and everyone said yes. At two in the morning, there was great exhilaration. Tulio and Herman had fifty-eight immediate supporters, with full buy-in. I visited the manufacturing floor the next morning, and the excitement was still there. Even those who had not attended the meeting approved of the decision.

Fears and Objections

Does concordance sound too good to be true? That reaction is not unusual. In fact, concordance is such a departure from the typical organizational decision-making model that it sometimes sounds attractive but not very feasible, and it elicits a range of fears in managers and employees alike, fears that are addressed in this section.

I'll Be Steamrollered

As a boss, I'm afraid the group will overrun me and do something I know will be disastrous, and I can't stop them. But everyone—including me, the boss—always has a veto. I can always prevent what I regard as a disaster. In the case of the paper manufacturer, the division manager was the highest-ranking member of the concordance group. He listened carefully for any proposal he was not willing to be responsible for, and would have said so if one had come to a vote.

The Others Are Too Immature

Some people under me are not smart enough or mature enough, or have not been here long enough or do not care enough, to make sensible decisions. In concordance, however, I treat people as if they *were* capable, and I usually find them more able than I imagined. The responsibility of being a member of a decision-making group increases everyone's concern for group goals. In the case of the paper manufacturer, the solution was much more satisfactory to virtually everyone than any solution that management alone would have come up with.

Nobody's Accountable

If I, the leader, decide to involve the group in a concordance process, my superiors will think I am surrendering power, that I am no longer accountable, and that they must now deal with a committee. In fact, however, with concordance decisions, I am just as accountable as when I am authoritarian. The concordance decisions *are* my decisions. I take full responsibility for them, just as if I had made them all alone. In the example of the paper manufacturer, the division manager, the one hierarchically responsible for the appointment, was fully responsible to his superiors for the final decision.[7]

I Don't Want to Jump In Too Fast

Out of my uncertainty I, as the leader, may decide to create a concordance model for "most" decisions—and I will decide which ones. But reserving the power to change even one decision may cause group members to feel futile, since they never know which decision I may take back from them. If I am unsure, it is better for me to say that I want advice only for now, and to wait until I am ready to create a true concordance model.

This Could Go On Forever

I'll use concordance, but if we cannot agree by a certain time, I'll decide. But if I reserve this right, I will have vitiated the concordance process; I'd be better off not even starting to use it. I can take care of my concerns about time by asking the group to agree to specific time limits at the outset. In addition, it is essential for me to say whether the decision-making process is concordant *before* the discussion, and to follow through. Of course, it is also essential that I keep my word, or else the whole process is undermined.

It's Just Another Company Ploy

Here's this week's game. Everybody knows that they are going to do what they want, regardless of what we say. Only when leaders keep the process fully concordant, allow group members to experience it at work, and allow concordance decisions to prevail will everyone believe it's for real.

Why Should I Give Up My Power?

As the group leader, when I become simply a member of the concordance team, I have to confront the change from role power to personal power. In role power, people do what I say because of my superior role. I acquire personal power only when people are influenced by me and my ideas and follow me for that reason, and so I must deal with any insecurities about my personal power before I agree to concordance. If I do not feel sufficiently competent to influence a decision through the quality of my ideas, I can make a perfectly reasonable choice not to try concordance.

I Will Be Too Influential

My influence as a manager will overwhelm the others. They won't be open, and so I had better stay out. If I truly want concordance, however, the group will have to discuss the issue of coercion openly. Typically, coercion diminishes when it can be talked about. If I take myself out of the group, the members will be missing important and unique input—mine—and the quality of the decision will be diminished. In the case, as the group grew comfortable with the process, their tendency toward automatic submission or resistance to the leaders quickly disappeared. The division manager and the plant manager both made several suggestions. Some were accepted, some were not.

Putting Concordance into Practice

The process of putting concordance into practice makes a difference in how well it eventually works. The organization has to consider several factors—such as whether the group or team is just being formed or already exists—and has to prepare leaders and participants. This section addresses those issues and provides a step-by-step set of guidelines for implementing a concordance model.

Introducing Concordance into Groups

New Groups It is simplest to institute concordance in a newly formed group. Members are just coming together for the first time, and there are no established roles, power struggles, old conflicts, alliances, or decision-making methods.

If I have an idea and want to start an organization to implement that idea, it is important for me to educate the others, not only about the concordance process but also about the content of my idea. Groups that do not understand the new idea have a tendency to revert to old and familiar decision-making patterns.

I may start the group by asking members to agree (concordantly) to let me make all the decisions at the beginning and let me decide when to turn the decision-making function over to the whole group. Their agreement makes the process concordant from the outset.

If I surrender my leadership of the group before the group members know what I mean, I run the risk of having my idea subverted before it is given a chance. If I hold on to my power beyond the necessary point, I run the risk that everyone will lose interest, and that I will have to do everything myself.

Sensitive timing involves being sure that people understand my idea, whether they agree with it or not. When understanding is reached, the time to surrender decision-making power has arrived. It also requires my self-awareness about the implications of surrendering control over "my" idea.

Established Groups I may wish to convert a group (of any size, even a large organization), with a history of using authoritarian or other methods, to a concordance process. If so, everyone will need a period of education. Group members have to learn what concordance is and take responsibility for their participation.

If any individuals choose not to participate, we can ask them to abide by the group's decisions. If they already do, we can consider them potential participants; they can always change their minds.

As the leader, I have to examine my own self-concept to make sure I am willing to exchange my institutional power for personal power and influence. Once these factors are dealt with satisfactorily, we meet to work out a transition from our current process to concordance. A period of testing one another's sincerity, exploring concordance, and consulting with experts on the concordance process is desirable. The transition plan may be the first concordance decision to be made by the whole group.

Guidelines for Using Concordance

Announcement Before the first meeting I, the group leader, circulate to all potential members of the concordance team an announcement saying that I want to establish a concordance process and a description of how it works.[8] To make the transition simpler, I ask each person two questions: What decisions are now being made without your participation that you would like to be included in? What decisions do you now participate in that you would prefer not to? The group's answers to these questions indicate how close the organization is to the inclusion criterion and where the first changes should be made. We discuss the answers at the first meeting.

The First Meeting   As the group leader, I introduce concordance into my work group: "I have the power (to the limits of my authority, responsibility, and accountability) to make all decisions for my position. Because I believe decisions will be of higher quality, more creative, and more fully implemented if I make them concordantly, from now on all my decisions will be made by our group, using concordance. You are free to choose to participate or not to participate directly. If you decide not to participate, I would like you to agree to carry out all of my decisions, which we will make with the concordance process. Since you already abide by my decisions, I presume that this will present no difficulty. I will continue to be completely responsible for all decisions, just as I was when I made them the old way. Those who choose to participate have all the decision-making power inherent in concordance. If some of you do not wish to participate now, you have the option to join at a later date, unless in the meantime the group decides otherwise."

Since any member's absence may paralyze the group, it is essential that group members make a rule for how to deal with the situation. Some groups agree that whoever appears at a meeting constitutes the decision-making group. Others decide that those present will make a concordant decision, communicate it to the absent members, and give them a specified time in which to raise objections. If they do, the group reconsiders its decision.

Early in the life of the group, it is a good idea to decide how meetings will be called and who will convene them. Often the group begins with a normal meeting time, and the group then decides the dates and times of future meetings.

Should the group appoint a leader? Some groups want to be leaderless. Some want someone appointed to steer the group. Some want to decide for each occasion whether they want leadership. The key is that the group decides concordantly.

Continuity   The group agrees that until a specific decision is made by concordance, current rules apply.

First Issues   It is sometimes easier to start with relatively simple issues, to give the group members experience with the concordance process. Once they gain confidence, they move on to more difficult issues. But beware: apparently simple issues often turn out to be more complicated than expected, especially in light of the fact that the first topic, regardless of its content, is the vehicle that the group uses to unearth and air unresolved issues. When that occurs, it is not the complexity of the issue that determines the difficulty of the discussion but rather the fact that this is the first issue discussed with the concordance process.

Decisions or Proposals   A good way to begin the concordance process is to ask all the people in the group to write down all the decisions they want made. The group then appoints a coordinator to compile these lists and post them as signup sheets in a central location, and members choose which decisions they wish to participate in. If someone feels that there are people who should be in a decision group, but they have not signed up, anyone else in the group may invite them to join.

The coordinator then contacts everyone and works out a starting date for each group. At a meeting of the entire group, the members decide whether each subgroup is a proposal-making group (PMG), responsible for analyzing the problem and bringing back options and recommendations to the whole group, or a decision-making group (DMG), responsible for reaching a final decision, which the whole group accepts. The entire group decides the timing and rules for the DMGs and the PMGs and sets priorities for which tasks will be tackled first.

Membership   DMGs and PMGs may be made up of full members or of members who wish to express their feelings but not participate in the final decisions. Each subgroup determines whether it will permit partial participation. In the beginning, the whole group typically meets regularly every week and then adjusts, according to the volume of work and the value of the meetings.

Preparation   PMGs become extremely important as the group progresses. Outside work by committees, resulting in the presentation of evaluated options based on appropriate background research, helps to focus the activities of the concordance group. This background work is usually not done as effectively by the large group.

Relevance   In the flow of problem solving, there are certain points at which a meeting of the whole group is most effective and certain points at which it is most effective to appoint DMGs or PMGs. It is important for the group to be aware of what phase of a problem the group is in and decide on the most efficient use of resources. Usually, work is best done by the total group when an issue is first presented, so that no relevant factors or considerations are overlooked. Work is usually best done by individuals or a subgroup when, after initial brainstorming and exploration, the group decides that it needs more research and information, and when the discussion would be more focused if a subgroup presented a set of options, an evaluation of the strengths and weaknesses of each, and a recommendation to the total group.

Progress   Progress toward concordance usually takes place along the openness criterion. Selecting the members of the decision-making group (inclusion criterion), and giving everyone a veto (control criterion) are procedures that may be introduced structurally. Openness, however, cannot be legislated. It increases only as people feel more comfortable in the group, and that usually takes time and testing. As the group becomes more open, decisions become sounder, more creative, and more efficiently and effectively implemented.

Impasses   When discussion reaches a stalemate, the levels of truth are useful for getting at real feelings and possible fears. As people become more open, the levels of truth become more valuable, since they reveal underlying reasons for a person's rigidity in holding to a position. Working down through the levels of truth is the most effective device for avoiding stasis because of one person's intransigence.

No Decision   If the group doesn't reach a decision, that is often the right decision. No decision may indicate that the group is not ready to decide, either because all the data relevant to making the decision are lacking or because people want more time to get used to a new idea. A decision based on incomplete discussion is likely to lead to difficulty with implementation.

About the Process

After the group has been functioning in the concordant mode for a while, it takes on some interesting characteristics. First, its decision-making patterns look quite similar to the ones used before concordance; for example, specialists continue making decisions in their areas. But there is a vast difference: since everyone has approved them, all decisions and decision-making practices enjoy complete support. Changing or refining any decisions that were not made concordantly, although they may be few, can make a tremendous difference in efficiency and morale.

Second, participants have a broader view of the organization. Before making a concordant decision, they must consider all the other aspects of the organization, as represented by other members of the decision-making group.

Third, a concordance group usually has a more relaxed atmosphere, since people know that at some point the group must ask them how they feel. Therefore, they do not have to worry about being steamrollered and can put their attention into listening to what other people have to say.

CASE: Concordance in a University Computing Center

This case demonstrates how concordance works in a real-life setting, as reported by the people who are using it. The case reveals some of the problems and resistance they encountered, as well as the ways concordance has improved communication and overall productivity.

The narrator is Chip, director of the computing center at a large eastern university.

To give some sense of the atmosphere surrounding this work, let me tell you how we actually reach a concordant decision. I will admit up front that we aren't always careful in following the process. We sometimes feel pressured to take shortcuts. However, when we do it carefully, it works very well.

We define the issue for decision narrowly, and we post it to the whole team or subgroup, with all the alternative solutions known already. This is an invitation to all those with responsibility in the decision area to consider participating. Defining the decision narrowly, and posting the alternatives already known, helps the team members decide whether they care to participate, saving the staff time.

When we get together, we often identify a moderator, particularly for large decision groups. The moderator's job is often crucial in saving our time. He or she keeps us focused, reminds us of aspects of the discussion we need to complete, and keeps track of time so that we have time to finish the meeting well.

The first thing we do when we get together is look around and check that everyone we thought was important to be here is here. If someone important is missing and didn't send a proxy with someone present, we may decide that we don't have the right people to make a decision. Next, we check to see whether any unexpected participants attended. If so, we listen to the feelings that drove them to attend.

Next, we ask everyone to tell us how they feel about being here to work on this issue. We ask people to speak when they are ready; we don't go around the table. We wait until everyone has spoken, and we don't interrupt or ask questions.

Now we are ready to get down to business. We ask all those with alternatives to present them in turn, with as few questions as possible and only for clarification, rather than comparison or debate. This is much like brainstorming.

Then the debate really begins. The moderator's job evolves from simply being a traffic manager to holding on to, and bringing us back to, important threads of the discussion that may be started and then left for the time being. When we start to hear quiet, we know that we have reached the end of one line of thinking. We may or may not be ready to make a decision.

We find out by making a proposal. Anyone may make a proposal at any time. A proposal is a carefully worded statement about our proposed decision. It is helpful to have it written down on a chalkboard or easel, so that everyone can see all of it. An important part of the proposal is to identify who will implement the decision. We work on the wording of the proposal until we have quiet again. Now is the proverbial moment of truth. We each listen to ourselves for a moment. Then we go around the table and ask each person to say *yes* or *no.* Anything other than an unequivocal *yes* is taken as a *no.* Responses like *okay* and *sure* and *go ahead* are taken as *no.* Whatever the vote, we go all the way around the table to get a sense of where we are.

If everyone does not say *yes,* we continue our discussion. We encourage those not voting *yes* to help us understand their feelings. We may conclude that we cannot make a decision at this time. That's all right. We may have realized that we really don't have all the people or information we need to make this decision. We affirm our intention to work on it later.

If everyone says *yes,* we have a decision. We then pause and each listen to ourselves again. Each of us asks: What is my body telling me about what I just did? Am I relaxed, or is some part of me still tense? Am I committed to the decision? If not, we go back to discussion.

Now that there are no more decisions to be made at this meeting, we take time to ask everyone to tell us how they feel about how the discussion went. Again, we ask people to speak when they are ready. We wait until everyone has spoken. Then we are done with the meeting.

After the meeting, the moderator posts, to the whole team, the proposals that were approved, and he or she may include some explanation of the key thinking behind each decision. This helps the team remain comfortable with the decision to delegate to proposal-making or decision-making groups.

There are some pitfalls to be avoided. In the information posted to announce the meeting, appearing to suggest a likely or preferred alternative sends the message that the team isn't really going to be heard.

There is nothing so distracting in a concordance meeting as someone who does not trust the group or some of its members. Lack of trust may be due to many things; generally, it is due to ignorance or injury. To some extent, we can address ignorance before decision meetings, through presentations to the staff and distribution of reports. And we can encourage individuals with fears about specific others to sit down with them, one to one, often with a moderator. But we need to be prepared to address these feelings as they come up during the decision meeting. We must be prepared to accept that we may not continue with the original purpose of the meeting, and that we need to spend time to hear these feelings before we proceed. This is one of the hardest choices to make, in our experience. Allowing for that possibility, we schedule large blocks of time when we call a meeting to make a concordant decision. If we listen well, we may be done early.

When group members, who are important to making the decision and getting it implemented, come and go, both within a meeting and across several meetings, they miss hearing important information. When a person reenters the process, the rest of the group often has to reiterate this information, leaving them with the feeling that they wasted their time. This applies even to eating during the discussion; when we are eating, we are not giving our full attention to what others are saying and how they are acting. The meeting moderator needs to schedule appropriate breaks, so that the group can stay focused during the discussion.

What does it take? Certainly it takes time. This is one of those "pay me now or pay me later" situations. We invest time in the concordant process to get the commitment of those who will implement the decision. In this way, the decision really gets implemented, and we avoid having to go back to argue the issue over and over again. A good sign that we have cut corners is that we are talking about the issue again, and usually in secret.

It also takes caring. Caring is not something you simply bring to the process; I could have as easily said that caring is something you get. Caring is what is happening during truly concordant decision making. The process works easily when we care, about ourselves as well as others—when we care enough to listen to our fears. The process exposes us to the care of others and encourages us to reciprocate.

The benefits are greater cooperation, efficiency, stability, and creativity. When we know everyone's feelings and take them into account in making decisions, we feel cared for, and we cooperate. People often have similar feelings about a situation. Responding to them in a group takes less time. And when I feel understood and feel good about what the team is doing, I don't spend time wandering around sharing my hurt and looking for understanding. The more information we have, the fewer crazy or disastrous decisions get made. And the more that people feel cared for, the greater the incentive to stay with the organization. I am much more energized when I think I will influence the result. I engage others more, and together we create a better solution than any one of us could have created alone.

Can this possibly work? Yes. When it works, the results are wonderful. Our problems are generally due to our not applying concordance completely. Usually this happens when someone in a position of authority under the standard rules (like the director) is afraid of losing control, with all the fears about his own incompetence and about having to deal with other people's hurt.

What decisions can a concordant group make? Any decision that any member previously had the authority to make.

Do we use concordance for everything? Not yet. But we are using it for some of the larger decisions, such as budget cuts and layoffs, hiring, and promotions. Two places where concordant decision making has worked for us are hiring a manager for the Computer Equipment Service group and hiring a group leader for the UNIX systems group. We have been getting used to it. I think we are ready to ask the whole team, "Are we going to operate our department by the principles of concordance?"

The goal of concordance is not simply to reach a decision. It is also to secure the commitment of those who will implement the decision. A group with lots of great ideas won't produce a quality product without that commitment to each other.

So why bother risking so much fear? Because we end up feeling better and doing a better job!

We have had serious financial pressures at the university, and central computing has suffered more than a 15 percent budget reduction, including a 10 percent reduction in staff, since the 1989–1990 fiscal year, when we started using concordance. Despite this, we now are providing nearly all the same services, we have added services, we are working with more energy, and we are better connected to our customers.

Concordance takes time and caring. But it has given us commitment to each other and has significantly increased our ability to produce quality services.

Pause for Reflection: Concordance

1. Would I feel different in a concordance group that I led, compared to one where I was not the boss?

2. Do I see advantages to the inclusion criterion (decision makers are those who know the most and those who are most affected)? Disadvantages?

3. How do I feel about the amount of time concordance takes? How would my organization respond? How would I convince my company to invest time in concordance?

4. Do I see any relationship between the concordance process and democracy? In what ways?

5. Can I see using concordance to discharge all my duties as a leader? What are my greatest objections or fears?

Conflict Resolution

In any group, even those most proficient at concordance, conflicts are bound to arise. Concordance provides effective techniques for resolving them.[9] The following guidelines are in the form of statements to be read to the members of the group, for their responses. (Parenthetical statements are instructions to the facilitator.)

1. *Issue:* State the issue to be resolved clearly, in written form.

2. *Blame:* Blame all the people you disagree with for blocking the solution to the problem. (This may be done as a free-for-all, or by having one person at a time blamed by the whole group, or by any other method the group decides.) Think of all the reasons it is the other person's fault. Be certain to get out all the reasons, even if you do not feel strongly about them or even if they are only partly true. Do not omit any, no matter how trivial. (Allow about five minutes.)

3. *Clarify:* Clarify all the statements you made. This is not a time for rebuttal or argument, but simply a time for clarity about what you meant. (Allow all legitimate questions, but *do not allow* any return to blaming or any defending. This should take about three minutes.)

4. *React:* Tell your reactions to what you heard—surprise, anger, sadness, delight, or whatever. (Allow three minutes.)

5. *Acknowledge:* State what you feel is right about what you said—in case you exaggerated—and what you feel is right about what was said to you. Do not resume the argument. Simply acknowledge the parts you feel are true. When the group acquires more personal insight and less defensiveness, members may begin conflict resolution. (Allow about ten minutes for this activity.)

6. *Reflect:* Shut your eyes. Reflect on what you have learned about your self-concept, especially those parts of yourself you feel least good about. Ask yourself, "Which of the things I accused you of are also true of me?" (Allow one minute.) "Which of the things I accused

you of do I think you feel about me?" (Allow one minute.) "What personal fears (being ignored, being humiliated, being rejected) do I have about this issue?" (Allow one minute.) "What do I want to accomplish personally (be paid attention to, look competent, be liked)?" (Allow one minute.)

7. *Explore:* Open your eyes. Discuss your answers to each of these questions. As each person speaks, if you feel the speaker is not saying everything, say what you feel is inaccurate. The speaker will reflect on the observation and either agree with you or say what he or she feels is right. (Allow ten minutes.)

8. *Collude:* Assume that we are all 100 percent responsible for the situation, and that no one is to blame. Shut your eyes. Reflect on your defenses, rigidities, and body state. In the spirit of problem solving, and not in the spirit of blame, take individual responsibility for creating the situation in which you find yourself. How do you elicit the situation you do not like? Do not withhold anything, regardless of how bad you think it will make you look. The worse you look, the more you learn—and, usually, the better people respond.

Turn to the person on your left and ask, "How did you collude to prevent a solution?" When you receive an answer, say "Thank you." Then that person turns to the left, asks the same question, receives an answer, and says "Thank you." Continue this procedure around the group until I stop you. After a few times, this question can be abbreviated to "How did you collude?" (Allow about seven minutes. Then say, "When you have run out of things to say"— pause—"that is the important time to continue." Continue for five minutes more.) Now stop and close your eyes.

9. *Significance:* What was the thing you said that had the most importance to you? (Wait ten seconds.) What was the thing someone else said that had the most meaning for you? (Wait ten seconds.) Did you think of anything and not say it? (Wait ten seconds.) Open your eyes and discuss all three of these issues. (Allow five minutes.)

10. *Resolve:* Return to the original conflict issue and continue the discussion until you reach concordance. Be aware of what you have learned about yourself. Whenever you feel that you or someone else may be caught in a personal defense, stop the discussion and focus on that issue. Use the levels of truth to clarify the situation. (Allow thirty minutes, or continue until resolution.)

In summary, conflict resolution becomes effective when it uses the principles of concordance; in particular, honesty and self-awareness. When team members share their thoughts and personal feelings, they have all the relevant factors that must be integrated to reach an optimal resolution. Ignoring the personal feelings of the members means the team is dealing with only half a deck. This idea is brilliantly captured in the anonymous adage, "How do I know what I think until I say what I feel?"

6

Redefining Leadership and Creating the Human Element Organization

The wise leader does not intervene unnecessarily. The leader's presence is felt, but often the group runs itself.... The leader's personal state of consciousness creates a climate of openness.... The leader who knows when to listen, when to act, and when to withdraw can work effectively with nearly anyone.... To know how other people behave takes intelligence. To know myself takes wisdom.... It puzzles people at first, to see how little the able leader actually does, and yet how much gets done.... Run an honest, open group.... It is more important to tell the simple, blunt truth than it is to say things that sound good.
—Tao Te Ching[1]

The attempt to train supervisors to adopt a single leadership "style" yields poorer results than encouraging them to create the essential conditions *in their individual ways* and with due regard for their own particular situations.
—Douglas McGregor[2]

This exploration of the Human Element in organizations has demonstrated how it applies equally to all of us. I respond to issues of inclusion, control, and openness and to the corresponding feelings of significance, competence, and likability because they are personally important to my self-concept and self-esteem. Those dimensions are perhaps even more critical for leaders who play a central role in nurturing—or preventing—the kind of open organizational atmosphere that leads to enhanced self-esteem.

The Human Element approach emphasizes that strong self-esteem leads to greater productivity through group and individual processes that open up interactions and free all of us to concentrate on our work rather than on complaints, power struggles, turf wars, sabotage, or apathy. As stated earlier, mastery of all the material in this book takes me a long way toward the goal of optimal leadership. If, as a leader, I understand myself and other people, the dynamics of groups and teamwork, and methods for helping individuals fulfill their potential and be efficient decision makers, then I am well equipped to lead. Managers and leaders who have helped their organizations take up the Human Element approach report improvement in the quality of work life, and they accomplish—or exceed—their financial and strategic goals. This chapter looks briefly at the implications of the Human Element approach for leadership and at the characteristics and challenges of putting it to work in an organization.

The Puzzle of Leadership

During my years of investigating and developing the Human Element model, I puzzled over leadership. Many diverse styles of leading seemed equally powerful. The "great man" theory of leadership, the leader as visionary, and the other major theories did not seem to explain the success of many different kinds of leaders. For instance, autocratic Vince Lombardi, homespun Joe Gibbs, and erudite Bill Walsh were all very different—and successful—football coaches. Werner von Braun used authoritarian ways to get a man on the moon, while self-effacing Mahatma Gandhi transformed India through nonviolence. And what commonality do Margaret Thatcher and Mother Teresa share?

The Leader as Completer

As is my wont, I looked for a simpler clarifying concept. I believe I discovered that concept in Elvin Semrad's notion of the *leader as completer*. By that, Semrad meant that the leader's role is to see that the team successfully carries out the functions essential to accomplishing its mission.

The concept of the leader as completer makes clear why some people succeed in some places and others do not. It accounts for the centrality of the leader's self-knowledge about what he or she does well and what other people should be assigned to. It reframes the popular John Wayne macho model, making it only one among many other leadership models that may work (another would be an Asian Taoist model, in which "he who leads least leads best"). It also explains why many different styles can work, since the behavior of the leader varies widely with the requirements of the group.

Successful leadership, of course, depends to some degree on technical and professional knowledge and skills, such as strategic planning, business law, finance, and so on, but these are not addressed here. Instead, the focus is on the approaches and processes that produce the highest-performing leaders. The leader as completer has the following tasks, characteristics, and personal qualities:

Completion   I know what it will take for my team to achieve its goals, and I see to it that we accomplish them to the best of our ability. I ensure that the best people for each job do it, and that the people most affected by a decision make it. I, like all other team members, do what I am best at, whether that means providing technical expertise, creating a vision, counseling, disciplining, coaching, resolving conflict, supporting, or inspiring. My job is to ensure that we as a team do whatever we must to satisfy the requirements for our success. A leader does not have to know how to do everything but must be aware of the essential elements of good teamwork and be able to let them happen, so that the team will be effective.

Leadership Style   Every leader is different and valued for his or her individual strengths. For example, if I as a leader am technically competent, it is important that I contribute my competence to the team effort. If I'm not particularly competent technically but am a very good organizer, then organizing becomes one of my roles.

Decision Making   As a leader, I adopt the decision-making model that will focus my team's skills on each problem to achieve the highest-quality decisions, and that will get them implemented immediately and thoroughly.

Success   My function as a leader is to help everyone, including myself, operate to our full potential, both individually and as a team. If my team is successful, I am successful.

Team Functions   I must know what functions my team—myself and everyone under my supervision—must perform in order to do our job best. For *external relations* (with the outside world, including customers, vendors, other departments, headquarters, field offices, competitors, consultants, media, and government agencies), I make sure our team has satisfactory and productive interactions. For *internal relations* among team members, I must be aware of interpersonal problems within the team and know how to get them resolved (see Chapter Three). I help everyone reach agreement as a team on inclusion, control, and openness issues in our internal relations. I am aware of the issues of atmosphere and role compatibility, the complementarity principles, the dynamics of groups, the stages of group development, blocks to teamwork, and methods for dealing with rigidities. For *task performance*, I make sure that we have the creativity, logical skills, and knowledge to develop and maintain a high-quality product or service. I see to it that we establish and clarify our goals, our vision, our long-range plans, and the values that inform our methods of working. I also recognize and integrate various cognitive styles, different methods of problem solving, and diverse backgrounds, to gain maximum advantage for each individual and for the entire group and to help eliminate the blocks to creative and logical thinking.

Self-Awareness and Self-Esteem Without self-awareness, all my actions as a leader are subject to self-deception and are therefore potentially ineffective or even dangerous. I must know how best to use myself and must be aware of threats, competitive feelings, or attractions that may distort my perceptions. In addition, I focus on the self-esteem of each group member and help create an atmosphere that enhances our positive self-concepts. I assume that we all work best when we feel good about ourselves. For example, to help team members feel fully *alive*, I strive to create an atmosphere of participation; for feelings of *significance*, an atmosphere of recognition; for *competence*, an atmosphere of empowerment; and so on.

Example An excellent example of the leader as completer is John Lucas, coach of the San Antonio Spurs professional basketball team. His appreciation of the importance of self-esteem is expressed by his assistant coach, George Gervin: "John believes in helping people. So if you have that influence and ability to get inside people, and help them take ownership in themselves, then you build up their self-esteem. . . . You feel good about yourself, you come out every night and play hard. . . . Lucas has turned the Spurs into a sort of NBA cooperative. Though he has tapped player David Robinson as the team's 'chief executive officer,' every player has a say. He often lets players handle the time-out huddles themselves. Lucas even lets players make personnel moves, not just help make them, but make them." In terms of the bottom line, after Lucas took over as coach, the Spurs went from winning 45 percent of their games to 67 percent, an impressive improvement.[3]

Understanding of People   If I am aware of myself as a leader, I can usually learn about other people through knowing myself well. I must have some understanding of people to know how they function best. I encourage full feedback, so that we help each other understand ourselves better. An open atmosphere enhances the feedback process.

Knowledge of Group Dynamics   It is essential that I know how teams operate, so that I can be sensitive to when they are not working well and know how to fix the problem. Using a process like concordance takes advantage of the whole team's abilities in deciding how best to function.

Task Abilities   I must know what is required, in terms of technical knowledge, creativity, and logical thinking, to accomplish the team's goal. Further, it is essential that I recognize when psychological factors are blocking individuals, or the group as a whole, and know what to do about it or how to get the job done through other team members.

Creating and Training the Leader as Completer

Leaders create themselves—they are not born or made. All leaders can use the "completer" model to improve their performance and that of their teams.

In training to improve my leadership ability, as a new leader I think about my personal history in groups. What roles have I traditionally played in groups throughout my life? What feelings do I typically elicit from people in groups? In what roles do I feel most comfortable? What roles do I have difficulty with? Then I can define the kind of leadership I would feel most comfortable with and effective at. To enhance my self-knowledge, I review my Pauses for Reflection in Chapter Three, on teamwork (complementarity and openness); in Chapter Four, on individual performance (work relations, individual decision making, and job fit); and in Chapter Five, on group decision making (concordance).

I gather feedback from people who have worked with me. An atmosphere of openness and self-awareness is crucial to making this feedback most valuable.[4]

All the team members and I have an open discussion of our strengths and weaknesses, usually beginning with each person giving his or her self-assessment and then hearing feedback from the other team members. This is usually an extremely valuable interchange. Many people expend a great deal of energy trying to hide their feelings of inadequacy, and some leaders find that they have clung to the belief that they are safe only if they are better than everybody at everything.

My team and I then systematically consider all team functions (outside relations, internal relations, problem solving, and task performance) and assess how well each function is now being accomplished and how these results could be improved. We match this evaluation with the assessment of team members' skills. If we do not match, we may train some of our members, acquire a new member, or change the work system. (The Pauses for Reflection that follow this section help assess the leader and the group in internal and external relations and problem solving.)

The best result of these discussions is to arrive at an accurate picture of where the team is and where it wants to go. The next step is to design a work schedule that uses this knowledge. One caveat is to be sure that both short- and long-term goals are considered. For the short term, assigning tasks according to members' current strengths is most efficient. For the long term, however, it is crucial to teach each person to expand his or her areas of effectiveness in order to accommodate the team's goals.

The ability to talk openly about how well work is being accomplished is an invaluable permanent tool that the team can use to make midcourse corrections, so that difficulties are recognized and dealt with immediately. If I am an experienced leader, I can use the Pauses for Reflection that follow this section to assess how well my current approach is working and how it can be improved. In answering the questions in the Pauses, I think of a current group or of a past group that I have led. If I have never led a group, I devise a theoretical group and imagine how it would operate, or I think of a group to which I have belonged.

Pause for Reflection: Internal Relations

In my group I feel...

Disagree 0   1   2   3   4   5   6   7   8   9   Agree

_____ Cell 15. I am fully alive. I use myself well. I am not bored.

_____ Cell 25. I decide for myself. I am self-determining and autonomous. I feel free and not coerced.

_____ Cell 35. I am aware of myself. I am aware of my unconscious and constantly try to become more aware. I do not deceive myself.

_____ Cell 45. I feel significant. I am an important person. I make a difference.

_____ Cell 55. I feel competent. I can cope with the situations presented by life.

_____ Cell 65. I feel likable. I enjoy my own company, and I like the person I am.

_____ Cell 11. Everyone participates fully in all relevant activities.

_____ Cell 21. Full expression is encouraged. People are not suppressed.

_____ Cell 31. People say how they feel. They do not withhold, and they do not lie.

_____ Cell 41. We all give one another recognition for work well done.

_____ Cell 51. Everyone who is qualified contributes to final decisions.

_____ Cell 61. Everyone's feelings are considered and paid attention to in all activities.

Pause for Reflection: Outside Relations

Disagree   0   1   2   3   4   5   6   7   8   9   Agree

_____ Cell 11. My group feels that outside organizations and individuals intrude upon them.

_____ Cell 21. My group has too much responsibility for events and activities outside its main work (such as visitors, supervision of others, work assigned to us).

_____ Cell 31. My group feels "out of the loop"—that is, not told the truth about outside events, never able to trust that others are not withholding or not lying.

_____ Cell 13. My group feels isolated, not included enough in the activities of outside organizations and individuals; we are not told what is going on.

_____ Cell 23. My group members feel subjugated—helpless to do our best work because of outside restrictions and limitations.

_____ Cell 33. My group has to deal with other people's problems and behavior more than we want to.

This is what I want to do about it:

Pause for Reflection: Problem Solving

Disagree   0   1   2   3   4   5   6   7   8   9   Agree

_____ 1. I anticipate problems, plan for the future, and organize resources to meet future events effectively.

_____ 2. I recognize problems when they occur and see them clearly.

_____ 3. When problems arise, I gather all available information relevant to solving the problem and listen to all sides before making a decision.

_____ 4. When confronted with a complaint or a claim, I check into the source of the assertion, to determine its reliability.

_____ 5. I am creative and imaginative in getting to the reasons behind problems and can sense aspects of the situation that most people miss.

_____ 6. I am flexible, considering many explanations for problems that arise, and creative in thinking of many approaches to solving a problem, in addition to the methods I know well.

_____ 7. When deciding what action to take, I consider all possibilities before choosing one, rather than doing the first thing that occurs to me. I am aware of the possible effects of my actions on others. I can anticipate people's reactions accurately.

_____ 8. I am well enough informed about the total organization to be aware of all the implications of my actions.

_____ 9. I know the goals of my unit and have a clear idea of which goals are more important than others. I can communicate the goals and objectives of the organization clearly to my staff.

_____ 10. I am not easily swayed by pressures that would interfere with accomplishing my goals. I stick to my convictions.

_____ 11. My decisions are reasonable, not unjustifiably wild or bizarre.

_____ 12. My decisions are also reasonable in not being excessively conservative, too safe, or unimaginative.

_____ 13. When the time is right, I make up my mind decisively and clearly.

_____ 14. I follow up my decisions to see if they work, and I profit from the knowledge of what works and what does not.

Defining the Human Element Organization

I am now in a position to look at the organization as a whole from the perspective of the Human Element model. What would such an organization look like, and how would I as a leader establish it?

The centrality of self-esteem and openness alone means that a fundamentally different organization must be created, with new values, a new philosophy, new methods of operating, and, most important, new kinds of relationships. The Human Element model offers all organizations the opportunity to change consciousness by helping people to be more self-aware.

The preceding chapters have discussed the components of the model at length. Here, they are brought together and integrated into the basis of a Human Element organization.

Assumptions

Truth   You and I tell the truth. Truth in the Human Element model contains tremendous power to improve organizational effectiveness by making teams, decision making, and individual performance more effective, faster, and ultimately more profitable for the organization.

Problem Solving   The focus is on problem solving, not on blame. Blame diverts energy from productive activities. I assume that everything that happens between you and me is 100 percent my responsibility and 100 percent your responsibility, and that no one is to blame.

No Moralizing The model does not judge who is right or wrong and what is good or bad, moral or immoral. Instead, it is concerned with behavior and feelings, with whether they are satisfactory or unsatisfactory, and with whether we want to retain or change them.

Relationships The model focuses on how we function and on the relationships between patterns of behavior and their consequences for our work environment.

No Self-Deception The Human Element approach is designed to help all of me be totally aware of my own patterns and their consequences. The enemy is *self-deception*. Once I decrease my self-deception (that is, increase my awareness), whatever I do is mine to decide, since I am aware of all the relevant factors and can select my behavior consciously.

Self-Awareness I am constantly seeking to know more about myself as a person, a leader, and a team member and am willing to acknowledge that I have a choice about changing myself.

Leadership My conception of leadership can be summarized in this way: "The good king or queen is one whose subjects (including the self) prosper."

Goals for Individuals, Their Relationships, and the Organization

In a Human Element organization, goals are based on the overriding aim of bringing about the greatest self-esteem for the largest number of employees. The assumption is that if all of us have high self-esteem, then the organization will be productive and successful.

Table 6.1. Organizational Goals of the Human Element Model.

Individuals feel...	Relationships are...	Organization facilitates an atmosphere of...
Alive	Energetic	Participation
Self-determining	Adult	Freedom
Self-aware	Honest	Openness
Significant	Acknowledging	Recognition
Competent	Cooperative	Empowerment
Likable	Friendly	Humanity

These goals specify the links among individuals, their relationships, and the organizational atmosphere. Obviously, all three are tightly interwoven: if the organization achieves the goals for individuals and their relations, then the open atmosphere will follow, which in turn will enhance the functioning of individuals. (Table 6.1 summarizes the interrelated goals.)

For the individual, the goal is continuously enhanced self-esteem along the six dimensions:

- *Aliveness:* I'm fully alive. I use myself well. I'm energetic. I'm not bored.
- *Self-determination:* I choose my own life. I'm self-determining and autonomous. I feel free and not coerced. I'm responsible for myself.
- *Self-awareness:* I tell the truth to myself and to others. I'm aware of myself. I'm aware that I have an unconscious and constantly strive to be more conscious. I don't deceive myself.
- *Significance:* I feel significant. I'm an important person. I make a difference.
- *Competence:* I feel competent. I can cope with the situations my life and my job present me with.

- *Likability:* I feel likable. I enjoy my own company, and I like the person I am.

For relationships among employees, and between employees and the people with whom they interact (including customers, vendors, consultants, and government representatives), the goal is to have them be as follows:

- *Energetic:* I am committed and put my energy and focus into my relationships.
- *Adult:* I take responsibility for my own actions and the reactions I elicit from others.
- *Honest:* All statements I make are true, and I do not withhold except in extremely rare instances (such as in guarding legitimate industrial secrets). My truth is one of the greatest gifts I can offer others.
- *Acknowledging:* I give others explicit recognition for the work they do.
- *Cooperative:* I find all avenues to maximizing cooperation and minimizing accusations and blame.
- *Friendly:* I consider people's feelings, as well as the business requirements. I perform in ways that others will enjoy, without compromising the integrity of the organization.

For the organization, the goal is to create an atmosphere that will fosters all employees' self-esteem, specifically by means of the following factors:

- *Participation:* The organization offers full participation in its business. I, the employee, do not want (nor am I required) to participate in all activities, but I do have the opportunity and am invited to do so. I'm kept informed of company activities and included in activities I wish to pursue.
- *Freedom:* I'm trusted to determine my own best courses of action.

- *Openness:* I'm fully open within the organization. I keep no secrets (except certifiable industrial or security secrets) and do not withhold. I answer all questions truthfully and completely.

- *Recognition:* I am known and recognized by the organization. As a policy, the organization routinely acquires an understanding of the abilities of each employee.

- *Empowerment:* I am fully empowered and do everything voluntarily. I participate in final decisions on all the issues that I know the most about and that most affect me.

- *Humanity:* The organization appreciates and knows me as a person and encourages social contacts.

Creating a Human Element Organization

As a leader in my organization, if I want to introduce the principles described in this book, here is what I do:

1. As quickly as possible, I provide training in these concepts for all my team members. (A team may mean one other person or the entire organization.) Then everyone will understand the principles of truth, choice, and self-awareness, as well as the three-dimensional model.

2. I call together all the team members and tell them that I am going to be a "leader as completer." That means I am committing to doing the following:

   - Making sure every essential function is being performed superbly

   - Being responsible for making sure the team's outside relations, internal relations, and task performance are carried out well

   - Knowing myself and designing the personal leadership style that works best for me

   - Knowing the members of my team well enough to know the best role for each one to play

- Learning to understand the dynamics of how teams operate
- Learning the functions that our team needs to perform well in order to achieve our mission, and figuring out how to inspire the team to accomplish them
- Having the sensitivity and flexibility to sense what functions the team is not accomplishing
- Being willing to do what is necessary, even though it may be personally displeasing
- Using the concordance process for all decisions, including determining how the team can function best

3. I set the following conditions for my leadership of this team:
- We all follow these practices: we don't lie, we don't blame, we don't withhold, we don't deceive ourselves.
- We all make every effort to increase our self-awareness, therefore reducing our self-deception.
- We all take individual responsibility for ourselves, so that every event between us is considered 100 percent my responsibility and 100 percent your responsibility, and no one is to blame.
- Our teamwork and conflict resolution are accomplished with the methods described in Chapter Five.
- This is our starting point: if these ideas are not working, we can use the concordance process to change them.

4. When new members wish to join or are invited to join the team, I and other team members show them the principles we operate by. If they are willing to operate under these rules— or if they can talk us out of them (concordantly)—they are welcome to join. If they join, they are given the same training that the others have had, as quickly as possible.

CONCLUSION

The Real Bottom Line

Where in my life did I stop dancing?
Where in my life did I stop singing?
Where in my life did I stop being enchanted with stories?
Where in my life did I become uncomfortable with the
    sweet territory of silence?

—*Angeles Arrien*[1]

Most of us stopped singing and dancing, and parts of us stopped evolving in general, at sometimes identifiable points in our lives. We stopped expressing ourselves fully, our expressiveness dampened by fear and weakening self-esteem. We cut off parts of ourselves. *The Human Element* is an attempt to synthesize old wisdom and new insights in the service of recapturing, unblocking, and expanding those blocked parts, and helping each of us be whole, to express all of ourselves fully.

I began this book with some history about myself and my search for simple but powerful unifying themes for the diverse events in my life. As someone who has pursued many different paths, with their ups and downs and twists and turns, I understand that it is not always easy to make the kinds of changes in oneself and in one's organization that this book recommends. Through my consulting, I have come to see that, regardless of the value of the Human Element ideas, resistance to change is much greater than I originally imagined. I have been chagrined by the difficulty of having my ideas heard, but I have also learned that this amount of resistance is not unusual. Resistance in itself does not guarantee the value of an idea, of course; poor ideas have also been resisted. But resistance must be addressed directly if the Human Element model is to gain currency.

The Human Element approach presents several notions that are difficult for some people to accept—in particular, ideas about truth, choice, and exploration of the inner world of the self. The strongest objections to the concepts of truth and choice have come primarily from a few people who take a very conservative religious view. They believe that there is only one truth, *the* spiritual path. They do not accept that each person may have his or her own truth, and that "the truth" can be defined as an agreement among observers. Similarly, the suggestion that I, not God (or at least that I in cooperation with God), am choosing my own life smacks of hubris to some people and is therefore unacceptable.

Others have objected that the workshop constitutes an invasion of privacy, and that was when I realized that the spirit of choice had to permeate every aspect of the training. In many groups, I have found people who did not like the Human Element approach or were not ready for it. I learned to respect their feelings and to let people proceed at their own pace, if they wanted to proceed at all. Respecting each person's self-determination ensures that the training does what it's supposed to do. If people attend only when they are ready, they usually take much more from the experience.

As I continued working, however, several questions arose. For example, if my training was good for developing leadership or teamwork, then why should it not be given to everyone whose job requires leadership or teamwork, just as training in running a computer is required for computer operators?

Several other drawbacks arose. When people were given a choice about participating and were forewarned that they might become upset sometime during the week-long workshop, some who had chosen the training began to wonder if they should go. This cautious approach often raised anxiety and doubt instead of alleviating concerns.

Further, managers who stressed the point that the workshop was voluntary were often looked at skeptically and accused of hypocrisy, since their employees did not believe that there would be no punishment for not attending.

Some managers ignored our request to keep the training voluntary. Curiously enough, the results for their groups were comparable to those for the volunteer groups, and no one criticized the managers who had required the workshop. On the contrary, they were often thanked profusely for this important experience. The voluntary basis of the training also restricted the degree of our influence because large companies could not simply order large numbers of people to go through our training. Thus some people in large organizations got the training, and others did not, which diminished the power of the experience.

For a while, I adopted an intermediate position, based on an admonition of my mother's: "You don't have to eat your spinach, but you do have to try it. If you don't like it, you don't have to eat it." This bit of wisdom contained the seeds of a satisfactory solution. I now believe that supervisors have the right and the responsibility to select people for required training that promises to improve job performance, including people skills. If any participant feels that our training or any part of it is too difficult or uncomfortable to handle, he or she can drop out at any point. Of the more than ten thousand people who have been through our training, one dropped out in the first meeting, and four or five left before the training was completed. This approach honors both the business objective of high-quality training and the human capacity for handling difficult situations. Nevertheless, some people remain wary: "We don't have the right to impose this on our employees."

In addition to personal objections to the Human Element approach, there have been objections based on observations about the process of change and the necessity of total overhaul of the status quo if change is to be effective. Even if a demonstrably revolutionary process is introduced into organizational life, there is no guarantee that the change will be adopted quickly, and there certainly is little likelihood that the change will result in any immediate improvement in productivity.

An excellent article by Michael Rothschild,[2] based on a paper by economic historian Paul David, explores the history of this phenomenon. Rothschild applies what he calls the "productivity paradox" to the computer revolution: "Although U.S. businesses plunked down well over $1 trillion for computer systems in the last decade, they have almost no measurable productivity increase to show for it and, therefore, they resist the changes." In his interesting historical analysis, the author offers a very convincing explanation: when a major innovation is introduced, it is typically fitted into the current environment. Citing the example of Edison's electric motor, the author points out that electric motors were first used as replacements for steam engines, but the support for steam engines, in the form of a system of vertical and horizontal shafts and belts, was retained. Only gradually did the support system change to accommodate and exploit the values of electric engines: "Finally, 40 years after Edison's breakthroughs, productivity growth took off. Where the annual labor productivity growth had hovered around one percent for the first two decades of the century, it jumped to more than five percent during the Roaring Twenties." Rothschild goes on to predict that all the investment in computers and telecommunications will create a similar productivity surge when corporations finally learn how to make full use of the new technology.

A similar phenomenon occurs on the human side in organizations. Although we have been able to measure improved productivity in specific areas, at this point it is difficult to achieve an impact on overall organizational productivity, for several reasons:

- Usually only part of the organization receives the training; the rest stays as it is.

- When people return from the training, the old atmosphere awaits them. Often it does not support their changes and may even be hostile to them.

- People who have not participated in the training, feeling like members of an "out" group, often oppose the new ideas.

- People who have not received the training are unsure of their new roles in cases where the organization does begin to change.

The new Human Element ideas are examined carefully. If they do gain acceptance, people will take more time to see all the implications of implementing the ideas and modifying other organizational practices to enhance the advantages that the innovations create.

As people in organizations become more self-aware, we should indeed see a productivity surge, perhaps one greater than any we have ever seen before. To experience the fruits of this surge, we need a kind of courage rarely spoken about in the annals of heroes: the courage to know ourselves, to be honest with one another, to handle the truth. Our current dealings with each other too often bring great pain and inefficiency. Through the Human Element model, we now have some understanding of how to relate to one another better and with greater pleasure. It is time to make use of our new insights by structuring our organizations around the people who work in them. Then we can enjoy the rewards of this new self-awareness, rewards that are not only psychic but also material.

In this book, I have attempted to take a step in that direction. I have presented theory, principles, and specific practical methods for using some of the wonderful breakthroughs in experience and research from the past forty years, breakthroughs that may result in an entirely different kind of organization. These principles can be summarized as three invitations. I invite you to explore what happens when we do these things:

- Diminish our defensiveness and communicate openly and honestly with one another
- Diminish blame and acknowledge how we collude with one another to create what happens
- Diminish self-deception and allow ourselves to look inward and know ourselves well

I hope that this book will contribute to the trend of developing more self-aware, open organizations and individuals with greater *self-esteem, and that our advancements in understanding the human* element will at least match our advancements in technology. As we realize the tremendous power of truth, recognize our awesome capacity to determine our own lives, and overcome our fear of looking openly and honestly at ourselves, we can attain limitless heights of productivity and personal fulfillment in our organizations, our relationships, and ourselves—the *real* bottom line. Then all our spirits may soar—together.

APPENDIX

The Human Element Tools

Books by Will Schutz

Profound Simplicity (1979; 3rd ed., 1986). As Will Schutz explored himself and the human condition—through encounter groups, bodywork methods, energy techniques, and spiritual disciplines—he discovered that each one, if pursued deeply enough, emphasized the same concepts of truth, self-responsibility, and self-awareness. This book weaves those principles into a foundation for a social philosophy.

FIRO: A Three-Dimensional Theory of Interpersonal Behavior (1958; 3rd ed., 1989). This book contains the original explanation of Will Schutz's FIRO (Fundamental Interpersonal Relations Orientation) theory. The book introduces the well-known FIRO-B measure (now updated and renamed FIRO Element B), provides a literature review, and describes the variables.

Related Books

The Human Element @ Work: A Fieldbook of Projects Transforming People and Organizations Around the Globe (2004); ed. by Rhonda Parkyns and Rosa Walden. This books tells of 14 different applications of The Human Element approach in a wide variety of settings, from coaching in the UK and Mexico, to developing teams at NASA and leaders at the Sydney Opera House, improving the teamwork of a Norwegian around-the-world sailing team, and ameliorating industrial relations in California schools.

Radical Collaboration: Five Essential Skills to Overcome Defensiveness and Build Successful Relationships (2004); by James Tamm and Ron Luyet. This is a "how to" book for building collaborative relationships, with several chapters devoted to The Human Element concepts and FIRO theory.

Instruments

FIRO Element B: Behavior. A result of the revised and greatly expanded FIRO theory, this instrument retains the attractive properties of FIRO B: it is short (15 minutes), simple, and self-scoring. At the same time, it offers additional features and clearer interpretations. *Element B* measures preferences in the areas of inclusion, control, and openness and provides a measure of the difference between perceived and wanted behaviors.

FIRO Element O: Organizational Climate. This instrument provides measures of satisfaction within an organization in the areas of inclusion, control, openness, significance, competence, and likability. Each measure is provided for the organization as a whole, and for teams, relationships, and individuals. The instrument can also be used to evaluate the effects of any organizational change.

FIRO Element F: Feelings. Based on the revised and enhanced FIRO theory, this instrument measures preferences in the areas of significance, competence, and likability in relationships. It is self-scoring and measures the difference between perceived and wanted feelings.

FIRO Element S: Self-Concept. Based on the revised and enhanced FIRO theory, this instrument measures feelings about the self in the three areas of behavior (aliveness, self-determination, self-awareness) and the three areas of feeling (self-significance, self-competence, self-like). It is self-scoring and measures the difference between perceived and wanted behaviors and feelings toward the self.

FIRO Feedback: Behavior and *FIRO Feedback: Behavior, Feelings, and Self-Concept.* These two instruments, used with *FIRO Element B, Element F,* and *Element S,* provide means by which the user can develop skills in giving and receiving feedback. The instruments provide measures of transparency and are helpful in increasing self-awareness by letting people discover how they are seen by others.

Team Compatibility Index (TCI). This instrument provides a structure for assessing compatibility—the ability of team members to work well together. The TCI provides measures of overall team compatibility, efficient use of personnel, and identifies trouble spots. The usefulness of the TCI is enhanced when followed by *FIRO Element W.*

FIRO Element W: Work Relations. This instrument provides a non-threatening framework for assessing and improving two-person work relationships. It is especially useful for long term relationships between two people who share common goals. Users may include supervisors and their employees, co-workers, doctors and patients, lawyers and clients, teachers and students, and members of temporary or occasional groups.

FIRO Element C: Close Relations. This instrument helps to explore relationships between spouses, lovers, or close friends using the FIRO dimensions of inclusion, control, openness, significance, competence, and likability. It provides measurement and a framework for discussion.

FIRO Element E: Self-Esteem. This instrument helps to uncover areas that contribute to low self-esteem and to explore the payoffs for low self-esteem. It reveals where blocks are, suggests how to remove them, and provides ideas for increasing self-esteem.

FIRO Element T: Openness (Truth). This instrument provides a structure, using progressively deeper levels of truth and openness, for an individual to explore a particularly difficult relationship.

Booklets

Concordance: Decision Making. A step beyond consensus, the information in this booklet provides a unique structure in which creativity, open dialogue, and logic encourage a team or organization to arrive at solutions that dramatically surpass those found through more commonly used decision making techniques. The concordance process maximizes quality solutions, creates commitment to the solutions, and produces quick, efficient implementation.

Interpretation of FIRO Element B. This booklet provides a step-by-step interpretation of *FIRO Element B* scores based on the revised and expanded theory and The Human Element principles. All the scores in the instrument including the difference scores are examined along with explanations for using the results to create positive personal and interpersonal change.

Conversion of FIRO-B to FIRO Element B. This booklet provides information about the evolution of FIRO-B to *Element B*, covering the developments in FIRO theory and their effects on the FIRO instruments. It also presents a description of the advantages of *Element B* over FIRO-B, as well as statistical characteristics of *Element B* as compared to those of FIRO-B. A simple method allows users to convert FIRO-B scores to *Element B* scores, thereby preserving all previously acquired information.

Guides

Guide to FIRO Element B: Behavior. This guide includes information contained in the *Interpretation of Element B* and *Conversion of FIRO-B to FIRO Element B* and provides detailed directions for administering *Element B*.

Guide to FIRO Element W: Work Relations. This guide gives detailed directions for administering and interpreting *FIRO Element W*. It details problems with, purposes of, assumptions of, and suggested improvements for performance appraisal and gives an explanation of the levels of openness.

Guide to FIRO Element C: Close Relations. This guide explains why *Element C* was developed and offers guidelines for its use. It provides detailed directions for administering and interpreting *Element C*, gives an explanation of the levels of openness, and offers suggestions for next steps.

Guide to the Team Compatibility Index (TCI). This guide provides an explanation of the *C-P effect* (the effect of team compatibility on productivity) and discusses uses of and approaches to the TCI. Step-by-step instructions for administering, calculating, and interpreting the TCI are included along with suggestions for next steps.

Wallcharts

FIRO Element Wallcharts are used for demonstrating learning points and facilitating discussions when conducting group sessions. They are 25" by 30" grids with space for scores for up to twelve people, for individual and group difference scores, and for transparency scores.

Wallchart for FIRO Element B. This chart is for recording *Element B* scores (on inclusion, control, and openness).

Wallchart for FIRO Element F. This chart is for recording *Element F* scores (on significance, competence, and likability).

Wallchart for FIRO Element S. This chart is for recording *Element S* scores (on aliveness, self-determination, self-awareness, self-significance, self-competence, and self-like).

Team Compatibility Wallchart. For use with the Team Compatibility Index, this chart has space for recording the operating patterns for a team of up to twelve people, their centrality (by pairs), their compatibility (by pairs), and calculations of team and individual compatibility indexes.

Levels of Openness Wallchart. This 25" by 30" poster enumerates the levels of openness (truth) and provides a statement and example of each. This is a tool for individuals and groups who wish to become more aware of and look more deeply into their own preferences for openness.

How to Order Materials

Online: www.BConNetwork.com

By phone: 1-800-INCLUSION (462-5874) (for the U.S. and Canada)
                 +1-650-871-4290 (International)

By fax: 1-650-871-4297

By mail: Business Consultants Network, Inc.
                 401 Marina Blvd.
                 South San Francisco, CA 94080
                 United States

Notes and References

Preface

1. Iacocca, L. *Iacocca: An Autobiography.* New York: Bantam, 1984.
2. D. Cole, quoted in E. Ramey, "Hands and Minds." *Human Resources Executive,* 1993, *7*(14), 21.
3. For information about Human Element workshops and all related books, films, and instruments, see the Appendix.
4. Rolfing is a method of deep massage aimed at relieving chronic muscle tension and releasing problems buried deep in the body. See I. Rolf, *Rolfing: The Integration of Human Structures* (Boulder, Colo.: Rolf Institute, 1977).

Introduction

1. Jung, C. *Collected Works.* Vol. 13: Alchemical Studies. New York: Pantheon, 1953.
2. The human potential movement, especially in the 1960s and the 1970s, centered on the Esalen Institute at Big Sur, California. It has been described in G. Leonard, *Walking on the Edge of the World* (Boston: Houghton Mifflin, 1988) and in W. Anderson, *The Upstart Spring: Esalen and the American Awakening* (Reading, Mass.: Addison-Wesley, 1983).
3. D. McGregor's *The Human Side of Enterprise* (New York: McGraw-Hill, 1960) was one of the pioneering books in the field. Somewhat more recent books include T. Peters and R. Waterman, Jr., *In Search of Excellence* (New York: HarperCollins, 1983); J. Naisbett, *Megatrends: Ten New Directions Transforming Our Lives* (New York: Warner Books, 1982); K. Blanchard and S. Johnson, *The One-Minute Manager* (New York: Morrow, 1982); R. Kanter, *The Change Masters* (New York: Simon & Schuster, 1983); W. Ouchi, *Theory Z: How American Business Can Meet the Japanese Challenge* (Reading, Mass.: Addison-Wesley, 1980); S. Covey, *Seven Habits of Highly Effective People* (New York: Simon & Schuster, 1989); and P. Senge, *The Fifth Discipline: The Art and Practice of the Learning Organization* (New York: Doubleday, 1990).
4. Schutz, W. "Some Implications of the Logical Calculus for Empirical Classes for Social Science Methodology." *Psychometrika,* 1959, *24*(1), 69–87.
5. Schutz, W. *FIRO: A Three-Dimensional Theory of Interpersonal Behavior* (3rd ed.). Mill Valley, Calif.: WSA, 1989.
6. Bradford, L., Benne, K., and Gibb, J. *T-Group Theory and Laboratory Method.* New York: Wiley, 1964.

262 NOTES AND REFERENCES

7. Assagioli, R. *Psychosynthesis.* New York: Viking Penguin, 1971.

8. Moreno, J. *Who Shall Survive?* New York: Nervous and Mental Disease Publishing, 1934.

9. Lowen, A. *Bioenergetics.* New York: Viking Penguin, 1976.

10. See note 4 to Preface.

11. Perls, F., Hefferline, R., and Goodman, P. *Gestalt Therapy.* New York: Julian, 1951.

12. See W. Schutz, *Joy: Expanding Human Awareness* (New York: Grove Press, 1967). See also *Joy: Twenty Years Later* (Berkeley, Calif.: Ten Speed Press, 1989).

13. Schutz, W. *Here Comes Everybody.* New York: HarperCollins, 1971.

14. Schutz, W. *Elements of Encounter.* Big Sur, Calif.: Joy Press, 1973.

15. Schutz, W. *Leaders of Schools: FIRO Theory Applied to Administrators.* San Diego, Calif.: University Associates, 1977.

16. Schutz, W. *Evy: An Odyssey into Bodymind.* New York: HarperCollins, 1976. Schutz, W. *Body Fantasy.* New York: Irvington, 1977.

17. Schutz, W. *Profound Simplicity.* New York: Bantam, 1979. (3rd ed. published 1986 by WSA.)

18. The primary exercises for body awareness are drawn from the brilliant work of Moshe Feldenkrais. His most relevant book is *Awareness Through Movement* (New York: HarperCollins, 1973). Tapes of his exercises are available from Feldenkrais Resources, P.O. Box 2067, Berkeley, CA 94702. Further information is available through Will Schutz Associates (see Appendix).

19. See Appendix.

20. In a survey administered by Kevin Berg to employees of a computer company, 150 people were presented with the following statement: "Most of my problems and frustrations at work are usually someone else's fault." Before the Human Element workshop, 31 percent of the employees strongly agreed with this statement. After the workshop, none of them agreed with it.

21. This is the first instance of the universal *I.*

Chapter One

1. Moyne, J., and Barks, C. (trans.). *Open Secret: Versions of Rumi.* Putney, Vt.: Threshold Books, 1984.

2. The virtues of simplicity were being extolled at least as far back as the early fourteenth century. William of Occam stated what came to be known as "Occam's razor": the assumptions introduced to explain a thing must not be multiplied beyond necessity. Later, Leibniz introduced a similar formulation about the "identity of indiscernibles," which means that entities indistinguishable from one another are really the same thing.

3. An excellent review of the concept is presented in R. Bednar, M. Wells, and S. Peterson, *Self-Esteem: Paradoxes and Innovations in Clinical Theory and Practice* (Washington, D.C.: American Psychological Association, 1989).

4. Bennis, W., and Nanus, B. *Leaders: The Strategies for Taking Charge.* New York: HarperCollins, 1985. Bennis, W. *On Becoming a Leader.* Reading, Mass.: Addison-Wesley, 1989.

5. J. Luft, personal communication.

6. Myers, I. *The Myers-Briggs Type Indicator.* Princeton, N.J.: Educational Testing Service, 1962.

7. Ouchi, W. *Theory Z: How American Business Can Meet the Japanese Challenge*. Reading, Mass.: Addison-Wesley, 1980.

8. Blake, R., and Mouton, J. *The New Managerial Grid*. Houston, Tex.: Gulf, 1978.

9. Covey, S. *Seven Habits of Highly Effective People*. New York: Simon & Schuster, 1989.

10. Senge, P. *The Fifth Discipline: The Art and Practice of the Learning Organization*. New York: Doubleday, 1990.

11. Facet design was introduced by Louis Guttman. A good description of it can be found in D. Canter (ed.), *Facet Theory: Approaches to Social Research* (New York: Springer-Verlag, 1985).

12. In the FIRO theory, *openness* was originally called *affection*. Affection is actually more a feeling than a behavior and is therefore not so parallel to inclusion and control as openness is (as the behavioral aspect of affection).

13. I use the term *collude* to mean "mainly unconscious cooperation."

14. Table 1.2, presented here in revised form, was originally developed by Gary Copeland, Ron Luyet, and Karen Copeland.

Chapter Two

1. As interpreted by John Heider in *The Tao of Leadership* (Atlanta, Ga.: Humanics, 1985).

2. Goldfarb, W. "The Effects of Early Institutional Care on Adolescent Personality." *Journal of Experimental Education*, 1943, *12*, 106–129.

3. Glueck, S., and Glueck, E. *Unraveling Juvenile Delinquency*. New York: Commonwealth Fund, 1950.

4. Chopra, D. *Quantum Healing*. New York: Bantam, 1989, p. 249.

5. Self-scoring paper-and-pencil instruments are available from Will Schutz Associates for measuring interpersonal behavior (*Element B*), interpersonal feelings (*Element F*), and self (*Element S*). See the Appendix for ordering information.

6. This approach to defenses, in its earliest formulation, was developed with Nancy Waxler for her Ph.D. dissertation ("Defense Mechanisms and Interpersonal Behavior," Harvard University, 1960), where she reviewed the literature on defenses and organized them into a smaller number. I have revised this approach over the years.

7. This list of clues, slightly revised here, was developed by Ron Luyet.

8. Since Wolfe, the concept of self-esteem has become even more a target of ridicule. See the cover story of *Newsweek* for Feb. 27, 1992: "The Curse of Self-Esteem: What's Wrong with Feelgood Government" (pp. 46–51).

9. An outstanding effort aimed at the root causes of social ailments is the Task Force on Self-Esteem established by legislation authored in 1989 by John Vasconcellos, a California state assemblyman. Vasconcellos believes that if the self-esteem of the citizenry is not strengthened, solutions to social ills will be without a solid foundation.

10. Gloria Steinem's book *Revolution from Within* (Boston: Little, Brown, 1992) is particularly important because it comes from someone strongly identified with the social revolution. Her appreciation of the inner revolution as well fills out the conditions for social change more adequately.

11. This list of characteristics, slightly revised here, was developed by Ron Luyet.

12. *Element E*, a self-scoring paper-and-pencil instrument for measuring self-esteem, is available from Will Schutz Associates. See the Appendix for ordering information.

Chapter Three

1. Redenbaugh, R., and Bell, C. "Quality and Business Processes: The New Coin of the Realm." *Action Technology*, 1990, p. 1.
2. Schutz, W. *Leader's Manual: Element B, Behavior and Team Building.* Mill Valley, Calif.: WSA, 1989.
3. Schutz, W. "What Makes Groups Productive?" *Human Relations*, 1955, *8*(4), 429–465.
4. Schutz, W. *FIRO: A Three-Dimensional Theory of Interpersonal Behavior* (3rd ed.). Mill Valley, Calif.: WSA, 1989.
5. Schutz, W. "The Sequence of Interpersonal Areas and of Leader-Member Relations in a Training Group." Unpublished paper available from Will Schutz Associates (see the Appendix for ordering information).
6. Elvin Semrad introduced the concept of "goblet issues" to me.
7. This fable was related by Sigmund Freud, citing Schopenhauer, in Freud's *Group Psychology and the Analysis of the Ego* (London: Hogarth Press, 1922).
8. Data are available on request from WSA.

Chapter Four

1. "Jack Welch's Lessons for Success." *Fortune*, Jan. 25, 1993, p. 86.
2. Gellerman, S., and Hodgson, W. "Cyanamid's New Take on Performance Appraisal." *Harvard Business Review*, 1988, *66*(3), 36–41.
3. The WRE process is typically conducted with *Element W: Work Relations*, an instrument that formalizes the theory and provides a convenient structure for the ensuing discussion. It is available from Will Schutz Associates. See the Appendix for ordering information.
4. This approach is simplified by the use of *Element J: Job*, an instrument completed by both the supervisor and the worker. It is available from Will Schutz Associates. See the Appendix for ordering information.
5. My favorite work on creativity is W. Gordon's *Synectics: The Development of Creative Capacity* (New York: HarperCollins, 1961), a classic in the field. As for logical thinking, any book on scientific method lists a series of steps; I was brought up on A. Kaplan's *The Conduct of Inquiry* (San Francisco: Chandler, 1964).
6. An excellent book on blocks to creativity is L. Kuble's *Neurotic Distortion of the Creative Process* (New York: Noonday, 1961). Recent comprehensive work also appears in M. Czikszentmihalyi, K. Rathmunde, and S. Whalen, *Talented Teenagers* (Cambridge, England: Cambridge University Press, 1993).

Chapter Five

1. Sherman, S. "A Brave New Darwinian Workplace." *Fortune*, Jan. 25, 1993, pp. 50–56.
2. Blake, R., and Mouton, J. "Reactions to Intergroup Competition Under Win-Lose Conditions." *Management Science*, 1961, *7*, 420–436. These authors take an approach that approximates consensus and perhaps even concordance. They define "decision by consensus" as a state of affairs in which communication has been sufficiently open and the group climate sufficiently supportive to make everyone feel that he or she has a fair chance to influence the decision.

3. This procedure contrasts with the Japanese convention whereby management decides which people are the appropriate ones to make a decision; see P. Drucker, *Management: Tasks, Responsibilities, Practices* (New York: HarperCollins, 1973). Drucker also states that the Japanese are cognizant of the importance of implementing any decision, building effective execution into the decision-making process. This statement has a connection with that part of the concordance inclusion criterion that requires the people most affected by a decision to participate in the decision-making team's deliberations. Also see P. Schwab, "People Support What They Help Create," unpublished doctoral dissertation, Union Graduate School, 1982.

4. Moberg, D., and Croucher, G. "Caterpillar Inching Along." *In These Times*, Sept. 1, 1992, p. 6.

5. Reade, L. *The Ship That Stood Still.* New York: Norton, 1993.

6. Schwab, "People Support What They Help Create."

7. This kind of confusion occurs often; see E. Jaques, "In Praise of Hierarchy," *Harvard Business Review*, 1990, *68*(1), 127–133: "None of the group-oriented panaceas face this issue of accountability. . . . If the CEO or the manager of the group is held accountable for outcomes, then in the final analysis he or she will have to agree with group decisions or have the authority to block them, which means the group never had decision-making power to begin with" (p. 128). The concordance model solves this dilemma: everyone has the same power that Jaques ascribes to the CEO.

8. Schutz, W. *Concordance.* Mill Valley, Calif.: WSA, 1987. (This publication evolved into the present chapter.)

9. Because conflicts come from rigidities, the conflict-resolution strategy is to dissolve rigidities. That is why this process could rightly be called *conflict dissolution.*

Chapter Six

1. As interpreted by John Heider in *The Tao of Leadership* (Atlanta, Ga.: Humanics, 1985).

2. McGregor, D. *The Human Side of Enterprise.* New York: McGraw-Hill, 1960.

3. Tom James, telephone conversation with author, 24 May 1994.

4. To facilitate evaluation of the current state of leadership in any organization or organizational unit, a form called the *Leadership Survey* is available from Will Schutz Associates. See the Appendix for ordering information.

Conclusion

1. Arrien, A. *The Four-Fold Way: Walking the Paths of the Warrior, Teacher, Healer, and Visionary.* San Francisco: HarperSanFrancisco, 1993. "Many indigenous peoples believe that whenever in our lives we stopped dancing, singing, being enchanted with stories, or began experiencing difficulty with silence is where we began to experience loss of spirit" (p. 41).

2. Rothschild, M. "The Coming Productivity Surge." *Forbes ASAP*, March 29, 1993, pp. 17–18.

Index